What people are saying about

Striking at the Roots

Striking at the Roots is a practical field guide for animal rights activists that covers a wide spectrum of strategies and tactics for dealing with the media, the courts, the streets, and those foul dark places of horror where animals are so cruelly treated, and where compassionate activists must reluctantly venture, in pursuit of effective intervention. If you are serious about helping animals, then you should seriously read this book.
Captain Paul Watson, founder and CEO of Sea Shepherd Conservation Society

Wow! An amazing resource just got more amazing! What's not to love about a book with kindness at its heart that offers guidance on activist topics from leafleting to self-care? With updated information, this sympathetic, engaged, and trustworthy guide has become even more inspiring.
Carol J. Adams, author of *The Sexual Politics of Meat* and *Burger*

Striking at the Roots is an eloquent and inspirational guide to action for animals. The power to change society rests with each and every one of us—it's not enough to change ourselves, we have an obligation to planet earth, to the web of life itself, to change others. This book motivates and informs, puts the passion into compassion, and will save lives.
Juliet Gellatley, founder and director of Viva!

With *Striking at the Roots*, Mark Hawthorne shows that anyone can help achieve remarkable victories for animals. Within these pages, longtime activists from around the world offer their practical advice on bringing your message to the public, staging a protest, getting a restaurant or dining hall to offer vegan options, avoiding activist burnout, and much more. From leafleting and letter-writing, to the legal system and even dealing with critics, this is an inspirational, must-read guidebook for effective grassroots animal advocacy. I wish this book had been around when I was a new animal activist!

Nathan Runkle, founder of Mercy For Animals

Brilliant, easy to read, full of real-life experiences and practical examples. If you want to make your life count, influence others and save a few thousand lives, this book is your roadmap. Give it to everyone you know!

Ingrid Newkirk, president of People for the Ethical Treatment of Animals

Striking at the Roots by Mark Hawthorne is an eloquent reminder that in this age of big organizations, big money, and big media, it's still the individual activist who makes the real difference. Clear, practical guidance on everything from letter writing to civil disobedience is combined with inspiring and edifying stories of people from around the world who are making their voices heard for the animals. A must-read for both the veteran activist and the person who wants to get involved but isn't quite sure how to get started. I wish it had been available when I got started as an animal activist, and I'm certainly glad it's here now. It ranks with the best guides to animal advocacy that have ever been written.

Norm Phelps, author of *The Longest Struggle: Animal Advocacy from Pythagoras to PETA* and *The Great Compassion: Buddhism and Animal Rights*

With *Striking at the Roots*, Mark Hawthorne gives activists the roadmap they need to create the most impact for animals. This is an essential tool for our movement.

Ari Solomon, host of *The VeganAri Show* and director of communications at Mercy For Animals

Striking at the Roots helped guide my advocacy when I first read it nearly a decade ago. I can't wait to see the next generation of compassionate crusaders shine a light in the dark and inspire people to choose more consciously with the advice in this new edition. We each have limited time on this planet. This book will help you make the most of it.

Michelle Taylor Cehn, founder of World of Vegan

There is not a single page of this book from which I did not learn something valuable!

Jeffrey Moussaieff Masson, author of *When Elephants Weep: The Emotional Lives of Animals* and *The Pig Who Sang to the Moon: The Emotional World of Farm Animals*

Mark Hawthorne once again reminds us of the power of one. *Striking at the Roots* is a complete roadmap for animal activists, from letter writing to guiding those who may find themselves arrested. It directs readers to available resources, organizations, and individuals. But it goes beyond the general guide book by including passionate stories from national leaders and grassroots activists from several countries. It also considers the emotional toll on activists by offering guidance for finding one's emotional level of activism and includes suggestions on maintaining some peace of mind while engaged in the struggle; this is a major contribution. *Striking at the Roots* is a compassionate and valuable tool for activists.

Dorothy H. Hayes, author of *Animal Instinct*

In *Striking at the Roots*, Mark Hawthorne manages to set before us the full horrors of man's inhumanity to animals without leaving the reader feeling helpless and puny. He has talked to campaigners in many countries, analyzing what works and, having done so, can signpost the way to positive action. His writing is lucid, shrewd and results-driven. He advises on everything from talking to the public at a street stall to effecting a change of policy at a major corporation. There is also guidance on how to survive emotionally the knowledge that, second by second, money and prestige come to those who mass produce, abuse and dispose of animals. His message is that the task we face is immense but that when people of compassion apply themselves skillfully, we have what it takes to change the world.

Andrew Tyler, former director of Animal Aid

Many people want to help end animal abuse but don't know where to start. This book is an excellent guide for everything from casual, spare-time activism to full-time careers.

Dan Piraro, creator of "Bizarro"

From publicizing an issue to taking action, from feeding a large group to running a rescue center, activists will find this guide from veteran animal-rights crusader Hawthorne detailed, straightforward and highly practical, even if your cause isn't animal rights. Drawing on his own experience and those of his colleagues, Hawthorne provides advice from a number of perspectives on a long list of methods: leafleting, letters and articles, protests, corporate campaigning, internet outreach, direct action and government lobbying. Though it's concerned throughout with inter-species justice, providing an adequate introduction to the principles, history and progress of the animal rights movement, as well as numerous animal rights resources, the book's tips on tabling, organizing protests, effective letter-writing and other matters are just as easily applied to any cause. Concise guidance, an empowering tone, and a large, global community of voices make this book eminently useful for anyone organizing a movement, though Hawthorne's optimism can belie the often difficult path to change.

Publishers Weekly

Striking at the Roots

A Practical Guide to Animal Activism

10th Anniversary Edition — New Tactics,
New Technology

Striking at the Roots

A Practical Guide to Animal Activism

10th Anniversary Edition—New Tactics,
New Technology

Mark Hawthorne

CHANGE
MAKERS
BOOKS

Winchester, UK
Washington, USA

First published by Changemakers Books, 2018
Changemakers Books is an imprint of John Hunt Publishing Ltd., No. 3 East Street,
Alresford, Hampshire SO24 9EE, UK
office1@jhpbooks.net
www.johnhuntpublishing.com
www.changemakers-books.com

For distributor details and how to order please visit the 'Ordering' section on our website.

Text copyright: Mark Hawthorne 2017

ISBN: 978 1 78535 882 1
978 1 78535 883 8 (ebook)
Library of Congress Control Number: 2017962505

A CIP catalogue record for this book is available from the British Library.

Design: Stuart Davies

Printed and bound by CPI Group (UK) Ltd, Croydon, CR0 4YY, UK

We operate a distinctive and ethical publishing philosophy in
all areas of our business, from our global network of authors to
production and worldwide distribution.

Contents

For a certain cow in India, who showed me
a kinder way of living.

There are a thousand hacking at the branches of evil to one who is striking at the root.
—Henry David Thoreau, *Walden*

Acknowledgements

The animal rights movement is comprised of some of the most supportive human beings imaginable, and I am indebted to many of them from around the world. My humble thanks to these activists for patiently enduring my endless questions and transforming them into the practical advice that is the heart of this book: Carol J. Adams, Pam Ahern, Bina Ahmad, Nick Atwood, Carolyn Bailey, Julianna Baker, Monica Ball, Gene Baur, Tara Baxter, Georgina Beach, Laura Beck, Beverly Lynn Bennett, Megan Bentjen, Marcy Berman, Martina Bernstein, Olga Betts, Jaya Bhumitra, Tony Bishop-Weston, Rachel Bjork, Shari Black Velvet, Jennifer Blough, Sarahjane Blum, Ken Botts, Andrew Butler, Jenna Calabrese, Jon Camp, Amber Canavan, Katie Cantrell, John Carmody, Ericka Ceballos, Alka Chandna, Tina Clark, Callie Coker, Jake Conroy, Mo Constantine, Jim Corcoran, Lauren Corman, Susie Coston, Fernando Cuenca, Aurelia d'Andrea, Jason Das, Karen Davis, James DeAlto, Margo DeMello, Joyce D'Silva, Adam Durand, Monica Engebretson, JL Fields, Kate Fowler, Camilla Fox, Lisa Franzetta, Bruce Friedrich, Leah Garces, Juliet Gellatley, Kathy Guillermo, Dian Hardy, Josh Harper, Michael Hayward, Robin Helfritch, Alison Hermance, pattrice jones, Aubrie Kavanaugh, Shannon Keith, Justin Kerswell, Aph Ko, Michal Kolesár, Nora Kramer, Sarah Kramer, Rachel Krantz, Hans Kriek, Keegan Kuhn, Camille Labchuk, Carrie LeBlanc, Tammy Lee, Julie E. Lewin, Gary Loewenthal, Karl H. Losken, Haviva Lush, Mia MacDonald, Clare Mann, Erik Marcus, Patty Mark, Liz Marshall, Helen Marston, Tim I. Martin, Caroline McAleese, Jo-Anne McArthur, Michele McCowan, Jennifer Mennuti, Marisa Miller Wolfson, Peter Milne, Judith Mirkinson, Dawn Moncrief, Liberty Mulkani, Jack Norris, Jill Nussinow, Glenys Oogjes, lauren Ornelas, Kassy Ortega, Wendy Parsons, Colleen Patrick-Goudreau, Bryan Pease, Fiona

Pereira, Thomas Ponce, Dana Portnoy, Lisa Rice, Dallas Rising, Matt Rossell, Nathan Runkle, Brenda Sanders, Jessica Schlueter, Jessica Schoech, Deirdre Sims, Jasmin Singer, Kelly Slade, Gary Smith, Samantha Smith, Maren Souders, Charles Stahler, Kim Stallwood, Jo Stepaniak, Andy Stepanian, Mariann Sullivan, Andy Tabar, Joyce Tischler, Eric Tucker, Kate Turlington, Jose Valle, Tino Verducci, Elaine Vigneault, Sarah Von Alt, Zoe Weil, Steve Wells, Sue Werrett, Anna West, Freeman Wicklund, Trevor Williams, Alfie Wood, Roger Yates, and Meg York.

My research also led me to experts not necessarily associated with activism, and I appreciate the insights of reporter Henry Lee, who was with the *San Francisco Chronicle* when I interviewed him in 2008 but has since moved on to KTVU-TV, and journalist Wendy Suares, formerly of WTOK-TV, now a morning news anchor at KOKH-TV in Oklahoma City. Thanks to Chip Heath, co-author of *Made to Stick: Why Some Ideas Survive and Others Die*, for reviewing my thoughts on "sticky" communication.

I am exceedingly grateful to Kymberlie Adams Matthews, Beth Gould, Sangu Iyer, and everyone else from *Satya* magazine for allowing me to express my thoughts about animals and activism in writing over the years and for kindly granting permission to reprint the standalone quotations found in each chapter. Sadly, *Satya* ceased publication in 2007.

Thank you to Tim Ward of Changemakers for taking this book on in the first place and agreeing that a new, expanded edition makes sense, and to Mollie Barker for her rigorous copyediting.

To my partner, lauren Ornelas—whose love, support, and compassion inspire me every day—thank you for your insights and input and for all your encouragement when I had my doubts.

Finally, my thanks to you, animal advocates everywhere, for embracing this book and letting me know how it's helped you in your activism. You are the reason I wrote this book in the first place.

Preface

What Are We Fighting For?

When activists speak out against animal suffering, they are generally referring to the exploitation of animals in the production of food, clothing, entertainment, consumer products, pharmaceuticals and pets, such as:

- Chickens in the meat industry who are bred to grow so quickly that their brief lives are filled with misery: fragile bones, lung congestion, limb deformities, and heart failure are common. An average adult man raised the way "meat" chickens are would weigh 1,000 lbs.
- Egg-laying "battery" hens who spend about two years packed into wire cages with other hens without room to spread a single wing. If she doesn't die from untreated illness or uterine prolapse pushing out an egg, the exhausted hen is slaughtered as soon as her egg production declines.
- Male chicks hatched in the egg industry who are immediately gassed, ground up while fully conscious or flung into garbage bags to eventually suffocate. (Some egg industry groups have said they will phase out these killings.)
- Pigs who spend their lives in crates so small they are unable to even turn around.
- Cows who are artificially inseminated each year so they will "give" milk. Their newborn calves are taken away, the females going back into the dairy system while many of the males are crammed into small crates and later sold as "veal" or "beef." Mother cows are slaughtered when their milk production declines.
- Ocean-dwelling animals who are scooped from the sea

by the billions each year to slowly suffocate or be boiled alive.

- Animals who languish in captivity for "entertainment" or "education." Zoos and marine parks don't help us understand animal behavior. They help us understand the behavior of humans who think animal cruelty is acceptable.
- Baby seals who are cruelly clubbed for their fur and frequently skinned alive.
- Bulls, horses, and baby calves who suffer the intense pain of spurs, electric prods, and cinch straps used to make them appear "wild" so rodeo cowboys will seem like heroes.
- Mother elephants who are killed so their babies can be exported and used in animal acts like circuses around the world. Other wild animals suffer the same fate.
- Companion animals who are bred into a hopelessly crowded pet population in which millions of them are abandoned, abused, neglected and euthanized every year.
- Rabbits, nonhuman primates, mice, dogs, rats, and other animals who are annually tortured and killed by the millions in the course of needlessly testing drugs, chemicals, and household products.
- Cows who have their throats slit and their skin ripped off while they are fully conscious in India and China, sources of most of the world's leather.
- Australian sheep who undergo "mulesing," a gruesome mutilation in which large chunks of skin and flesh are cut from their backsides without any painkillers. Sheep no longer producing enough wool are crammed onto export ships and sent to the Middle East for slaughter.
- Birds and mammals hunted for "sport" who may suffer prolonged, painful deaths when they are injured but not killed by hunters. Animals in "canned" hunts, meanwhile,

are killed in an enclosed area by hunters who pay to shoot these "trophies."

- Fur-bearing animals who are caught in traps or raised in fur farms and then gassed, suffocated, or electrocuted (done anally or through the mouth so the blood doesn't ruin the fur).

- Chimpanzees, bears, lions, and other wild animals who are physically and psychologically abused so they will perform tricks for human amusement.

- Horses and dogs used for racing who are treated as "running machines," not sentient beings with needs of their own. These animals are routinely killed when they are no longer deemed profitable.

Foreword to the 2008 Edition

Is Activism the Meaning of Life?

Right now, raccoons are chewing off their paws to escape from steel-jaw traps.

Right now, baby chicks' beaks are being burned off by the egg industry.

Right now, animals are being beaten and whipped in circus training schools.

Right now, millions of dogs, cats, sheep, pigs, chimpanzees, rabbits, mice, fish, and other animals are being abused in myriad ways by "scientists."

Write now.

This reminder about the horrors suffered by other animals every moment—and for the most frivolous of human whims—graces PETA's guide to letter-writing. The reminder serves two purposes: First, it keeps any problems in our own lives in perspective. Second, it reminds us of how easy it is to take action on behalf of other animals. Writing a letter is just one powerful way among many that we can expose abuse and make positive changes for animals. Letters can literally mean the difference between life and death, as Mark Hawthorne discusses in this important book.

Anyone who shares his or her life with a dog or cat understands that the human species is not the only one whose members are worth knowing as individuals. My wife and I share our lives with the world's most perfect cat, Gracie, and she motivates us as activists. Every day, when we return from work, she greets us at the door, often rolling over so that we can scratch her belly. We know that she feels a full range of emotions—from joy and sadness to fear and self-confidence. She helps us remember that other animals are individuals who have needs, desires, and the capacity to experience rich emotional lives.

Although we are less likely to know them personally, other animals—whether they are mammals, birds, or fish—are just as intelligent and interesting as any dog or cat. As philosopher Henry Beston writes in *The Outermost House*, "In a world older and more complete than ours, [other animals] move finished and complete, gifted with extensions of the senses we have lost or never attained, living by voices we shall never hear. They are not brethren, they are not underlings; they are other nations, caught with ourselves in the net of life and time..."

Three more keen observers of other species are Dr. Jeffrey Masson, author (with Susan McCarthy) of *When Elephants Weep: The Emotional Lives of Animals*; Dr. Jonathan Balcombe, author of *Pleasurable Kingdom: Animals and the Nature of Feeling Good*; and Dr. Temple Grandin, author of *Animals in Translation: Using the Mysteries of Autism to Decode Animal Behavior*. All three books are highly recommended for their ability to help us tear down the barriers that we have constructed between ourselves and other species.

Recognizing that other animals have the same basic capacities as human beings is not anthropomorphism; it is simply common sense if we take the time to observe other species. It is also what science is increasingly beginning to acknowledge. Grandin shows, for example, that other animals "have the same core feelings people do" and that "all domestic animals need companionship. It's as much a core requirement as food and water." All three authors discuss the fact that other animals love to play and that adult animals will, like human animals, often allow children to "win" when they're playing. Grandin discusses her belief—which is based on ample scientific rationale—that the psychological trauma of fear in animals is even worse than physical pain because it is thoroughly debilitating in a way that physiological pain is not. This should give us all pause when we consider the lives of animals in factory farms, fur farms, vivisection labs, circus training camps and so on. Try to imagine their abject fear.

All three authors—and many more—show that every time we think that there is something unique about the human species, further research proves that—as Darwin taught us—humans are not unique in our various capacities; whatever differences exist between humans and other animals are differences of degree, not kind. Because some scientists continue to deny Darwin's observations and to focus on trying to find differences between humans and other species, Grandin argues that perhaps they are the ones who have real trouble learning. Time and time again, contrary to the assumptions of certain scientists, we learn that animals can anticipate the future, delay gratification, dream, play, use language and tools, and do everything else that we thought they couldn't do. When scientists fail to identify animals' capacities, scientists have failed—not animals.

In April 2007, *The New York Times* reported that chimpanzees have better short-term memories than do human beings; chimpanzees have consistently far outperformed humans on short-term memory tests. But it's not just chimpanzees who have impressive capacities that defy the common misconception of animals as beings who lack self-awareness. Consider these recent quotes from mainstream media stories:

- "Chickens do not just live in the present, but can anticipate the future and demonstrate self-control, something previously attributed only to humans and other primates, according to a recent study."
  —*Discovery*
- "Elephants can recognize themselves in a mirror and use their reflections to explore hidden parts of themselves, a measure of subjective self-awareness that until now has been shown definitively only in humans and apes, researchers reported yesterday."
  —*The Washington Post*

- "Rats appear capable of a complex form of thinking before known to exist only in humans and other primates—the capacity to reflect on what they do or do not know."
  —*University of Georgia news release*
- "[Pigs] have proved they are at least as clever as chimpanzees with their first forays into video games."
  —*The Daily Telegraph*
- "...scientists have now confirmed what pet lovers have always known: that each animal has its own distinct personality. More than 60 different species, from primates and rodents to fish and even insects, have been scientifically documented to exhibit individual differences in characteristics such as aggression or shyness."
  —*The Independent*

Anyone looking for more of these kinds of stories will find a steady stream of them. We now know that chickens, pigs, fish, rats, mice, and all other vertebrate animals are interesting individuals in their own right. Of course, they also feel pain in the same way—and to the same degree—as human beings. Civil rights icon Dick Gregory explained, "Dr. King taught us that the fight against oppression is never an easy one. It is even harder when you have no voice.... Because I am a civil-rights activist, I am also an animal rights activist. Animals and humans suffer and die alike. Violence causes the same pain, the same spilling of blood, the same stench of death, the same arrogant, cruel, and vicious taking of life. We shouldn't be a part of it."

Walker Percy suggests in *The Last Gentleman* that insanity is the most rational response to reality. What do we do about the fact that more than 1.3 billion human beings are living on less than a dollar a day? What do we do about the war in Iraq or the genocide in Darfur? What do we do about vivisection laboratories, factory farms, and slaughterhouses? It seems reasonable to assume that it is the insane among us who are fully grasping—and accepting responsibility for—both the degree of suffering in the world and the inability of any of us to put an end to it. The rest of us are suffering a psychological malady that is summed up nicely in one word: "denial."

But is the final word really that we're all in denial? I think that it's true that denial and insanity are the two options for human existence only if you neglect another possibility: changing reality and making things better—or at least less horrible. That is the subject of Mark Hawthorne's vital book: how to improve the lot of animals, who are the most exploited and least considered beings on the planet. Animals exist with us in the world and are more like us than unlike us, yet we devour their corpses by the billions for a momentary palate sensation, we steal their fur and skin from them for vanity, and we drive them insane and injure them in laboratories to "test" another toothpaste—or simply to find out what will happen when we hurt them.

In this book, you will find ample corroboration for Alice Walker's thesis in *Possessing the Secret of Joy*: The secret of joy is resistance to evil. The point of human existence, Walker contends in perhaps her most powerful novel, is to move beyond ourselves and fight to make the world a kinder place. Refusing to support cruelty and suffering is crucial, but the next step— resisting injustice—is even more important. Mark gives us the tools that we need to put this thesis into practice.

It is not enough to withdraw our support of cruelty. If it were, the most ethical lifestyle would be that of the hermit in the mountains—or whoever consumes the least resources. But there is another important factor that must be considered: our impact in the world. For example, if you adopt a vegetarian (or better yet, vegan) diet, you will save approximately 100 animals every year. That's wonderful, but consider this: If you convince one *more* person to adopt a vegetarian diet, you (in that moment) double the positive impact of your entire life as a vegetarian. I'll repeat that, just in case you were skimming: Handing *one* leaflet to *one* person who changes his or her mind on the basis of that leaflet will *double the positive impact of your entire life of choosing exclusively vegetarian options.* And we can do a lot more than distribute just one leaflet.

The story in this book that I find the most inspiring is the one about Nathan Runkle picking up a brochure at a table, studying it, conducting further research, and then launching Mercy For Animals, an extremely effective animal rights group that has saved millions of animals from abuse. As I write this, Nathan has just broken the news of an undercover investigation into a turkey slaughterhouse that will awaken millions of people around the world to the dark underbelly of their Thanksgiving dinners. One brochure, taken from one table, did it. One hour of someone's time literally changed the world for millions—if not billions—of animals.

This book is packed with tips and advice that will help all of us become better advocates for animals. It will help us take our own compassionate lives and multiply them exponentially by reaching out more effectively and influencing other people. Mark's words will give us ideas and tools that will allow us not just to double our positive impact but to multiply our positive impact by thousands. The sky, as they say, is the limit.

Make no mistake: Activism is changing the world right now. In addition to the growing body of evidence that other animals are interesting individuals—just like the dogs, cats and human beings we know a little bit better—big changes on the health and environmental fronts are also taking place.

As just one example, in December 2006, the UN hammered home the point that eating meat is bad for the environment by releasing a 408-page analysis of the environmental impact of raising animals for food. The report concludes, "The livestock sector emerges as one of the top two or three most significant contributors to the most serious environmental problems, at every scale from local to global." Raising animals for food is the number-one source of greenhouse-gas emissions, releasing more gases into the atmosphere than all the world's planes, trains, trucks, and automobiles combined. Other studies have made the same point.

On the health front, we have pro-vegetarian books from respected researchers and physicians, including Drs. Dean Ornish, Caldwell Esselstyn, Neal Barnard, T. Colin Campbell, Andrew Weil, and many more. The American Dietetic Association, the American Medical Association (AMA), and even the US Department of Agriculture now conclude, based on scientific evidence, that vegetarian diets are healthier than diets that include meat. *Not one* respected physician or nutritional or medical association (not one) says that eating any meat or animal products, ever, is essential for good health. The dietary regime of the sole well-known pro-meat doctor, Robert Atkins, was denounced by the AMA as "dangerous." As if in tacit endorsement of the AMA's statement, Atkins keeled over dead at 260 pounds (118 kilograms). Some "diet."

As we work to make the world a kinder place, it helps to keep constantly in mind that we in the animal rights movement have science and rationality on our side. We have justice on our side, and we also have public opinion on our side. Our goal is simply to help people understand the ways in which their own actions may not be congruent with their ethics. Everyone opposes cruelty, but the general public has no idea how animals used for food, clothing, experimentation, and human entertainment suffer. Our task, then, is not to change people's ethics; it's simply to educate them about the reality of other animals' suffering as vigorously as we are able, using the tools provided by this book.

We can do it, and we can do it in our lifetimes. Not long ago—a mere historical blink of an eye—society believed things about government and human behavior that are diametrically opposed to what we believe with equal certainty today. Just 200 years ago, no one would have believed that we would abolish slavery in the developed world, give women the right to work and vote, abolish child labor, and establish largely democratic systems of governance. "But the Bible dictates the treatment of slaves, women, and children," they would have protested. "It is natural to treat other people this way; it's how we've always done it," they would have said—much as many people argue today about humans' relationship to other animals.

The animal rights movement is young, and we have new savvy and new tools. We also have a growing following among the world's youth. I have no doubt that in 100 years—if we are all as active as we can be and work as hard as we possibly can—human beings will look back on past generations' mistreatment of other animals with the same horror that we now reserve for historical injustices like slavery and other deeply immoral transgressions against human beings.

Our ethics concerning animals are changing, and this book will play an important role in accelerating that change. It is deeply empowering to know that by wearing T-shirts, putting bumper stickers on our cars, adding an auto-signature to our emails, or doing some other very small things, we can save lives. The more deeply that we're willing to devote ourselves, the more good we can do. This book gives us the tools and the motivation, and nothing is more important.

Dr. Martin Luther King taught us that "The arc of history is long, but it bends toward justice."

Thank you for being a part of the movement toward a more just world.

Bruce Friedrich
Vice President, International Grassroots Campaigns
People for the Ethical Treatment of Animals

Introduction to the 10th Anniversary Edition

To a considerable portion of the public, the words "animal activist" conjure an image of someone throwing red paint onto fur coats, or perhaps protesters yelling outside a meat shop. The reality, however, is much less dramatic. True, it's not uncommon to find flamboyant protests and theatrics. But most people who are engaged in animal advocacy don't fit into a stereotype. Many of them are quietly yet persistently writing letters to editors or handing out vegan literature. They're sharing animal rights documentaries and books with their family and friends. They're volunteering at animal shelters and sanctuaries. And they are asking their local restaurants and campus dining halls to carry more vegan options. The consequence of this activity is that not only are people finding animal advocates to be rational, compassionate individuals, but the public consciousness about animals is genuinely shifting.

Filmmaker Gabriela Cowperthwaite didn't even consider herself to be an activist, yet she was so moved by the plight of killer whales in captivity after taking her kids to SeaWorld that she produced and directed *Blackfish*, the 2013 documentary that galvanized the animal rights movement and forced the marine park company to make drastic changes, including an end to their killer whale shows.

Although SeaWorld executives dismissed *Blackfish* as propaganda, they did not anticipate the power of social media. Deeply moved by the film, which focuses on the captivity and misery of the orca Tilikum, campaigners and celebrities alike began discussing the practice of keeping animals in tiny tanks and using them for entertainment. Audience engagement spiked online when *Blackfish* was shown on CNN, with well-known stars publicly denouncing SeaWorld, and animal rights organizations fanning the flames with a barrage of posts to their followers. (Tilikum died in 2017, after 34 years in captivity.)

I, too, was caught off guard. In 2008, when *Striking at the Roots* was first published, I knew little about social media and its value as a resource for activists. Facebook had been launched four years earlier, and YouTube in 2005. Twitter arrived in 2006. Instagram was still three years away. As I compose this introduction, these are the four most-popular social networking sites in the world, in the order I listed them, and they have radically altered how activists agitate for animals. You can bet that a decade from now the social media landscape will be just as unpredictable as it is today. And who knows what emerging tactics and technology— such as virtual reality headsets that take viewers inside animal enterprises—will be standard tools in the activist's toolkit?

One thing this rapid growth taught me is that a new, revised edition of this book was needed. I continue to hear from activists from around the world who tell me how they use this book, and I want these advocates to have the best tools available. Indeed, the idea for this book came from my own experiences trying to find ways to get active for animals. I couldn't find a comprehensive resource that would teach me how to be active on my own, so I created one by interviewing more than 120 activists from around the world. It's really their voices and their ingredients for success you'll find in this book—though this edition includes the insights of 140 activists.

Among the questions I pondered when I began writing was, what is animal activism? To me, animal activism is compassion in action. Most people abhor cruelty to animals. The trouble is, they almost never see it, and when they do, they think it's the exception. Of course, when they do see it, most people are shocked. The job of the activist is to access people's innate compassion by showing them that the horrors of animal exploitation are everywhere. When they realize they are supporting abuse they actually oppose, people are inclined to re-examine their behavior, and that's a start.

Striking at the Roots: A Practical Guide to Animal Activism is intended for the person who agrees with the premise that animals are mistreated in our society, believes that the public has a moral obligation to speak out against this cruelty, and who wants to be directly involved in opposing animal exploitation in its many forms. By "striking at the roots," activists are challenging speciesism—the belief that some species (especially humans) are superior to others—and advocating ethical veganism. As such, this is a guide to the most pragmatic opportunities available for speaking and acting on behalf of animals. We will examine tried-and-true models of activism and explore some modern tactics that are gaining traction among advocates with a talent for using technology.

While revising this edition, a number of activists and organizations have been removed. Generally, this was because the group mentioned no longer exists or the suggestion offered by an activist has been replaced with more current advice.

Moreover, the changes that have occurred since the first edition of this book include employment. Bruce Friedrich, for example, left PETA, went to work for Farm Sanctuary, and has since cofounded his own nonprofit, the Good Food Institute, and Jon Camp left Vegan Outreach in 2016 to work for The Humane League. In most cases throughout this book, if someone is no longer at the same position they were in 2008, but the advice they offer is still relevant, I've kept it as is. Their job affiliation—assuming they were on staff with an animal rights group—is not as important as their experience.

Being an advocate for animals is not always a popular activity, but that should not dissuade you from doing what is right. Every social movement that had any impact—whether it's the abolition of slavery, the suffrage movement, civil rights, the child-protection movement, or reforms for farm workers—was initially backed by a person or a group thought to represent the minority opinion, and those opposed to them tried to provoke the fear that overturning the status quo would lead to chaos: the end of slavery would result in economic ruin, granting women the right to vote or banning child labor would weaken national strength, passing laws against child abuse would dissolve families, and so on. Animal rights activists are now hearing the same sort of nonsense from those who profit by abusing animals. According to animal exploiters, the only way to feed the world, cure diseases, or advance scientific knowledge is by using animals. To them, animals are not sentient individuals with their own interests, but commodities to be used for human profit, amusement, convenience, or taste.

The following pages will guide you through the fundamentals of grassroots activism. We will begin with what I and many other animal advocates consider one of the easiest models of activism, and then we'll progress, chapter by chapter, through the more involved tactics and meet some of the activists who find them successful. Appendices will cover milestones activists have won for animals, animal rights groups worldwide, recommended books, your civil rights, a cruelty-free shopping guide, suggested actions you can take today to help animals, and other relevant material.

What animals experience in slaughterhouses, factory farms, research labs, marine parks, zoos, fur farms, rodeos, and the like is unspeakable. Most people don't want to know. Yet we must speak about it. We must share the truth of what happens in these animal enterprises. Only when our friends, our family, and the public are awakened to the reality will hearts and minds be changed.

Let's get started.

Chapter 1

Animal Tracts: Leafleting

What you do makes a difference, and you have to decide what kind of difference you want to make.
Jane Goodall

Fernando Cuenca of Seattle tells a story that may be familiar to many readers. "When one of my closest friends found out I went vegan," he says, "he looked at me straight in the eye and said, 'Don't ever talk to me about that.' So I didn't." In fact, Fernando said nothing to him about his ethical lifestyle for more than a year, but one day his friend asked him why he no longer ate meat. "I gave him some literature I had at home and told him he could read it. When I saw him again the next week, he thanked me for sharing the information with him and quickly went vegan, then later he quit his job and went to work for an animal rights organization. His mom, his sister, and his nephew also went vegan. He married a vegan, and they are raising a vegan son."

Fernando's story illustrates the quiet power of animal rights literature, and other activists share his enthusiasm.

"Leafleting is my favorite type of outreach, honestly," says Elaine Vigneault, who estimates she's handed out tens of thousands of booklets and says she's enjoyed very positive interactions. "I've been told, 'Hey, I saw you here on campus last year, and I have been trying to go vegetarian ever since,' and 'This is great—more recipes to add to my collection,' and even 'Thank you for doing this; people need to know the truth.'"

Mo Constantine recalls the moment she and a friend were leafleting on the upper west side of Manhattan. A woman wordlessly took a leaflet and kept going, but she was so moved by the literature that she stopped mid-stride and quickly turned around. "When she came back, she seemed shocked by what she had read and asked if she could please have more [leaflets] to pass out to her friends and family, so we gave her a stack of them," says Mo.

Revolution in Print

By a happy coincidence, leafleting is both one of the easiest models of activism and one of the most effective. It is also about as old as the printing press, with religious leaders, monarchs, and elected officials from centuries ago publishing heated language designed to sway public opinion and stimulate change. It was a list of questions and propositions for debate written by Martin Luther and supposedly nailed to a church door in 1517, after all, that started the Reformation in Europe. In the 18th century, "pamphleteers" were the bloggers of their day, distributing hastily printed tracts that helped foment revolutions in France and the United States. Of this period, perhaps the best-known pamphlet is Thomas Paine's *Common Sense*, which took a decidedly radical stance on political issues and led to the US fighting for independence from Britain.

This tradition continues today as activists use leaflets to advocate for the liberation of millions of nonhuman animals. Leafleting has been a tremendous boon to the animal rights movement, since it does not have the budget to wage an advertising war with those industries that exploit animals; McDonald's currently spends about a billion dollars a year on ads, many times the combined budget of every animal protection group—and that's just one example.

Getting our message out there often means face-to-face meetings with the public. The good news is this personal interaction is tremendously successful at affecting the hearts and minds of people, and this can be much more effective than advertising or legislation; after all, an ad can be ignored and a law repealed, but once someone is enlightened about the harrowing abuses that occur every day within animal agriculture, biomedical research, circuses, puppy mills, and more, it is unlikely that a compassionate human being could forget what they've learned. You probably won't convince someone to give up eating meat or wearing leather overnight, but on the other hand, you just might. At the very least, you are planting seeds of change.

Leafleting is often described as a numbers game, working to influence as many people as possible. An average leafleter at a busy spot, such as a concert or packed festival, can pass out 150 to 200 leaflets in an hour. In that same amount of time, a superb leafleter can pass out as many as 500 leaflets—about one leaflet every eight seconds. If you commit with a friend to hand out leaflets for an hour each week, you will reach about 30,000 people a year with the message of compassion for animals.

While an activist can leaflet in support of any animal cause, from spreading the word about animal shelters to asking local residents not to visit the circus that's coming to town, leafleting in support of veganism is probably the most popular tactic. That makes sense, because every person you convince to adopt a vegan diet saves about 100 animals a year and doubles your impact as a vegan. Think about that: Each person you sway to embrace veganism is just as important to animals as your lifetime commitment to not consuming animal products.

"I consider the cost of the outreach effort in measuring its effectiveness," says activist Tammy Lee of Bay Area Vegetarians, a grassroots organization located near San Francisco. "Leafleting is a very inexpensive form of advocacy—all that is involved is the cost of literature, whereas other forms of activism do have fees associated, like tabling space, or running commercials, or having a program on TV. What's great is that leafleting can be a very spontaneous activity, and effective even with small increments of time."

Some of the best places to leaflet are busy street corners, healthy-living festivals, street fairs, outside concerts, and on public college campuses—especially if you are a student or can pass as one. Indeed, the learning atmosphere of a college, with students challenging old beliefs and embarking on new experiences, is ripe for positive, life-affirming changes. "At the moment, I don't think the animal protection movement is even reaching 10 percent of college students," says Erik Marcus, who uses his site Vegan.com to promote activism. "Given that leafleting requires no special background and is something that anyone can do, I can't think of a better starting point for new activists who want to make a difference."

One of the key points to remember when handing out vegan literature is to not complicate the issue by engaging in too much rhetoric about animal rights, if you can help it. Most people already oppose animal abuse, so when leafleting, it is a more efficient use of your time to focus on how animal factories and slaughterhouses abuse animals, rather than constructing an abstract argument about how animals' rights are being violated.

Rather than daydreaming about perfect and absolute solutions, activists need to push for the most rapid progress. Above all, we need to continually assess what differences we are making. Are we accomplishing all that we can to reduce the total universe of animal pain and suffering? Clearly, we have the tools. Do we have the will?
Henry Spira
Satya **magazine**, June 1996

Voices of Experience

I asked longtime leafleters Rachel Bjork, Jon Camp, Robin Helfritch, Gary Loewenthal, Jack Norris, and Kassy Ortega to offer their insights on various aspects of leafleting. Following is their advice, along with some of my own.

On starting out:

- "Without question, the first booklet is the most difficult to give out," says Jon. "Some find it best to make their leafleting debut with another person—either an experienced leafleter or someone starting out for their first time as well."
- "Leafleting in pairs, especially for the first few times, is always more fun," agrees Kassy. "The first time can be a little scary, but having a friend can help. First-time leafleters should seek out an experienced leafleter to show them the ropes."
- Some don't have that option, however, as they might not know of any others interested in doing this. "My suggestion for them is to just take the plunge and give out that first booklet," says Jon.

On a new leafleter's concerns:

- "There are a few main concerns with individuals considering leafleting," says Jon. "One is that they will be asked a bunch of questions and they will not know how to adequately respond to them. The good news for these people is that the vast majority of individuals will either take a booklet or say 'No thanks.' And for those who do wish to ask questions, we don't need to be encyclopedias. Our answers to most questions can be as simple as, 'Animals suffer unnecessarily in factory farms and slaughterhouses. We can reduce this suffering by opting for more vegetarian fare.'"

On negative responses and rude people:

- "Take a deep breath and *let it go*," says Rachel. "You are making a difference in the lives of animals by getting the information out there. Getting angry about other people's apathy won't make them change, but it will make you unhappy and more liable to burn out from activism. The animals need you, and happy vegans make much better activists than angry ones."

- "Some new leafleters worry that individuals are going to be rude," says Jon, "yet only a very tiny number of people are, and we can always just respond to those few by telling them that we're sorry that they don't agree with us but to have a nice day."

- "I've found that if faced with a rude person, it's best to not engage them and move on," says Robin. "It's a waste of precious time that you could be leafleting to and having conversations with other people who may be more open to your message."

- "I generally try to diffuse people's anger by affirming their feelings," says Jack. "If they're angry about something, I'll recognize their anger. Often, they have misinterpreted something that I believe and when I set the record straight, they feel less attacked and thus feel less like attacking. I try to find common ground—and usually the common ground is that people agree that unnecessary suffering is bad."

- "Some might make a nasty or belittling comment, but those who do are a very small minority," adds Jon. "Leafleting is a statistics game—if you give out X amount of booklets, you're most likely going to reach many receptive individuals and help animals significantly. I've found it best to not let nasty comments get to me, just smile it off, and focus on the good we can do. One thing that animal advocates have on our side is a sense of compassion and kindness. Responding to nasty comments with kindness presents us with a great opportunity to make people think, and oftentimes, individuals who make a rude comment at first will come up later and apologize and ask for a booklet."

Jenna Calabrese (pictured left) says being positive and polite are important elements of effective leafleting. Credit: Vegan Outreach

Additional leafleting tips:

- The more we look like our audience, the more approachable we will appear. For example, wearing a college T-shirt while leafleting at a university.
- Smile and make eye contact. Friendliness goes a long way.
- Avoid wearing dark sunglasses, which hide your eyes. (If you need to shade your eyes, wear a hat.)

- Lean in while presenting leaflets. This conveys an air of confidence and will increase the number of leaflets taken.
- "Take advantage of potentially like-minded people," says Rachel. "If someone walks by saying 'I'm a vegetarian,' don't let them go at that. Ask, 'Have you ever thought about taking the next step and ditching milk and eggs?' They may not have. If someone says they work in a shelter, you can say something like, 'I love animals too, that's why I'm vegan.'"
- Try to place the leaflet directly in front of the passing person's stomach so it's less effort for them to take the brochure from you if they choose to.
- "One thing I found out is that people are more likely to take a leaflet if it looks like you're taking a fresh one off the stack," says longtime activist Gary Loewenthal. "Also, I try to stand in a place that's level or a tiny bit higher than where the recipients are."
- Be extra polite. Use phrases like "thank you" or "have a great day" to those who take literature, which tells people we are well-meaning individuals concerned about the issue, rather than "animal rights extremists" whom the public is all too eager to dismiss.
- If you leaflet on private property and are asked to leave, do so immediately.

Animal advocacy is, in a certain sense, standing up to tell true life stories that are not being heard; true life stories that most people are ignoring. The first step in animal advocacy is to help people see things differently. Animals are somebody, not something.

Tom Regan
Satya **magazine**, August 2004

Other Leafleting

Veganism isn't the only topic your leafleting efforts can focus on. Fur, circuses, vivisection, rodeos, trophy hunting, and companion animal issues are just a few additional animal rights concerns about which activists can educate the public by handing out printed materials. Indeed, it's a good idea to not only have a stack of literature handy while protesting, but to have one or two people in your group actively distributing information about your campaign to passersby.

Tara Baxter handed out leaflets in front of Whole Foods Market locations during a campaign to stop them selling bunny meat, for instance. "I always smiled and said simply, 'Would you like to read more about why we are out here today?' Almost everyone took the leaflet. There were also people who just stood with signs. And some people were more comfortable with a megaphone. I have a sales background and a good handle on the issue at hand, so I always liked the leafleting part. I think shoppers wondered what the fuss was about but didn't necessarily want to stop and have their experience interrupted, so someone asking them if they'd like to know more gives them the choice rather than feeling talked at."

Likewise, at an Empty the Tanks demo protesting animal captivity, I stood on the sidewalk with scores of activists in front of a marine mammal park. Most of us held signs with slogans like, "This pool is a prison." When drivers paused to ask about our protest, we offered them a pamphlet on the cruelty of captivity and what they can do to help end it.

You might also leaflet in front of a movie theater to raise awareness about cruelty issues that may be related to a film being shown. When the movie *Kangaroo Jack* was released, for example, lauren Ornelas stood outside her local theater and distributed leaflets concerning the sportswear company Adidas and their use of kangaroo skins for soccer shoes, and she leafleted against fur outside a theater showing the live-action version of

101 Dalmatians, in which the villain wants to make a coat out of puppies.

In addition to handing out leaflets, you can post them on bulletin boards in public areas such as apartment buildings, companion-animal supply stores, laundry facilities, libraries, recreation centers, gyms, student unions, supermarkets, co-ops, and veterinary offices. Your leaflet will stand a better chance of staying in place if you can get permission before posting it in a public area. Often, vegan and vegetarian restaurants and health food stores will allow you to leave a small stack of pamphlets near the register or in a designated literature rack. Leaving a stack of leaflets is a great idea because everyone who picks one up is actually interested in the topic—you're reaching the lowest-hanging fruit, and with almost no time expenditure on your part. If you leave some there, be sure to check back frequently and restock the supply—the leaflets go fast!

Some activists like to set up a table in a public area with lots of foot traffic, such as outside a grocery store, and offer a variety of pamphlets on animal issues (permission is usually required for setting up a table, and a permit may be needed). This model of activism takes a little more time and effort, and we'll address it in Chapter 3.

Getting Started

Like any model of activism, leafleting takes a certain level of commitment. "It's important to take things slowly at first," says activist Jenna Calabrese. "Some great activism has been done in just 30 minutes on a campus. We want leafleters to be able to continue to do this for years to come, rather than burning out within the first few months because they tried to put in eight-hour days right off the bat."

Although it is a very easy tactic, walking around handing out booklets to passersby can sometimes feel routine, and you may encounter a few impolite people. As Jon Camp points out, it's important to remember how much good leafleting does for animals.

"In just a matter of an hour," he says, "we can oftentimes reach hundreds of individuals with this information." He adds that if even one individual stops eating animals, their compassionate decision equates to less animal suffering every year. "This is not including the number of people who will be more empathetic to farmed animal issues and such. In short, this is a highly effective and efficient use of time. So while it might be easy to dwell on the worst-case scenario, the likeliest of scenarios is always that leafleting will be relatively painless and that as a result, many more individuals will consider the animals' plight."

To emphasize his point, Jon likes to share his favorite example

---

A Few Words about a Few Words

A common sentiment within the animal rights movement is that "animals do not have a voice," often expressed as, "We are the voice of the voiceless." Yet cows moo, pigs squeal, elephants trumpet, badgers growl, dogs bark and howl, chickens cluck, cats meow and hiss, deer bellow, tigers and lions roar, mice and hamsters squeak, turkeys gobble, sheep and goats bleat, and I hope you live your entire life without ever hearing a rabbit scream. Those are but a few examples. Animals may not be heard—they may not always be able to act as agents of change on their behalf (though they frequently resist)—but they are certainly not voiceless. They are constantly communicating their fear and pain when they are being abused. So, let's be better allies for these animals and recognize when they are voicing their preferences; characterizing them as "voiceless" reinforces the false premise that animals are "mindless objects" without desires of their own.

of how powerful vegan leafleting can be. Some years ago, as a student at the University of Illinois, Matt Ball was distributing vegan literature at his campus when he was approached by two men: a dairy farmer and a fellow student named Joe Espinosa. Rather than berating the dairy farmer for exploiting animals, Matt used a very respectful tone and discussed the positive aspects of veganism. Joe was so impressed by Matt's civil approach that he got some information himself, went vegan, and has gone on to hand out more than half a million booklets (and counting) on behalf of farmed animals. "So," says Jon, "Matt's decision to get out that day and speak up for the animals has yielded some enormous benefits!"

Benjamin Loison (pictured left), founder of Bite Back in Belgium, leafleting to students at the University of Brussels. Credit: Bite Back

What to say while leafleting:
What you say as you leaflet will depend on what you're handing out, and every activist has their own style. For example, Robin likes to match what she says with where she's leafleting. "If I'm leafleting outside a circus or other places of animal exploitation, I might say, 'Would you like some information on helping

animals?' If I'm leafleting at an Earth Day event, I might change it to 'Would you like a free brochure on living sustainably?' If I'm leafleting in a general area, such as outside a subway, I might use something more basic, like 'Would you like some free information on compassionate living?'"

Other icebreakers include:

- "Would you like a brochure on ethical eating?"
- "Did you get one of these?"
- "Info on animal cruelty?"
- "Like some information on why we're out here today?"

Robin adds that being authentic is a must. "If you do get the opportunity to have a conversation with someone, being sincere and yourself is especially important, so that they feel like you're

---

Be a Broken Record

Sometimes, even answering an omnivore's direct question like, "Why are you a vegan?" can make them feel defensive—even hostile. Often they are only asking one question so they can move on to the next, which might involve protein or Hitler or a desert island or plants having feelings. In her book *Living Among Meat Eaters*, Carol Adams suggests that we cope with confrontational omnivores by knowing ahead of time how we'll answer questions about our veganism, and then become "a broken record," repeating the same response if the person keeps asking. "I learned what happens to animals, and I did not want to be a part of it," you might say. "Whatever the statement is," writes Carol, "simply repeat it over and over again, being sure not to interrupt. Don't sound haughty in repeating it; simply make it a statement of fact."

---

talking to them as a regular person, and not giving them a rehearsed sales pitch," she says. "I always remind myself that I was once a non-vegan, until I learned the information that propelled me into veganism. When I remember that, it's easier for me to see people as I formerly was: a person who didn't know this information until the day that I did, and to speak to them with kindness."

One Final Suggestion

Sometimes the public comes to you. For this reason, Bruce Friedrich keeps a few vegan leaflets by his front door. On Facebook, Bruce shared one of his encounters with a Jehovah's Witness who came to his house:

Knock on door. I answer.

JW: "Can I give you this brochure about a free convention at FedEx field next week? We'll be talking about salvation."

Me: "Absolutely. Thank you. Can I give you this booklet about eating a cruelty-free diet?"

JW: "Thank you." Flips it open. "Oh, Bill Clinton eats this way? Will it help me to lose weight?"

Me: "It might. Clinton lost more than 20 pounds when he did it. It's also compassionate to animals."

JW: "I love animals, and I need to lose weight. I will read this and definitely try it. Thank you!"

Me: "You're welcome. You won't be sorry."

You'll note that Bruce didn't promise that switching to a vegan diet would lead to weight loss; he emphasized the compassionate side of veganism.

Chapter 2

Animal Writes: Letters, Articles, & More

Injustice anywhere is a threat to justice everywhere.
Martin Luther King, Jr.

Like many people, activist Maren Souders loves to travel by train. But on a long-distance ride from Salem, Oregon, to San Diego, California, Maren was disappointed to discover that Amtrak had no vegan meals in their dining car. She'd even asked for vegan meals in advance, but once onboard, the attendant said they had no record of her request, so she made do with side salads and baked potatoes—not exactly the dining experience she was hoping for. "I was disappointed and frustrated," she says, "but I wanted to take that energy and turn it into something positive rather than simply stewing in it."

Maren launched a petition, surpassed her goal of 15,000 signatures, and sent the results to Amtrak. The company's silence told the activist she needed to up her game, so she asked the supporters of her petition to send constructive letters by email or post to key contacts at Amtrak, including Tom Hall, vice president of customer service. "And about six or seven people—all around the country, none of whom I knew personally—stepped up and did that," she says. "And amazingly, without knowing each other, they seemed to naturally stagger it so that Tom Hall would have received about one letter per day for a week." After that week, she heard from Mr. Hall, who told Maren that not only had he read the letters, but Amtrak would be adding vegan menu options to all their dining cars in their next menu-change cycle. He even asked for her input. "The petition alone wasn't enough, but the letters were invaluable," she says.

It's important to note here that it wasn't the number of letters that mattered—only about a half dozen people wrote—but the content. Moreover, they represented a cross-section of the country, which no doubt appealed to a company with a national ridership, and the letters were passionate yet polite. Indeed, courtesy is a key element of activism, and letters afford us the opportunity to choose our words carefully. "Although anger gives backbone to compassion, legitimate emotional responses to animal suffering and abuse must be transformed into a mature and compelling statement of the problem, why it matters, and what you want the recipient to do about it," says Karen Davis, who probably spends more time writing than any animal activist I know.

Many people consider writing an art—and a lost one at that. Long gone are the days when we regularly drafted letters to friends and family to stay in touch. We rely so much on technologies like text messaging and spell check that, left to our own devices, composing a complete sentence can be a daunting experience for some. But don't let this wonderful way to campaign for animals slip past you. Writing letters to editors, policymakers, and companies is not difficult, and this tactic can be very effective.

"Letter-writing appeals to advocates who may not feel comfortable with public speaking or making phone calls," says Anna West, senior director of public relations for The Humane Society of the United States. She adds that letters can have far-reaching effects. "When you send a letter to the editor of a newspaper or magazine, you are not only sending a message to those editors that animal protection is an important issue that readers want to see more coverage of, but if your letter is printed, you can potentially educate hundreds of thousands of people. Sending emails to TV news programs about their coverage of animals can prompt producers to do more news stories about animal protection issues."

"There is no one right way to write for animals," says

author and activist Jasmin Singer, who offers a wide variety of suggestions. "Commit to writing a letter to the editor once a week in response to an animal or food story. Start a food blog, but include the ethical imperative of veganism in each post, sandwiched between a recipe and some food banter. If you're a writer, pitch animal stories to magazines, and make sure to tailor the pitches to the beat of the publication; if it's a health publication, for example, pitch a story on the rise of veganism. If you have a way with words and you're looking to volunteer for an organization, offer your skills in creating content—for their website, e-newsletters, etc.; some of this kind of writing can be dry, but small organizations are frequently thirsty for the help. If you're a student, whenever possible, write your term papers about animal-related issues, tying them to the topic of your class using whichever inroad you can find."

In this chapter, we'll explore these suggestions—and more.

Letters to the Editor

Since the Letters page is one of the most highly read sections of newspapers and magazines, a letter to the editor is one of the best tools animal activists have for making our message heard. Letters to editors are easy to write, and every community has at least one newspaper. Sending letters to the editor is effective because they:

- Reach a very large audience
- Can be used to rebut information not accurately addressed in a news article or editorial
- Create an impression of widespread support or opposition to an issue
- Are widely read by community leaders and lawmakers to gauge public sentiment about current issues.

There are essentially two kinds of letters to the editor: "soapbox" letters in which the writer expresses an opinion but is not responding to something in the paper, and letters that are in direct response to an article, editorial, or another letter that recently appeared in the publication.

As president of United Poultry Concerns, a nonprofit haven for domestic fowl, Karen Davis has devoted her life to working toward a better future for chickens, turkeys, and ducks. The Virginia-based sanctuary is the focus of most of her waking hours, and yet this former English instructor understands the importance of effective communication, so she also writes brochures, white papers, articles, opinion pieces, letters to editors, and books such as *More Than a Meal: The Turkey in History, Myth, Ritual, and Reality*. Karen estimates she spends about 98 percent of her activist time and energy formulating ideas, strategies, and calls for action in the medium of words.

"A lot of time is spent researching the information needed to craft an effective piece of writing," she says. "For me, even a letter to the editor is a painstaking process in which every word, phrase, and sentence is carefully weighed for content, clarity, concision, rhythm, sound, and style. Form and content are inseparable parts of the process."

While not every activist spends as much time as Karen crafting a letter, it is important to think carefully about the message you want to convey and do so in as few words as possible, especially for a letter to the editor. Being knowledgeable about the subject helps, which is why Karen advises that activists learn all they can about the issues and arguments surrounding animal rights. "When you take time to learn about the issue, you can add relevant details to your writing that enrich it beyond mere venting and generalities. This makes your letter more interesting and increases your credibility."

She observes that our culture pays particular attention to "what science says." When writing letters or opinion pieces, Karen often quotes poultry scientists, and she cites these examples:

- "Bruce Webster of the University of Georgia says factory-farmed chickens are 'treated like bowling balls.'"
- "Bird specialist Lesley Rogers writes: 'I am convinced chickens are not animals that should be kept in mentally and socially deprived conditions. They are as complex as the cats and dogs we share our homes with.'"

Google Alerts

An easy way to find out if your letters have been printed is by setting up a Google Alert at www.google.com/alerts. Just enter your name in the search field, choose how often you'd like to receive the results, and then enter your email address. Links to letters signed by you and published in newspapers that are searchable on Google's news page will be emailed to you automatically.

Tips for Getting Your Letter to the Editor Published

- Be concise. Start with a strong introductory sentence and follow it up with short, clear facts. Focus on the most important issue rather than trying to cover everything. Most newspapers publish letters that are no more than 300 words.
- Always include your first and last name, mailing address, and daytime and evening phone numbers in case the newspaper or magazine wants to verify that you submitted the letter (though generally only the larger publications will contact you). Only your name and hometown will appear in print.
- Stay professional. Polite, proofread letters are far more

effective than personal attacks.

- Mention anything that makes you especially qualified to write on a topic. For example: "As a cancer survivor, I understand the importance of a diet that avoids animal flesh."

- Readers care about how an issue will affect them personally. Including information on the local economic or other impacts of an issue will draw readers' interest.

- It is just as important to respond to positive stories, like pro-vegan articles, as it is to respond to the negative ones, such as a pro-animal testing article. Generally, people writing letters to newspapers are more likely to voice complaints rather than give compliments, so complimentary letters may be valuable and more likely to be printed.

- Letters to editors sent via email arrive promptly and don't need to be re-typed. Type your text into a word processing program and then paste the letter into the body of the email—do not send attachments.

- Remember who your audience is. Direct letters to readers, rather than the newspaper or author of the piece you are responding to. Write your letter so that it makes sense to someone who did not see the piece. Avoid long sentences and big words that the average reader may not understand (unless you're writing to a scientific or technical publication).

Stay humble. None of us knows everything about living a compassionate life. Remember that you have much to learn, too, and invite others to teach you what they know just as you hope to teach what you know.

Zoe Weil

Satya **magazine**, June/July 2005

Tips for Effective Animal Rights Letters to Editors

- Tell readers something they might not know—such as that most hens are confined in battery cages or how dairy cows are treated to produce milk—and suggest ways readers can make a difference (stop buying eggs and dairy products).
- Include information about the issue(s); do not assume that readers already know. For example, rather than writing "Foie gras production is bad," be specific: "In order to create 'fatty livers,' foie gras producers subject ducks and geese to an invasive feeding technique that forces into their stomachs up to 30 percent of their body weight every day. That's like a 200-pound (91-kilogram) man being forced to swallow 60 pounds (27.3 kilograms) of food a day."
- Watch your language. Instead of referring to an animal with an inanimate pronoun ("that" or "it"), use "who," "she," or "he." Also, use "animal advocates" rather than "animal rights groups," "farmed animals" rather than "farm animals," and "painkiller" rather than "anesthesia." And avoid industry terms such as "cattle," "hog," and "livestock"; use "cow," "pig," and "farmed animals" instead.
- Use positive suggestions to help readers make a difference. For example, rather than simply writing "Boycott the circus," you can suggest events that don't use animals, such as Cirque du Soleil, or direct them to websites like circuses.com.
- Do not use overly dramatic language, which may turn some readers off. Let the facts speak for themselves.
- Use an affirmative voice. For example, rather than writing "Vegans are not unhealthy," write "A vegan diet can protect against certain cancers, and it's been linked to a lower risk of heart disease."
- Promote the friendly side of veganism and animal

advocacy, and refrain from insults, which will hurt your credibility and perpetuate a negative opinion of animal activists.

- Like humans, animals have a wide range of emotions; try to depict this in your letters and help people understand how similar animals are to us. For example, "Like all animals, pigs feel pain and fear..."

Gary Loewenthal has gotten countless letters to editors published over the years, and he offers some simple advice: "Keep it short and tight. Pick out a couple of points. Briefly refer to the piece to which you're responding. Read it out loud. You'll find weaknesses. Read it to someone else out loud. You'll find issues. Eventually, you feel it's 'good enough.' It won't be perfect. Connect with what's in people's hearts. Cite ironclad sources that you think will resonate, if applicable. End with an uplifting closer, which could be, or could include, a highly doable suggestion that readers can do."

Don't be discouraged if your letter is not printed. Every letter you submit educates the editorial board of newspapers and magazines worldwide and paves the way for future letters to be printed. Monica Ball estimates she writes about eight letters a week to editors. "Of course, only a small percentage are published," she says. "Nonetheless, I feel it's important to write the letters because it keeps topics alive in editors' minds and lets them know there is interest in animal rights and animal welfare issues. Also, even when my letters aren't published, they may play a role in getting someone else's letter on the same topic published. And any letter published represents potential for change and is a small victory for animals."

Letters to Legislators

Like newspaper editors, public officials get lots of letters. But unlike letters to editors, letters to a senator, assemblyperson,

Letter Goals

Karen Davis suggests that whether your letter is to an editor, a company president, or a politician, keep it to three short paragraphs: 1) statement of the problem, 2) why it matters, and 3) what you want the reader to do about it. "Your goal is to get the reader to know, care, and change," she says. Equally important is keeping the letter concise, making your point clearly and succinctly. It also helps to include a vivid image in the letter, such as "When chickens are being starved in their cages, they're so stressed that their combs turn blue," or "Many factory-farmed turkeys are so crippled they have to walk on their wings to reach food and water."

Member of Parliament, etc., could have an immediate and long-lasting impact on a piece of legislation to protect animals. Think of a letter (or email or phone call) to a politician as a vote: The more they receive in support of or opposition to one issue, the more interest the legislator is likely to pay to that issue. Public officials appreciate hearing about the concerns of their constituency, and they have the power to make changes. For example, Compassion in World Farming (CIWF) and the Royal Society for the Prevention of Cruelty to Animals organized a massive letter-writing campaign to Members of Parliament in 1991, which led to a ban on sow stalls (gestation crates) in the UK.

Most activists agree that when writing to an elected official, it's best to take the time to draft something either by hand or using the computer (or typewriter). Don't rely on a pre-printed piece created as part of a specific campaign. "Members of Parliament prefer a personally written letter over postcards that people just sign and post," says Joyce D'Silva of CIWF. "They take the issue more seriously. And a letter usually requires an answer—or they might not get the vote next time round!"

If you want to go the extra mile, especially if you know officials will be voting on an animal issue soon, send a follow-up email or call the legislator's office after sending your letter. Karen Davis recalls urging council members in San Diego to vote to ban foie gras. "A council meeting was scheduled for the next day," she says. "So I wrote and emailed a letter, which I then printed out on [United Poultry Concerns] letterhead and faxed to each council member. Then I called each council member to introduce myself and to alert them that I had emailed and faxed a letter about the upcoming meeting on foie gras. That way, I covered my bases and felt reassured that I'd done what I could under a time constraint, and I like making direct contact with people I'm trying to influence."

Karen will even send a letter by express mail or some other method requiring a signature, and she believes a letter on an organization's letterhead can carry a weight in the corporate or legislative domain that an email does not. "As in all things," she says, "the situation should dictate by what means you send your letter."

When we were debating gestation crates in the Westminster Parliament in 1991 at the time of the first Gulf War, several Parliament Members stood up and said, "I've had more letters from the people in my constituency on pigs than I have on the war!" This is because we wrote to everyone saying that if you only write one letter this year, write this one. And they did! It's the case of democracy actually working for once.

Joyce D'Silva
Satya **magazine**, June/July 2005

Of course, the average activist probably doesn't even have imprinted stationery, let alone work with an organization, and that's fine—grassroots activism does not require a big budget. A sincere letter to your elected official, addressing one piece of legislation or a single issue that concerns you, is a powerful method for speaking up for animals.

Here's a suggested format for a simple letter to a public official:

Paragraph 1: Introduce yourself in two or three sentences ("I am a college student and avid hiker who recently learned of a plan to shoot non-native deer in our state as a way to reduce their population....").

Paragraph 2: Develop your point and position on this issue ("You may not know that there are non-lethal ways to control wildlife population, including...").

Paragraph 3: Conclude your position on this issue and ask the legislator to support it ("Furthermore, the National Park Service has not demonstrated that the eradication of these beautiful animals is even necessary.... I hope you will agree that there is no reason to kill the deer and will do what you can to ensure that a more humane solution is found").

Sign-off: Ask for a reply ("Thank you for your time, and I look forward to your response").

Tips for Effective Letters to Legislators

- Include your name and address on both your letter and envelope.
- Deal with only one issue or one piece of legislation at a time.
- If you live within the boundaries served by your elected official, let them know you are a constituent.
- Remember that your legislator's job is to represent you. Be respectful, but don't be afraid to take a firm position.

- Avoid detailed personal stories.
- Handwritten letters seem to hold more sway with legislators. The action of writing a letter by hand tells the official you feel passionate about the issue.
- A typed letter, or one written on a computer, and signed in ink invokes a similar feeling of deep personal concern.
- Politicians know it is easy to create mail-merge documents, and form letters tell the recipient "I am not vested enough in this issue to write an original letter to you."
- Proofread your letter for grammar, spelling, and punctuation errors.
- Ask for a reply. Ending the letter with "I look forward to your response" will let them know that you want a reply. (But don't be surprised if the reply you receive looks like a form letter. The legislator may have received numerous letters on the same issue you contacted him/her about and may have a prepared response.)

Activist Tim I. Martin believes that letters to editors and legislators work in concert to achieve advances for animals. "Policymakers often have a vested interest in what readers write to editors," he says. "A series of letters to legislators, multiplied using the power of the press, can have more leverage in getting those leaders to open up their ears, if not their hearts and minds. Letters to the editor are a good example of leverage, in addition to getting a lot of exposure for a small effort."

"Needless to say," adds Karen, "not all policymakers are receptive and not all letter-writing campaigns succeed. Getting Congress to move on an animal protection bill, especially a farmed-animal protection bill, is very hard, even with many letters over a period of years. The thing about writing letters and making phone calls is that you improve your communication skills. You become more confident, and confidence is crucial to effective activism."

Phone It In!

When the matter is urgent—such as an issue legislators will be deciding on in a day or two—it's best to call your elected official right away. Don't feel nervous about calling; you'll only be speaking with one of the official's aides. Just identify yourself as a constituent and voice your opinion, such as asking them to support (or vote against) a specific bill.

Honorifics

Show respect for policymakers by using the proper form of address in your letters:

Members of Congress:
The Honorable John/Jane Doe

Member, Senate:
Dear Senator Doe

Member, House of Representatives:
Dear Congressman/woman Doe

Prime Ministers:
Dear Prime Minister Doe

Other officials and elected representatives:
Dear (Title) Doe

Opinion Pieces

Opinion pieces, known as "op-eds" because they generally run opposite a newspaper's editorial page, are another popular venue for advancing the interests of animals. Op-eds are written by a reader on a topic that is relevant to the newspaper's audience. Because op-eds run longer than letters and the paper prints only one or two in an issue (sometimes more on Sunday), getting one accepted and published is a little trickier. Since they are longer than letters to the editor, they offer an opportunity for a better-developed argument. Op-eds are formatted like an essay, with the writer taking a position and elaborating on that position in about 700 words—longer if the writer is well known or represents a well-known organization.

"To improve your chance of publication, it's important to know something about the publication you're submitting your piece to," says Karen. "I think it can also help to call the editorial page editor in advance and present your idea to him or her and make use of whatever advice they give, before submitting your piece. My writing has benefited enormously from editorial advice and editing."

Kathy Guillermo, a writer for PETA and author of countless op-eds, recommends emailing the editor a day or two after submitting a piece. "If you get no response to that," she says, "then call the editor and ask if the piece was received and if the editor had time to read it. Always be very polite and professional. Sometimes a phone call can make all the difference because it can prompt an editor to take a look at a piece that he or she hadn't noticed before." Kathy cautions writers not to get upset if their submission isn't printed. "Understand that editors have many issues to deal with and though we know that our issue is literally a matter of life and death, not everyone else sees it as urgent. And if your op-ed isn't chosen this time, your next piece may be, so it's not a good idea to burn any bridges by, say, accusing an editor of being biased or unreasonable."

For Karen, a rejected op-ed simply means she rewrites it a bit. "Over the years, I've published many guest columns about the plight—and delight—of chickens and turkeys. I've also written letters and op-eds that were turned down. Usually in such cases, I rework the piece and eventually submit it elsewhere with success. Also, it's good to establish a relationship with an editorial page editor. Not to ramble on and take up their valuable time, but a brief friendly phone call about your submission can increase your chance of being published, and you may be pleased to learn on occasion that the editorial page editor cares about animals and values your concerns."

Tips for Getting Your Op-Ed Published

- Let readers know your view by getting to the point. The first sentence should reveal what you intend to write about.
- Make your argument accessible to a general audience, not just an academic one.
- Bring a local connection to a national issue if possible.
- Know something about the paper you are sending your piece to and the type of pieces they print, and adjust accordingly.
- Check the newspaper's guidelines online for their rules regarding op-eds.
- Include a call to action—something that the readers can do, such as visiting a vegan website for more information or calling their legislator to voice concern.
- As always, use correct grammar, spelling, sentence construction, and other essentials of composition. Lack of attention to these details discredits the author.
- Editors receive fewer op-ed submissions right before major holidays and toward the end of summer, so these may be opportune times to get yours published.
- Unless you're submitting to a news service, your op-ed should be an exclusive to the publication—no simultaneous submissions. (Though by all means send it to another paper if the first editor declines it.)

Blogs

See Chapter 8.

Articles

There's something extremely rewarding about writing for a publication or website: having an idea for an article, pitching your idea to an editor, writing the piece, and then seeing it in print or online, knowing that thousands of people will be reading your words. It's especially gratifying to me when the piece I've contributed helps educate people about animal abuse or focuses on a solution to it, like veganism.

A good place to start is with the publications and sites you already enjoy. Which of these publish articles, media reviews, interviews, and profiles with a perspective on animal rights? Such outlets are always looking for contributors who can bring a fresh viewpoint to activism, animal issues, veganism, etc.

Journalist Aurelia d'Andrea has held virtually every role in the world of vegan publishing, from freelance writer and guidebook author to guest editor at UK Vegan Society magazine *The Vegan* and editorial director at *VegNews* magazine. Today, as the latter's travel and beauty editor, her job description includes fielding queries from writers eager for a byline in a nationally recognized vegan magazine. In an average week, however, she rejects far more pitches than she accepts. "It's most often a case of the writer not knowing the magazine and, more significantly, not knowing our audience," says Aurelia. "That's rule number one for freelancing pros. Understand who you're writing for."

If you want to catch an editor's eye, she says, show them that you understand the publication's readership and aren't just shooting pitches blindly into the publishing ether. In the end, it saves both writer and editor precious time and energy. "Bring that magic combination of solid writing skills and a well-informed story idea, and you're hired. Not just for this story, but for future assignments, too," says Aurelia. She adds that most editors prefer working with writers whom they know to be reliable and who consistently produce high-quality work. "Those are the writers who get added to the go-to pool and get first-pass options on plum assignments."

Once you land the gig, no matter how big or how small the assignment, it's critical to respect deadlines. "Magazines, newspapers, books, and even blogs and newsletters are published according to an editorial schedule, and when you miss your deadline, it affects the entire production cycle," says Aurelia. "Even if I love a writer's work, it's just too risky to hire them again if they don't meet that all-important deadline." A late or missing story hits vegan, animal rights, and other cause-oriented publications especially hard, since they are often nonprofit entities where staff carry larger workloads, work with smaller budgets, and generally lack resources that other publications have access to.

"Ultimately, as both writers and editors, we want to use our platforms to advocate for causes we believe in," says Aurelia. "Standing up for animals comes with responsibilities, and taking your job seriously is the first step toward using your position to make a positive difference in the world."

Activists with an interest in direct action might find a home for their writing in *Bite Back* magazine, which publishes articles and interviews about protests and campaigns around the world. "Our readers are activists," says editor Nick Atwood. "We like articles in which lessons learned are shared with other activists. Some of the most inspiring activism on behalf of animals is happening outside the US, but it's not often covered by English-language media. It's exciting when we get a chance to share these stories with a new audience."

Anyone familiar with the magazine will see that the articles are smart and easy to read. "*Bite Back* is not the best place for a scholarly, academic article about an animal rights issue," says Nick. "We often publish articles about the rescue of animals or acts of sabotage by the Animal Liberation Front." The magazine accepts articles written under pseudonyms or submitted anonymously. "Before submitting an article, become familiar with our magazine. Read a few back issues. Shorter articles have a better chance of making it into *Bite Back* magazine. Also, it's a bonus if you are able to provide unique photographs that we could use to illustrate the article. Consider teaming up with a photographer, especially if you are writing about a local campaign or protest." Like most editors, Nick recommends that writers create a piece with a publication in mind, rather than writing an article and then searching for a place to have it published.

But animal activism requires that we reach beyond our comfort zones, so also consider publications and websites outside the movement for story submissions. Shari Black Velvet, for example, started her eponymous magazine in 1994 to cover the UK's music scene. "*Black Velvet* is first and foremost a rock music magazine," she says. "However, as I believe in animal rights, I have included a couple of animal rights-based interviews over the years and a lot of the time try to mention if a musician is vegetarian, vegan, or a supporter of animal rights."

Because animal exploitation is literally everywhere, you will likely find an animal rights angle for any outlet, and the more mainstream it is the better. A health publication may be interested in a submission having to do with animal testing or a discussion about soy, while a travel magazine may publish your article on veggie vacations or a profile of a local animal sanctuary that's open to the public. The website Bustle.com focuses on news and issues related to women, so it offers a wide variety of possibilities. Founding editor Rachel Krantz says there is a growing audience for stories on veganism and animal rights, but whether it's Bustle or some other site or publication, she recommends identifying editors who write about animal rights issues or veganism and then referring to their piece in your pitch.

"Point out what you liked about it—something that makes it clear you actually read it and that's genuine. If you can mention something sincerely that you really appreciated, whether it be an article on the website or, better yet, one that they themselves wrote, that's going to be a great way to ingratiate yourself from the beginning and flatter them a little bit and make them more open to what you have to say next."

Other tips from Rachel:

- Pitch to publications and websites you already read. "I think a lot of times people tend to be too aspirational, thinking they're going to make their first pitch to the *New York Times*."
- Don't be afraid to write about your own experiences—and keep it sincere. "If you don't have access to healthy foods, I say write about that, so people can learn more about how this is connected to food deserts and privilege. It shouldn't only be people writing about why this is so great. It's okay for it to be complicated, because I think that resonates with people. They appreciate people talking about it honestly."
- If you're a person of color, you may have an advantage. "There's definitely not enough people of color in mainstream media talking about being vegan. As an editor, that's something I would totally want narratives of. Just talk from a personal perspective about how, for example, being Latina informs your concern for a more just food system."
- Don't be afraid to include other social justice issues. "The intersectional argument for veganism is so strong. It affects public health, the environment, workers' rights, human rights in general, and it's a feminist issue."
- Keep it newsworthy. "For example, if you're interested in writing about the ways in which moving to a plant-based diet is the best thing you can do, in terms of lifestyle

changes, to protect yourself against breast cancer, Breast Cancer Awareness Month would be a great peg. And you want to make sure that you're pitching to an editor saying, 'Breast Cancer Awareness Month is coming up and I have this article about ways a plant-based diet can help protect you against cancer.'"

- Connect the dots. "Even if you think you're writing a health article [in the example above], there's no way to talk about the health argument here without also talking about what happens to the animals. 'Why does it raise your cancer risk so much? Well, because you're ingesting a ton of pregnancy hormones because cows are kept pregnant their entire lives.' Health content in general does well, so look at how you can pitch based on these health awareness days or some big study that comes out."

- Do your homework. "Every place is going to have their own guidelines, so it's important to research what a website's preferences are and follow them exactly, because you don't want to disqualify yourself just because you're submitting to them based on the way you've done it for other places. Most sites will have that information available online."

- Fact check everything. "People are looking to discredit vegans, and if we misstate something, we're going to be discredited right away."

Guest Columns

Articles appearing in the editorial section of a newspaper or magazine written by someone not on the staff of the publication are typically called "guest columns." Usually between 400 and 800 words long, guest columns can be an important way to sway public opinion. Visit the publication's website or call them to find out what their guidelines are for submitting a guest column.

A typical guest column might:

- Offer a solution to a common concern or problem (perhaps an animal welfare issue that concerns your community)
- Use your expertise to discuss a recent animal-related trend or news event
- Share a personal experience that is likely to interest many other people.

If you're really feeling ambitious, meet with the editor of the newspaper and ask if you can provide a regular column, possibly once a month, or an occasional column on subjects of interest. There are so many topics that involve animals that you should have plenty of material for future columns. Avoid jargon or an academic tone in your column, and work to sound like yourself. Use a conversational tone.

A variation on the guest column is the guest post, which is published on a blog. Many major publications offer these, and it's best to submit a guest post to a blog you're familiar with. These are typically between 800 and 1,000 words and, like guest columns, should be original pieces that have not been published elsewhere.

Although every publication is different, most editors like to see a brief proposal first, not the full article. Let the editor know why you want to write a column or post for that publication or site—something that tells them you're familiar with the stories they cover. Include a potential headline in your pitch and two or three sentences explaining what the article is about. If you do not receive a reply within a week, follow up with the editor. If you still receive no reply or they decline your idea, pitch it to another publication!

If you find yourself able to contribute on a regular basis, be prepared to meet deadlines. Also, keep a journal and write down any ideas you have, even if they sound ridiculous—you never know what is going to inspire a terrific column.

Student Papers

Some students dread writing papers. But think of them as a great way to learn more about animal issues, educate others, and hone your advocacy skills. Persuasive papers (also called argument essays) and research papers are opportunities to express your own observations about animal exploitation and cruelty—and propose remedies for these issues. I'm not here to tell you how to write a student paper, but I can suggest a few things to keep in mind when considering animal rights for your topic. The goal of a persuasive essay/paper is to demonstrate knowledge and facts about a topic and to present this knowledge as an argument for a specific viewpoint. A research paper, on the other hand, is built on facts and will probably require, as the name suggests, more research.

Whatever the assignment, your instructor will set the parameters, and they will either let you come up with your own subject, allowing you to address the topic of animal rights directly, or will assign a specific theme, in which case you might need to think creatively. Because animal use is so pervasive in our society, though, you will probably have little trouble coming up with an angle. For her undergrad class Feminist Research Methods, for example, Jocelyn York wrote a persuasive paper arguing that feminism should also address animal issues. In law school, Jocelyn's partner Meg York wrote papers on animal topics. "I wrote about the Animal Enterprise Terrorism Act, ag-gag laws, and how methods of addressing interpersonal violence must expand to include consideration of companion animals," she says. "And when I was 14, I wrote about how dissection was wrong, and I was excused from biology class."

Remember that a paper filled with nothing more than emotion will not be very convincing (nor is it likely to earn you a very good grade). You will need to use facts from the most up-to-date and accurate sources you can find. And don't simply rely on animal rights organizations or websites to provide information—try to find original sources, such as surveys, well-documented books, and studies in peer-reviewed journals. Let the facts speak for themselves. Writing "Circuses are cruel," for instance, is not as persuasive as stating "According to a study from the University of Bristol, UK, wild animals used in circuses spend 91 to 99 percent of their lives confined to cages, wagons, or enclosures typically covering a quarter the area recommended for zoos." Doing your own research about animal exploitation is not only rewarding but an excellent education in animal rights.

Occasionally, a teacher will ask a student to read their paper to the class. Don't panic! This is a wonderful opportunity to share your views and educate your fellow students (as well as giving you some public speaking experience). Practice reading your essay out loud—first to yourself, and then to someone you trust to give you honest feedback.

Volunteer Your Skills

Finally, if you're truly inspired by the writing muse, consider using your skills to help a local animal organization with their written material. This could be a newsletter, email alert, press release, bylined op-ed (you "ghost write" the piece for someone else), brochure, fundraiser letter, website text—just about anything. A funny thing about nonprofits, though: they are not always prompt about responding to people who volunteer their time and services. If this happens to you, try not to take it personally. Charity organizations are notoriously understaffed, and animal groups are no exception. It's best to call and speak to someone rather than email them with your offer to help.

Good writing is indeed an art, and it has incredible power. Whether you can compose brief letters to editors or longer pieces for newspapers, magazines, an animal rights group, or even for school, your ability to translate your passion for compassion into words will raise awareness and help advance the interests of countless animals.

Chapter 3

Animal Talk: Tabling

I have publicly expressed opinions on such conditions in society which I considered to be so bad and unfortunate that silence would have made me feel guilty of complicity.

Albert Einstein

The first time Nathan Runkle visited an animal rights information table, set up inside a local shopping mall, he went away with more than a handful of pamphlets—he went away with a new lifestyle. The information was presented by an animal rights group in Ohio called People/Animals Network, he recalls, "and I took a bunch of literature. I remember reading it and feeling sick to my stomach. I had never heard of factory farming or vivisection or veal crates or battery cages. It was so clear to me then that this was the problem." Nathan promptly researched and presented a report on animal rights to his class and went vegetarian. He was 11 years old. Four years later he founded Mercy For Animals (MFA), one of the most highly regarded animal rights organizations in the world. Mercy For Animals is among a handful of groups actively investigating how animals are bred, raised, and killed for food, and Nathan has become a vocal thorn in the side of agribusiness. And to think it all began because some activists were tabling at the mall.

As Nathan will attest, tabling (also called "holding a stall" in some countries) is one of the most effective outreach activities you can do for animals; it will put your knowledge of animal exploitation and its remedies to good use.

To table or hold a stall is simply to arrange a selection of leaflets, fact sheets, stickers, and other printed information on a folding table, or something similar, for the public to take with them. Your table can also display a banner and even show a video—anything to attract people and help them understand the extent of animal abuse in our culture. You remain at the table, answering questions and selling related merchandise, if you have any. Most of the larger nonprofit animal rights groups will supply you with all the literature you need. Although it takes a little more time than handing out leaflets, tabling gives you the chance to share a lot more information, collect names for your database, and give people a glimpse of what animal activism is all about—not the skewed image they may have gleaned from negative press stories or a website devoted to animal exploitation.

"There are a lot of things I love about tabling," says Jennifer Mennuti, who tables for a variety of animal rights groups. "I think the best thing is that people who approach the table are usually interested in the topic and receptive to guidance and receiving resources. As opposed to leafleting, where the recipients often don't know what they're receiving and there isn't much opportunity for interacting. Tabling offers the opportunity to listen to people to best know how to help them."

Opportunities for tabling are as varied as the tables themselves: concerts, school events, health food stores, parks, festivals, and shopping centers are among the many places you can set up a table.

"Having a stand or table is always so beneficial whatever way you look at it," says John Carmody of Animal Rights Action Network Ireland. "We tend to organize national tabling events from time to time, and in this we have a fantastic display of literature which is always displayed in a really cool, eye-catching way. We love to use a banner to highlight the group's name, but what gets people going is a fantastic DVD that shows many exciting demos and events we have held. My number-one tip for having such a successful display is to be hugely warm, friendly, knowledgeable, and always understanding with the other person in order to ensure they don't feel alienated."

There are several ways that individual activists and their friends can get in on the tabling fun:

- You can volunteer with an organization that regularly tables at local venues. If you've never tabled before, this is a great way to get your feet wet. Search the Web for vegan groups in your area and ask them about upcoming events.
- Many animal advocacy groups such as Mercy For Animals, VegFund, and Viva! have everything you'll need to table in your neighborhood, including literature, displays, posters, and signage.
- Set up your own table. Ask a like-minded, outgoing friend to join you and the experience will be more enjoyable. One person can stand behind the table while the other mingles with the flow of foot traffic, handing out leaflets and directing people to your display.

Bruce Friedrich says some of the best locations in the US for setting up activist tables are government-owned property like metro stations, public streets, and even some convention centers. "They may try to tell you that you can't table there," he says, "but they have no right to." Even government-owned zoos have to let you pass out anti-zoo literature, right at the entrance, if you like. "They'll try to shunt you to the sidewalk," Bruce says, "but legally, they can't do that."

Getting Permission

Pick a good location for your table—one with plenty of foot traffic—and then investigate whether or not you'll need permission to table there. For example, if you'll be holding your stall at a concert or other performance, contact the show manager. To table on campus—either at your school or another one—check with the student activities office. If you want to table at a shopping center or outside a theater, you'll need permission from the manager, as this is private property. (UK-based Animal Aid says that in practice, many people do stalls in the street without getting permission, and as long as the police do not deem you to be causing an obstruction and they do not get any complaints from businesses near the stall, you may be okay.)

You may not need permission to table in a park or other public space, but it's best to first check with a city official, such as the local council or mayor's office, before setting up your stall. Be sure to ask:

- If you need a permit to table in your chosen location
- If there are rules regarding the sale of merchandise at your table (if there are restrictions, you can simply ask for a donation instead)
- If there are any restrictions on what you can display or make available to the public.

When asking for permission, let the person know you will bring all your own material and will take care to clean up afterward.

Mercy For Animals frequently tables at events. Note the sign-up sheet and the volunteer mingling with foot traffic. Credit: Mercy For Animals

Setting Up

Having an attractive table means more than just being organized or making sure your banner is straight. Though having quality leafleting and data sheets is always a good idea, Nathan Runkle stresses the importance of not having too many pieces of literature to choose from. "We like to keep the table relatively simple," he says. "When I first started doing activism and tabling, I thought, 'The more literature the better. We'll have a thousand brochures on everything!' Not only was it difficult to transport all those different brochures, but we found that usually when somebody comes up to the table they would only pick up one or two pieces of literature." So, Nathan and his team consolidated their materials into a 32-page vegan starter kit (labelled "vegetarian"), as well as an 8-page version and a quarterly magazine. "Basically, everything we want to get across in just a few important pieces of literature. We focus on what is going to be compelling—what we want people to walk away with."

Nathan suggests that a vegetarian or vegan starter kit, available from many of the larger animal rights groups, is a tabling must. "This gives people the tools and resources they

Holiday Tables

For extra impact, time your tabling effort to coincide with a holiday and then draw a connection between them. For example, you might table against veal on Mother's Day to protest the dairy industry's practice of taking calves from their mothers immediately after birth, while Easter season is a perfect time to address the horrors of egg production or to educate the public about the many ways rabbits are exploited—and urge parents to do their homework before giving their children bunnies as Easter gifts!

need to get started right away. And these things work," he adds. "I was recently at a check-cashing place wearing an MFA shirt, and one of the girls who worked there said she'd stopped by a table at an animal rights event last year, picked up one of the DVDs, and watched it and hasn't eaten meat since then. So, tabling really does have an impact."

Tabling Items

In addition to a table, you'll want to have:

- Driver's license or school ID
- Literature: vegan leaflets, stickers, data sheets, and other pamphlets
- Name and phone number of your contact person at the venue
- Banner, if you have one, to go along the front of your table
- Sign-up sheets and clipboard
- Tablecloth—large enough to cover anything stored beneath the table
- Shirt and buttons (badges) with an animal rights message
- Pens
- Clear sticky tape
- Rubber bands
- Paperweights (if tabling outside)
- Donation can
- TV with DVD or other screen for showing videos
- Lamp (if the venue is at night or indoors)
- Extension cord and power strip, or a power generator to run a TV
- Petition (if you'll be collecting signatures for an issue)
- Drinking water (non-plastic, reusable bottle, please—great for stickers!)
- Wheeled cart (trolley) large enough to haul your literature and other material—but small enough to fit under the

table (the collapsible kind works great for this).

> The last thing animal advocates should do is give people another reason to ignore animals. If we present ourselves as self-righteous and pure, and view everybody else in the world as impure, we are just going to turn people off. I can't even count the number of people who have been turned off to animal rights when we behave this way.
>
> **Tom Regan**
> *Satya* **magazine**, August 2004

Table Manners

Chances are people walking by your table are going to be sizing you up as well as your display, so look approachable. This means you're standing straight, you're not eating or smoking, and you're giving the impression that you're happy to be there: a smile goes a long way and will make people more relaxed. Also, if you're tabling outside, avoid wearing sunglasses, if possible—making eye contact is important! If you must shade your eyes, wear a hat.

Greet people who approach your table, and be attentive to those who express an interest in whatever issue your table is addressing. Ask visitors to add their name and email address to your sign-up sheet. If you're tabling for an organization, tell people who add their name that the group will be emailing them with news and alerts.

Don't feel dismayed if someone asks a question for which you don't know the answer. Be honest: tell them you don't know, but you will find out. Get the person's email address, or make a notation next to this information on the sign-up sheet if they've added their name. Later you can research the question and respond—even with links to online details.

Be patient and treat everyone with respect. Remember that you too were once unaware of the egregious abuses animals suffer. Learning how you made the connection between animal exploitation and your consumer behavior may help someone else see the relationship and make changes in their lifestyle as well.

"We often get the 'What's all this, then?' questions," says Roger Yates, who formed the Vegan Information Project to advocate for the philosophy of veganism in Ireland and regularly holds stalls in Dublin. "I think that vegans often make a mistake in opening by giving a list of things they won't—or worse, when they say 'can't'—eat. First, that emphasizes the dietary aspect of veganism, and second, it's a fairly negative initial engagement."

Roger advises activists to instead say things like, "We're here to promote the philosophy of veganism, which stands for justice, peace, and nonviolence," or "We are animal rights advocates, and that means that we believe that other animals are rights-bearers and what we do to them when we use them are rights violations." Both statements place the emphasis on the philosophy and not the diet, he says. "If people say something like, 'Ah, yes, but there's a lot of stuff you can't eat,' we say, 'No, we *could* eat that, but we *won't*'—again bringing things back to ethics."

Vegan Information Project covers their table in a weatherproof canopy, including sides and a back, creating what Roger calls a "gazebo stall" in an effort to move away from the simple folding tables most activists have used.

Although you'll want to keep an eye on your table at all times—tabling with a friend makes it easy to take bathroom breaks or see the rest of the event—you don't necessarily have to stand behind it. If he notices that people seem too intimidated to approach his table while he's there, Jack Norris of Vegan Outreach will stand somewhere else. "I just stand far enough away so that I can keep my eye on the table, but without it being obvious that I'm staffing it," he says. "Maybe 10 yards [about 9 meters] or so. And I return when someone starts to look around like they want to talk to someone."

Do not linger speaking with those who obviously stopped by your table to argue; it only wastes your time and makes other visitors to the table uncomfortable. Of course, people may not be inclined to give up habits like meat-eating right away— don't mistake such reluctance for belligerence. Someone who is genuinely interested may still disagree, and perhaps you'll say something to them, or they'll walk away with a pamphlet, that will engender more contemplation on the issue. But if someone is clearly being confrontational, you won't be helping the animals any by arguing your point. Remain calm, stay focused, and simply say you're sorry they feel that way. Sending them off with a smile and "Have a nice day" may feel less satisfying to you at that moment, but you're doing more good in the long run.

"Be enthusiastic, but listen," advises Gary Loewenthal. "And I mean really listen to others' objections. Don't use pat answers. Ask if your response was helpful. Let them talk. Relate to them, and they'll relate to you. If someone has a shirt that shows a sailboat, ask them not just about sailing—which is fine—but how one sails on a calm day; people enjoy talking about things they know. You'll be surprised how often they take literature from the table afterward. Thank people. Dress basically like they do. Don't exaggerate. Know your material. This requires constant studying; there really is no substitute. Don't be afraid to say 'I don't know.' Finish the conversation with a tip that you think they will think is doable, and say 'Thanks' or 'Good luck,' maybe even shake their hand. Be sincere. Make this real, not an act."

This is true for any activism, but being genuine is especially relevant to animal activism, because part of the challenge of changing hearts and minds is overcoming a person's cognitive dissonance—the discomfort they experience in simultaneously holding two conflicting thoughts, such as, "I don't want to contribute to animal suffering" and "I like eating animals." To overcome these contradictions and lessen the dissonance they feel, animal-eaters not only justify their actions in many ways ("Eating animals is natural," "I only eat 'humane' meat," etc.), but they often avoid taking in new information that doesn't fit with their pre-existing beliefs (what psychologists call the "confirmation bias"). Another way to look at cognitive dissonance is to think of it as the voice of a person's conscience. Deep down, most people understand that eating animals, for example, is unethical, but they are hindered by habit. The activist seeks to cut through that interference, and being sincere and compassionate as you converse with people who stop at your table, and really hearing them, is one of your best tools for achieving this.

The stall from Dublin-based Vegan Information Project includes literature, vegan food samples, and merchandise. Credit: Roger Yates

After Tabling

If you've been tabling at an event, concert, or other organized venue, thank everyone when it's time to go home: the venue owner, manager, staff members, and anyone else you dealt with, such as the band's tour manager. If your tabling was on behalf of an organization, they will have given you specific instructions, which will probably include returning the donation can, sign-up sheets, any petitions, and the table sign. They will also tell you how to send in any donations you have collected or funds from merchandise you may have sold on their behalf.

Talking With — Not At — Someone

Bruce Friedrich has a great technique for engaging strangers in conversation about animals. He wears a shirt reading "Ask Me Why I'm a Vegetarian." When someone asks, rather than launching into an angry diatribe about animal abuse, Bruce asks the other person, "Do you eat meat?" The person generally says, "Yes," to which Bruce responds, "Why?" The person will answer with something like, "Well, I like the taste." Bruce will then ask, "Well, what do you know about factory farming?" Thus, Bruce has initiated a respectful dialogue.

Sticky Tables

In researching this chapter on tabling, I discovered a book called *Made to Stick: Why Some Ideas Survive and Others Die* by Chip Heath and Dan Heath. This 2007 bestseller is touted as a must-read marketing text, but the principles behind it are as applicable to animal advocacy, and indeed can be applied to teaching, the work of spiritual leaders, environmental advocacy, or persuading volunteers to donate time to a nonprofit. Moreover, I believe *Made to Stick* can be used to emphasize the critical role of the individual animal activist.

The Heath brothers were inspired by Malcolm Gladwell's *The Tipping Point*, which refers to the idea that certain behaviors and ideas are "sticky" and catch on with society. But Chip and Dan take the idea a step further, and they give many examples of ideas that have become viral and part of our culture's collective consciousness. A professor at Stanford University, Chip had spent a decade asking why bad ideas sometimes win out in the social marketplace of ideas—and what idea could be worse than any of the inhumane ways we treat another species and damage our planet? He wondered why a false idea could displace a true one, and what made some ideas more viral than others. As an entry point into these topics, he dove into the realm of "naturally sticky" ideas such as urban legends and conspiracy theories.

What these ideas have in common, according to the Heaths, is a Simple, Unexpected, Concrete, Credible, Emotional Story. So, how can we apply this "SUCCES" strategy to animal activism and not only make our message resonate with the public, but make it *stick*? What can we say to someone while tabling that will have a lasting impact? Anyone who has tabled has encountered a broad mix of society. Some people go slack jawed in utter shock at the sight of an undercover video, while others politely (or maybe not so politely) walk away, preferring ignorance. How can we employ the Heaths' principles to increase our tabling (or other outreach) effectiveness, transforming it from the realm of mere rhetoric into an easily comprehensible message that will inspire the public to take action? The key to success is in the delivery: making the core message understandable and memorable in the way that retains essential elements.

The good news is that most tabling displays are doing a lot of these things right. Take a table exposing animal agriculture as an example. It has, for most people, an unexpected message: the suffering of animals raised and killed for food. It has simplicity: go vegan to not support animal abuse. It uses concrete images that vividly illustrate exploitation and cruelty. The person tabling appears credible, provided they have done their homework and maintains a respectful attitude. And what could be more emotional than the misery of innocents? I believe that whatever the animal rights issue, such displays are fairly typical, though I realize I am generalizing here—every activist or group presents their table or stall a little differently.

What I suspect could use more development among most animal outreach efforts, especially tabling, is the principle of stories, and it's in this area that the activist can truly shine. Effective stories can act as a catalyst for change, elevating an idea into something tangible. We certainly have no shortage of compelling stories. Among the most famous stories concern pigs, goats, and cows who have managed to flee an abattoir, transport truck, or auction yard, eluding their pursuers in a frantic bid for freedom. Animals like the two Tamworth pigs, who became international celebrities after escaping a UK slaughterhouse and spending a week evading recapture, attract media attention and teach the world that (surprise!) farmed animals do have feelings and don't want to die. These clever pigs, incidentally, named Butch and Sundance, were given a home for life at a sanctuary in Kent and even became the subject of a BBC movie, *The Tamworth Two*.

The key to using stories is keeping them simple and making sure they reflect our core message. Of the types of stories the Heath brothers discuss, I believe "springboard" stories—so called because they provide the listener with a leap in understanding and stimulate action—offer animal activists the most promising opportunity to change the public's perception and behavior toward animals. Springboard stories communicate ideas and accelerate change. As the Heaths put it, "In addition to creating buy-in, springboard stories mobilize people to act." True stories with happy endings work best, since people want to feel they can make a difference. A story about failure—though perhaps effective in other circumstances—is not going to empower somebody.

One of my favorite stories involves a rabbit named Emmeline. As I write this, Emmeline—a large, healthy, affectionate rabbit with a thick coat of spotless white fur and a mischievous personality—is living in comfort with two human guardians,

Heidi and Tara. But two years earlier, she was passing her days and nights in misery on a meat farm, crammed into a cage with other bunnies. Being confined to an outdoor cage or hutch can be devastating to an animal's health, especially a rabbit destined to end up on someone's plate, so it's not surprising that Emmeline and five of her cage-mates became sick—so sick that the owner of the business simply dumped the bunnies in a nearby park and left them to die. (Three of the six did just that.)

Seeing what were clearly domesticated rabbits in the park, an activist contacted Tara, and they assembled a rescue team. After three weeks of gaining the rabbits' trust with food, Tara and her fellow volunteers came to the park with a large mobile enclosure to "corral" the animals. "Emmeline put up the strongest fight," says Tara. "She wandered away from the rescue site, and a volunteer had to head her off and try to get her hopping back toward the corral. Eventually, the three bunnies were rescued and brought to SaveABunny, a local nonprofit, where they were found to have terrible mite infestations, sore hocks, painful bite wounds, and eye infections."

Emmeline also had a few mysterious-looking sores that were thought to be abscesses but turned out to be sites of parasitic botfly infestation. "Botfly infestation is deadly," says Tara. "The fly larvae can puncture the skin and release a terrible toxin, rendering the bunny in shock and then eventually dead." Extreme care had to be taken for the surgical removal of the larvae. After the surgery, Tara and Heidi brought Emmeline to their home to recover, with Tara spending the first night with her in a bathtub. "She took a very long time to wake up and eat," she says. Although Emmeline regained her health and could be adopted, for months back at SaveABunny she had no luck finding a loving home. Until Heidi and Tara realized how attached they had grown to Emmeline and adopted her.

"Because we had seen where she came from and were part of her actual rescue, we felt a special and immediate bond with her," says Tara. "I was very protective of her experience. When she came to live with us, we spoke softly around her, moved carefully, gave her space to retreat to, and did all we could to earn her trust. We tell her every day what a good friend she is and how grateful we are that she's with us. She's a beloved family member, and now we can't imagine life without her. We can only imagine what she's seen in her short time before we rescued her, and we are in awe of her will to survive. The way to honor her is to give her the best life possible and to respect her as an individual."

Oh, and one of the rescuers was a real estate broker who notified the city that the man who dumped the rabbits was operating a meat farm on land not zoned for agriculture use, and his business was shut down.

Another example I love comes from Vermont-based VINE Sanctuary, whose donor newsletter told the story of how one of their residents, a pig named Truffles, came to live with them. "We don't know how Truffles ended up on Craigslist as a piglet," the story begins, "but we do know that a kindly elder couple who ran an informal sanctuary welcomed her into their home 12 years ago. For nine years, she lived with them, first in the house and then in the barn, where she forged close friendships with roosters, hens, and guinea fowl." As the narrative unfolds, we learn that the couple is eventually unable to care for Truffles and her feathered friends, so VINE welcomes the pig and the birds into the sanctuary. But Truffles was elder herself and had never known another pig. VINE staff wondered how she would respond.

"Truffles soon became an integral member of our multispecies community. Her pen became a refuge within a refuge for the most vulnerable birds, such as a bow-legged turkey called Lily, who hung out with Truffles whenever she needed a break from her more rambunctious brothers." Although Truffles is a zealous guarder of food, the article explains, she willingly shared meals and treats with roosters and hens. "Sometimes, we worried that she wouldn't get enough of her own breakfast because so many hens were dipping their beaks into her bowl!"

She also charmed sanctuary staff and visitors and was especially fond of belly rubs. "Her enjoyment of life was infectious. It was impossible to see Truffles walking around the pasture wagging her tail without breaking into a smile."

Everyone at VINE understood that their time with Truffles could be short—she was already elderly when she arrived at the sanctuary. It turns out they had three years with this fun-loving pig. "Truffles arrived in July of 2014, and we said farewell to her this past Tuesday, due to kidney disease. She fell asleep with the taste of watermelon in her mouth, surrounded by both human and avian people who loved her."

I am not suggesting that telling compelling stories is the definitive strategy for approaching activism. But it may help the public embrace the concepts of the animal rights movement and think, genuinely and deeply, about the suffering of animals— and then make changes in their lifestyle. There is a tenet in the advertising business regarding the power of emotionally connecting with a message: People remember only one-third of what they read and one-half of what they hear, but they retain *100 percent* of what they feel. All I am proposing is that we implement a new tabling tactic—a fresh way of framing our argument that inspires a more emotional connection—and see if we increase our success. I observe progress in the movement, but making our position, and our tables, sticky would advance the interests of animals even more quickly.

Tips for Effective Tabling
Effective animal activism, whether it's tabling or any other model of outreach, educates the public about the atrocities animals suffer. Consistent exposure to the truth reinforces our message and helps consumers understand not only how serious the issue

A committed activist who won't burn out needs three important things: facts, confidence, and passion. When we know our subject and can articulate our issues, our confidence grows along with our credibility, and we become stronger and more effective every time we speak. But facts by themselves may not be persuasive. If we lack or fail to convey passion for our subject, we will have a hard time getting people's attention.

Karen Davis

Satya **magazine**, July/August 2001

of animal exploitation is, but their role in it. Such knowledge can be shocking to a compassionate person, who may never have considered how, for example, their "harmless cheese habit" directly impacts the lives of cows used for dairy, all of whom end up slaughtered when they are no longer deemed to be profitable commodities. Outreach is often a slow and multifaceted process, and tabling is just one of the many essential models for informing the public.

You have many opportunities to table, whether you volunteer for a nonprofit or set up a stall by yourself at a local event. Whatever the case, here are some final suggestions from activists with a lot of tabling experience.

"Be friendly," says pattrice jones, cofounder of VINE Sanctuary. "You don't have to smile if you don't feel like smiling, but you should be warm and welcoming." VINE volunteers table at many events, so pattrice created some guidelines for them to follow. When talking about veganism, she says, tablers should firmly walk the fine line between admitting that it can be difficult to be vegan and giving people an "out" for continuing to hurt animals. "We're not smug, preachy, or clueless vegans. We don't call ourselves 'cruelty free' or say that it's always 'easy' to be vegan. We do, in fact, understand the many factors that lead people to not yet be vegan. At the same time, we are representing the interests of nonhuman animals who have every right not to be the ones to pay the price for inequality among human beings. 'I statements' can be helpful: 'I hear what you're saying... I too worry about [whatever people-oriented problem they have raised]... at the same time, I'm not comfortable with [bring the conversation back to what is done to nonhuman animals]....'"

She also advises tablers not to let themselves get sucked into long conversations that keep them from attending to other visitors at the table. "Invite any crank or troll to visit us online to continue the conversation and then firmly turn your attention to the person who has walked up to the table. For sure, do not let someone stand in front of the table, blocking people from seeing it, while engaging you in some petty argument or asking you spurious questions about eating insects or whatever. Find some way to politely move them along. Or specifically ask them to step to the side, so that other people can approach the table." Remember: we're not trying to win arguments; we're trying to win hearts and minds.

Another group, United Poultry Concerns, has created some tabling do's and don'ts that we can all learn from.

Do:

1. *Familiarize yourself* with the subject at hand. READ the information you are passing on to the public. NEVER pass out information that you have not personally read. Be prepared to discuss many aspects of your topic including impacts on animals, humans and the environment. Be sure to emphasize positive lifestyle changes.
2. *Know your table* arrangement and the range of your information. Be ready to answer questions and provide additional references.

3. *Keep your table clean and well organized.* Keep all food and drinks off your table. If you need to eat or drink while tabling, take a break away from the table. If a visitor sets a food plate or coffee cup or other "stuff" on your table, kindly remove it and hand it back.

4. *Dress for success* and for your tabling environment. Look comfortable yet professional. Wear clean, neat vegan clothes. Look similar to your visitors. Wear your message, but *do not overdose* on animal rights leisurewear.

5. *Be proactive.* Smile and make eye contact when visitors pass by your table. Be friendly and ask them if they know about your cause or if they would like some information about your cause. Always offer a brochure to a visitor who seems hesitant. People who would otherwise walk away without taking anything will almost always take a brochure if you ask them nicely if they'd like one, and hand it to them.

Don't:

1. *Don't compromise* your cause. NEVER "apologize" for caring about an animal. Stay focused.

2. *Don't attempt to address unfamiliar issues.* Simply indicate that you are unfamiliar with the issue. Urge the visitor to contact your lead organization, or volunteer to get in touch with them at a later date.

3. *Don't be an obstacle to the public.* Never stand between a visitor and the exhibit table. Always maintain a positive and professional attitude. Never insult your visitor. Keep a cool and collected tone at all times.

4. *Don't spend time arguing with people who seek to distract you* from your cause. Determine when a discussion is getting out of hand or going nowhere, and politely excuse yourself. Do not digress to disputes about abortion, politics, and the like. The animals need 100 percent of your time when you

are tabling and leafleting for them.

5. *Don't spend time chatting with fellow activists* and missing opportunities to reach out to passersby. NEVER look or act bored. Save the gossip, gab, and dullness for *after* the event.

Remember: Be friendly, be focused, be informed, and be attentive. Oh—and have fun!

Chapter 4

Animal Attractions: Protests & Demonstrations

We must always take sides. Neutrality helps the oppressor, never the victim. Silence encourages the tormentor, never the tormented.
Elie Wiesel

The circus was coming to town, bringing animal acts with it, and SAFE—Save Animals From Exploitation, a national charity in New Zealand—was ready. They staged a protest action just outside the venue and gave it a Big Top theme, with an activist dressed as a ringmaster and other activists costumed as animals in a cage. Loud calliope music further made the protest appear to be affiliated with the circus, which is exactly what SAFE was hoping for.

"People attending the circus thought we were part of it," says Hans Kriek of SAFE, "and we handed out hundreds of orange balloons with anti-animal circus slogans on them to children about to enter the circus. It was impossible for the circus to stop this, as taking balloons from children would not go down well!" The result was an arena filled with orange balloons protesting animal exploitation—and there was nothing the circus could do about it.

Not every protest needs to be this complex. Indeed, a protest can be as simple as one person holding an anti-captivity banner outside a marine park, for instance. They can also involve hundreds of people marching and chanting slogans to voice their disapproval of, say, a planned factory farm in their community. Because protests are often the "face" of the animal rights movement—the form of activism the public seems to see the most—it is frequently the activist's first taste of campaigning.

Although some activists may regard protests and demonstrations as unrelated efforts—and they may have subtle or distinct differences—for the purposes of this chapter let's assume that protesting and demonstrating on behalf of animals are similar enough activities to be interchangeable. They both involve planning and a clear message to the public and the target (e.g., a research facility or store selling fur).

Anger is one of the major pitfalls of being an animal activist and it does burn you up inside. But what starts out as anger has to get transformed into something that's more positive for you and for what you're trying to do.

Mary Lou Randour

Satya **magazine**, July/August 2001

Bird's Eye View of a Protest

Among the many forms of animal cruelty that activists work to end is foie gras, which is the product of an invasive technique to force-feed ducks and geese until they have become so obese their livers are engorged with fat. The diseased livers of the slaughtered birds are considered a delicacy in many high-end restaurants, which have attracted protests from outraged activists who regard foie gras as a frivolous appetizer inseparable from the egregious abuse of animals.

In 2004, animal advocates sponsored a California bill that banned the production and sale of the extravagance in 2012. But a number of animal advocates from a grassroots group called Santa Clara County Activists for Animals (SCCAA) were not content to wait eight years for the law to take effect, and they decided to make a difference in their community. "We located all the restaurants in our area that sold foie gras," says lauren

Ornelas, who led SCCAA at the time, and then they researched each one to determine which business they would target. "One of the restaurants in San José was tied to a restaurant in San Francisco that was very pro-foie gras. We realized it didn't make sense to target a restaurant that had already dug their heels in and even had another location."

The group settled on Le Papillon, a popular upscale business located at a busy intersection in San José, and sent them a very polite letter explaining the cruelty that is involved in foie gras. They also included a video depicting abuses at the two foie gras facilities in the US: Sonoma Foie Gras in California and Hudson Valley Foie Gras in New York. "The reason we sent a letter is that if they were to respond in writing, we'd have proof that they received the letter and we could use whatever they wrote in defense of their position to be better prepared—we wanted to be able to answer that," says lauren, who is also the founder of the nonprofit Food Empowerment Project. "This is important for *any* campaign where you're targeting a business that can survive without whatever it is you're asking them to stop, whether it's a restaurant selling foie gras or a department store selling fur or an amusement park with live animals. It's important to try to get that letter response so you know how to counter their argument, but also so you can tell customers and the media that you already know what your target's argument is."

Another reason these letters are important, explains lauren, is that they can save activists a lot of time. "When I write these letters, I assume that the entity does not know as much as they should about the issue. You're doing that because you don't want them to feel challenged—you're giving them a way out. 'You're running a business. You probably have no idea what's involved in this. Here's some information.' They probably do know, but you still give them that out. Protesting is something you do toward the end of your campaign. You want to try to convince them before you have to step onto the sidewalk. If you can do that with a letter or a phone call, that's better, because you get what you want without having to expend much energy."

In this case, SCCAA received no response to their letter, even after months had gone by. "At this point we called the restaurant and spoke with the manager, who told us we needed to speak with the chef, who told us we had to speak with the manager. It went back and forth like this until they finally told us they weren't going to stop selling foie gras."

So, the group began the next phase of its campaign. "I had a serious talk with the SCCAA members and explained that if we protest, we have to commit to being out there until the restaurant stops selling foie gras. You don't want to ever seem weak. We want animal exploiters to see us as a force to be reckoned with, and if you're out there one weekend and not the next, then there's no consistency. When you set yourself up as a constant presence, they will take you more seriously. We agreed we would be out there every Saturday."

They began their weekly protest by holding signs. "Every campaign requires an escalation in tactics," says lauren, "so we had to figure out ways that we could escalate the strategy as a small organization. We started out with signs without any images and a flier we made ourselves with cute pictures of ducks that we handed out at the restaurant. We had four people out at the restaurant every Saturday night; we picked Saturday nights because that's their busiest night of the week." The group wasn't getting much response from management, so eventually SCCAA started holding signs that read "Honk if you love animals," so the diners inside would hear the support from passing cars, and they began using signs that depicted ducks being force-fed. "We were lucky to get banners from Animal Protection and Rescue League, which we used in front of the restaurant."

To add to the escalation, SCCAA would also occasionally stage a lunchtime protest during the week in addition to Saturday night. "The lunch customers were not the restaurant's regular crowd, and they were overwhelmingly supportive," says lauren. "They were shocked at the cruelty." The evening regulars, on the other hand, were not always kind. "They were hateful of us. Rude. But occasionally there would be someone who would come back out and say, 'We told them we were upset that they were serving foie gras.'"

lauren says she realized the campaign was working when the restaurant started to become aggressive. "They would try to block us from reaching their customers and stood in our way, so I knew we were starting to bother them." SCCAA members were so harassed that they would walk one another to their cars after each protest. "We wanted to make sure our people were safe."

At one point during the campaign, the restaurant's owner told lauren he would never remove foie gras from the menu. "They were digging in their heels," says lauren, "but we were resolved to be out there until the law banning foie gras went into effect."

After seven months, realizing the activists were not going away and were within their rights to demonstrate, Le Papillon relented and informed SCCAA they would no longer be selling foie gras.

Reflecting on the campaign's success, lauren points to several important factors that made victory possible. "In order to be effective, activists need to begin by doing their research," she says. "They need to make a decision to commit to it. Sometimes campaigns can take a long time, but you don't start something and not finish it. Consistency is really key." She adds that if she were doing the campaign today, social media would play a major role, both in organizing the demos and informing the public.

And lauren reminds activists that even a small group can win campaigns. "It's not always about numbers," she says. "Having a few activists in front of a store or restaurant can mean you reach more people, rather than having a huge group that people avoid. Don't be nervous. When you do these things, even if there's just a few of you, know your position well, and do your research in terms of your rights as well as the issue so that you have the confidence that you're speaking on behalf of justice and what's right. Don't ever waver on that. Don't ever let them feel you doubt your rights or the issue you're talking about."

Post script: California's 2012 foie gras ban was immediately challenged by foie gras producers, and it was overturned in 2015. In 2017, a federal appeals court reinstated the ban, though as this book goes to print, some chefs and companies that profit from foie gras have vowed to continue fighting it.

(L to R) Ryan Frazier, lauren Ornelas, and Carol Evans protest a restaurant selling foie gras. Credit: Santa Clara County Activists for Animals

Media Attention

There is no question that news coverage has played a critical role in countless protests, and it's one reason some animal rights groups use sensationalism to convey their message, often

---

Everyday Protesting

You can protest each time you shop for food and clothing: just go vegan. By removing your support of industries that profit from sales of meat, eggs, dairy, fur, leather, and other products made from animals, you are saving lives and protesting against the use of such products.

---

objectifying women in the process.

Wendy Suares of KOKH-TV in Oklahoma City is one of many reporters who acknowledges the power of sensational protest images. "In those cases," she says, "the issue isn't as controversial as the protesters' methods. Like getting nearly naked and locking themselves in a cage. That act alone guarantees publicity." But it wasn't sensationalism that motivated Wendy to report on a low-key demonstration when she was a journalist in Mississippi. Activists were gathered outside the University of Mississippi Medical Center to protest the cruel treatment of an eight-year-old rhesus macaque named Mowgli. Animal advocates from across the country had formed an alliance to save Mowgli from invasive experiments and certain death, and many of them stood quietly outside the center holding signs of protest. "That was a situation that not many people knew about," says Wendy, explaining her interest in the story. "It was something new and controversial—the idea that tax dollars were going to support such procedures on a monkey that had previously been abused. I also was interested because the effort behind the protest was coming from across the nation." (Although using tax dollars to fund animal abuse may be controversial, sadly, there's nothing new about it, and Wendy's remark highlights how much public education activists have yet to accomplish.)

"There are a number of factors that go into covering animal rights protests," says Henry Lee, a reporter with KTVU-TV news in California. "Are there multiple protesters? Is the protest affecting traffic or commerce? How unusual is the method of protest? Is there conflict between protesters and police or protesters and ordinary citizens or employees of targeted companies?" He says reporters also take the length of a protest into consideration. "Is it a drawn-out demonstration, with an activist perched somewhere and vowing not to budge, eat or stop doing some other action until his or her goals are met? Or is it a quickly fizzling event that could potentially be missed by late-arriving media—or wasn't properly announced to the press beforehand? Having said that, there is a balance that must be considered. Some media outlets might tire of any protracted protest where nothing new occurs. In the news business, reporters look for unusual, novel things to cover."

Activist Patty Mark says a good banner or protest sign can make all the difference. "I've never forgotten what a top journalist told me over a coffee in 1979: 'Patty, never look like Lucy's Lemonade Stand.' The more professional looking we present, the more professional our message appears." Patty also recommends that activists never exaggerate the message. "Always be honest to the public and the media," she says. "It is most important for the animals that we always maintain our credibility. Make sure the public and media always know they can trust what you say and that your facts are spot on. If you don't know something for sure, don't say it. The media will come back again to those groups and activists they know do their homework and present well."

Many activists make the mistake of just emailing a press release or media advisory and hoping the news media shows up. (A press release includes more information than a media advisory, which is used when you want to keep the specifics secret until the actual event.) Gary Smith, who runs an animal rights-focused PR company called Evolotus with his wife, Kezia Jauron, says press releases need to be factual and without propaganda. "Journalists will dismiss press releases that are unprofessional or nonstandard."

Another big mistake: Not responding to the media. "Believe it or not, the first thing I tell activists is to answer their phone when media calls," says Gary. "I can't tell you how many times I've read in a local story that media reached out to an organization or activist for comment but was unable to reach them. Also, when you promise a journalist that you will get them information, make good on that promise. Creating relationships with media only helps you and your organization down the line." If you don't have local media contacts, Gary suggests going to those media websites and finding email addresses for their newsrooms. "It's a good idea to send your release with a note at the top a few days ahead of your action or event and follow up the day prior." And don't overlook small neighborhood media outlets. Even a paper with a circulation of just 10,000 readers will reach 100 times more people than you're likely to reach simply passing out leaflets for an hour.

Activists can't be expected to be public relations professionals, so if the idea of sending a press release is intimidating—and your campaign can afford it—consider hiring someone who specializes in working with the media. Gary adds that doing PR badly can not only harm your own efforts, but it can make animal activists in general look bad. "It can erode the public support we so badly need in order to make change. It also makes my own job harder in the long run. So, we really caution people against the assumption that all publicity is good publicity. Frankly, sometimes media attention is neither necessary nor strategic, and again, this is where a professional can help you gain the wisdom to know the difference."

For their campaign to pressure Whole Foods Markets to stop selling bunny meat, Tara Baxter, Marcy Berman, and Margo DeMello invested US$1,000 to have a public relations service disseminate their press release to media outlets throughout the

United States. "Within 24 hours, we were seeing news stories from across the country about how upset people were that Whole Foods was selling bunny meat," says Tara. "It was even mentioned in Conan O'Brien's monologue! It was exactly what we needed in order to get the news out before our planned Day of Action, where hundreds of activists showed up at over 50 stores to protest." Tara acknowledges it was a lot of money to spend, but says it was worth it. "There is no way to reach that many markets as quickly and effectively. We had enough newsworthy information to include in the release, including an upcoming nationwide protest, so it was picked up thoroughly and the press snowballed from there."

(Tara adds that the campaign wasn't saying that one species deserved protection over another; they were trying to prevent Whole Foods from creating consumer demand, which would spread to other stores.)

Of course, media attention goes well beyond having a protest covered on TV or in a newspaper, large or small. Unfortunately, many of the animal rights stories you see in the news perpetuate the view of activists as extremists or even "terrorists." Getting events that counter this misconception covered by the press can both disabuse people's negative perception of animal activism and foster compassion for animals. One example I will explore in Chapter 11 concerns a coalition of activists who rescued 1,800 hens from a battery-cage farm; the ensuing media exposure raised public awareness and even caused people to forgo eggs ("I had no idea hens lived like that," was a common refrain).

"Media is crucial to the success of most campaigns," says Hans Kriek, whose roles at SAFE have included executive director, campaigns director, and media spokesperson. "Animal activists do not have the financial resources that industry has to get their message out. The media provides a free vehicle but is independent, so expect coverage to include both sides of the issue. Always prepare before you go to the media. Knowing your facts and being able to provide footage can often make a huge difference to get the story taken up by the media."

SAFE has positioned themselves as experts the media can turn to with questions about animal rights or welfare. "SAFE is well respected by the media, as we have provided them over the years with many stories that had real merit to them," says Hans. "We have helped the media by providing them information and footage and knowledgeable spokespeople. The media is always looking for new stories and rely on us to identify fresh animal welfare and rights stories. SAFE is often asked to provide expert opinion on a wide range of animal issues."

Small Can Be Big News

"I think one of the main misconceptions many activists have is that you need significant numbers in order to have a successful protest, but that simply isn't the case," says activist Andrew Butler. "One outstanding and extraordinary example of that is Brian Haw, whose nonstop, one-man protest outside the British Houses of Parliament, which began on the 2nd of June 2001, not only drew international attention to his anti-war message, it also won massive support for the right to protest in Britain. The government even enacted a new law to remove him from Parliament Square, but to no avail. He's still there—a constant reminder of what one person can do to educate others."

In February 2004, Andrew engaged in a similar, albeit shorter, protest. "I went to Stockholm to protest against an artist named Nathalia Edenmont, whose 'art' involved killing and then chopping off the heads, tails, and paws of mice, cats, and rabbits, arranging them on vases, her fingertips, or flowers, and then photographing them for exhibition," he explains. "I went to the gallery where the photographs were being shown, took out a sign reading 'Cruelty Is Not Art' and said I would remain there 24 hours a day until the exhibition was removed." After five snowy days and nights of Andrew speaking to everyone who came to the gallery and many people deciding not to patronize it, the exhibition was taken down. "I think you win support and sympathy simply by acting on what you hold to be morally right and true," he says.

Patty agrees that a small protest can have impact and stresses it can make for a great photograph, too: "For instance, we had an activist sit in a Perspex box filled with red seawater on the St. Kilda beach in January, which is summer in Australia, to protest Japanese whaling in Antarctica. It took only a few of us to get the box to the beach and fill it with water, but the photographic shot, which got a lot of media attention, was basically only *one woman activist* sitting in the red water holding a simple sign saying 'STOP WHALING' with the appropriate website on the sign. Photographers loved the image, and you don't even need an interview as long as the photo makes it in some papers with the website on the sign." Bruce Friedrich, meanwhile, recalls a protest when he was with PETA: "We had one person dressed as Satan at a poultry convention with a sign reading 'See You in Hell, Chicken Abusers.' It made the front page of the *Atlanta Journal-Constitution*."

Can a small demonstration be considered successful even if it garners no media attention? If it is benefiting animals, yes. Peter Milne, for example, turned a few slaughterhouse images into posters and asked his friend Mitchell Asquith to join him in regular low-key demonstrations on the streets of Brisbane, Australia. They couple this with some leafleting, and Peter reports they have changed a lot of hearts and minds. He recalls one woman who frequently walks by their display. "I offered her a leaflet," he says. "She looked at me and said, 'Since seeing these posters I don't eat meat anymore.'"

Getting Media

Tips for attracting positive media coverage:

- Make sure you have a good, newsworthy story first
- Produce interesting media releases
- Become skilled at assessing media and choosing your battles
- Have an excellent media spokesperson
- Master the art of snappy sound-bites and exciting visuals
- If on TV, make sure activists in the background are engaged in the protest, not talking among themselves

Tips for Effective Protesting

Before engaging in a protest, clearly understand the actions you want the organization or company you're targeting to take; contact them and see if your grievance can be settled without a demonstration. As we saw in Chapter 2, businesses that rely on good relations with the public may be inclined to resolve an issue without you even having to pick up a protest sign. If your opponent won't agree to end their abuse of animals, it's time to plan and carry out your protest. "Protests need to be part of a wider campaign; they are not the campaign in itself," says Hans. "Protests require a lot of energy, so it is best to do fewer protests but do them really well. Think of an angle that the media would be interested in and try to make it look colorful and engaging. Always keep protests peaceful—sometimes a little humor goes a long way!"

Before the protest:

- Pick a good day. If media is important to your effectiveness, avoid holding your protest when the media will likely be busy covering major stories, like elections or big events. Weekdays are ideal, and earlier in the week is generally better for media attention. If reaching the maximum number of people is your goal (such as at a restaurant that serves foie gras), go at a key time like Friday or Saturday night; the media will likely never come, but that's not important in this case.

- Pick a good location—one that is easily accessible to reporters and protesters. Consider traffic issues and work schedules.

- Once you've chosen a location, check with the local police or city hall to determine where private property stops and public property begins. You need to protest on public property, such as the public sidewalk along a city street or in a public park. (In the United States, the First Amendment protects your right to free speech, but if you cause an unnecessary disruption or you incite violence, you can reasonably expect trouble from police.)

- If appropriate, disseminate a well-written press release or media advisory (be sure to proofread it!) to the local newspapers and television news stations a day or two prior to the protest. This should briefly outline the issue you are protesting and state where and when (the exact time) the protest will be. Include the name, phone number, and email address of a contact (someone who can be reached during the event as well) in case the reporter has questions.

- The day of the event, issue a press release early in the morning that provides more information on the event and the reasons for it. Again, make sure to include a cell number of someone who will be accessible to media during the event. Print a few extra copies of the release, as well as any background material, that you can distribute to reporters who arrive.

- Ensure that all participants are familiar with the issue(s) you're protesting. Brief everyone on your goals and main message points. Passersby and the media may direct questions to any activist, so everyone must be prepared!
- If you expect more than 10 participants, prepare a few simple chants; these will help keep the energy high and communicate your message. Weigh the value of chanting against the value of passing out literature, since chanting may cause passersby to avoid your event.
- Assign all protesters a task. Ask someone to be in charge of taking photos, people to hold your banner (if you will have one), and ask another person to keep the chants going. Ask everyone else to hold posters and/or pass out leaflets.
- Designate one spokesperson to talk to the media. This person should be well educated on the issues, prepared with brief statements to the press, and able to stay on message. It's best if the media spokesperson doesn't have to worry about anything other than talking to and keeping track of the media. Use the media spokesperson's name as the contact on the press release or media advisory, and ensure everyone at the protest knows to tell the media to speak with the spokesperson; the media will usually honor that request.
- Dress conservatively: You want to appeal to the masses, so it's best if you look like them.
- Do not wear any clothing or accessories made from animals, such as leather shoes or belts, to the protest. If the public regards you as hypocritical about defending animals, it will detract from the message. In fact, avoid wearing vegan clothing that looks like leather, lest someone accuse you of being a hypocrite.
- To ensure everyone is present when the media arrives, ask all activists to be at the protest 15 minutes before you've

told the media that the protest will begin.

- Have a sign-up sheet ready so participants can add their names and contact information. Keep this paperwork hidden from view so protesters remain anonymous.

During the protest:

- Be polite at all times. Some people would love to stereotype animal rights activists as "radicals" so they can avoid the truth about animal exploitation. You're less likely to be typecast if the public perceives you as polite and rational.
- Concentrate on the protest. This should be about the animals; people can socialize after the event.
- Hold protest signs prominently.
- Double the chances that your signs will be seen by photographers and passersby: Make them two-sided.
- If you have enough people, chant!
- Never say, "We're disappointed by the low turnout" if fewer activists than you'd hoped for show up; instead, remain upbeat: "We're thrilled to be out here, and we're getting so much support from the public!"
- If you are leafleting, look friendly and approach people. Make it easy for them to take a leaflet; don't expect them to ask for your literature (see Chapter 1).
- Body language is important: Do not sit or lean.
- Activists should not be eating, smoking, or chatting on mobile phones.
- The main organizer should always be stepping back to confirm everything is in place.
- Take down the names of the reporters who show up, along with their media affiliation.
- Take photos, especially shots of the group with signs visible. Deliver a few of the best images (along with a brief description of each) to the media that didn't attend.

After the protest:

- Make sure everyone who attended the demonstration has added their name and phone number (or email address) to the sign-up sheet, and then contact them later to thank them — and ask if they'd be interested in protesting again.
- Create a press release that recaps the protest and disseminate it to the media outlets or reporters who did not attend. Don't merely cover the same points as the pre-protest press release — include news about what happened, how the public was educated, etc. You want the reporter to know there's a story here!
- Better yet, call the media that weren't able to attend and discuss the high points of the protest. They may run a story even if they weren't there.
- Follow up with reporters who showed interest in your protest, sending them any other information they may have requested.
- Write a letter to the editor. Pick up the newspaper the following day to see how your protest was covered; regardless, write a letter to the editor about the issue and thank the community for their support (even if they weren't very supportive).

Give Peas Some Chants

Chanting a slogan is a street protest tradition and is perhaps epitomized by the ubiquitous and defiant anti-Vietnam War mantra "Hell no, we won't go!" It was catchy, it rhymed, and it reflected the anger of the time. Animal rights protests can also be enlivened by memorable, rousing chants that convey the message of the protest in a few words and get activists energized. Often, one person leads the chant by calling out a question, and the rest of the group responds. An example is a standard chant adapted for our movement, which is, alas, rather boring: "What

When to Downsize

Prepare two banners for your protest—a large one (10 or more feet/3 meters long) and a small one (about 6 feet/1.8 meters long). Use the smaller banner if only three or four activists turn out for the protest—a few people holding a large banner emphasizes the low turnout.

SAFE spokesperson Shanti Ahluwalia talks to the media during a protest challenging New Zealand's government to change how authorities investigate animal cruelty complaints. Credit: Jo Moore / SAFE New Zealand

do we want? *Animal rights!* When do we want them? *NOW!"* Some additional chants I've come across include:

- "Animal abusers: Total losers!"
- "Make compassion the fashion! Don't buy fur!"
- (Outside a restaurant that serves lobster) "If you want to get some peace, make the lobster torture cease!"

- "Namibia, Namibia, you can't hide! Stop the seal pup genocide!"
- "1-2-3-4, open up the cage door! 5-6-7-8, rise up and liberate!"
- "KFC, what do you say? How many chickens have you killed today?"
- "Don't breed, don't buy, while shelter animals die!"
- "Fur trade! Death trade! Fur trade out!"
- "How do you sleep at night? For the animals we will fight!"
- And this succinct little chant directed at the president of US poultry company Perdue Farms: "Cluck You, Frank Perdue!"

Brainstorm chants with fellow activists until you all agree on a few you like. The time-honored "Two, four, six, eight..." motif is a good start, provided you can come up with something suitable that rhymes with "eight," such as "tolerate" or "eliminate." Example: "Two, four, six, eight, rabbits we will liberate!" But a chant that states the issue and includes a call to action is best: "Vivisection is our foe! Let those helpless beagles go!" Envision your chant ending up on radio or television. What message do you want the public to remember?

Active Voice

Whether your protest is modest or dramatic, large or small, keep things professional. Create posters with messages and images that reflect the chant—and check your spelling! "Be creative and think visually," says Patty. "Always step back from your action and look at what you see, because what you see is what the media photographers will film and photograph. Even take a photograph of a mock-up of your action to see how it looks in a photograph—you'll be surprised how easy it is to pick up things doing this. 'Oh, dear, I didn't notice that we couldn't see the main sign or that so-and-so was standing in front of the cow's head.' Study your protest as you would a rough draft of an article you are writing."

"I know a lot of people don't like protesting, but I think it's an important act and an important experience for people to have," says longtime activist Mia MacDonald. "Yes, you can feel powerless out there, but you can also feel powerful. I look back on some of the small protests where I and others at times might have felt awkward, self-conscious, ineffectual, cold, strange, or whatever, that I now think really had an impact or contributed to the reframing of animal issues and animal activism that's going on today. I don't think the increased media attention to the animal angle or to animal concerns and those promoting them is unrelated to all those protests in the 1980s and 1990s."

While it's true that some protests may require a lot of planning, the attention they garner can help put pressure on the organizations and companies you target—and animals will reap the benefits. "Whether it's getting a business to stop selling fur or the public to vote for an initiative to ban gestation crates, all protests should be focused on getting something done," advises Sarahjane Blum of GourmetCruelty.com. "It's paramount that you can give a concrete answer to anyone who asks 'What can I do?'"

Keep Your Cool

When protesting, it's inevitable you will encounter someone who's not as interested in learning about the animal rights cause as in arguing with you. Maybe your protest makes them feel guilty about eating meat or wearing fur. Maybe they're just having a bad day. Whatever the case, it's important that you not engage in an argument. Animal Liberation Victoria's Patty Mark puts it this way: "Even if someone in the public becomes aggressive or abusive, do not return their verbal violence with more anger or violence. Our main message is nonviolence and we must demonstrate this at all times, even though this does get hard to do! Animal activists are animal ambassadors, and during any actions, tabling, or protests we must do the best job we can to represent them in the strongest way possible. Depending on your age group there are various ways to approach this. If you are younger, think how you would want your parents to defend you: how you would want them to act, what you would want them to say. If you're older, think how you would want a lawyer to defend you in court. Are you prepared? Have you got your facts straight? Always speak with authority, conviction, and determination, but *always with respect* for whoever you are talking with. Try to develop a type of empathy even with those least willing to listen to your message."

Activist Dian Hardy recalls a particular protest at a livestock auction yard in the Bay Area that got out of hand. She organized the protest to draw attention to the lack of any legislation that protected animals at auctions, and activists from her group, Sonoma People for Animal Rights (SPAR), were joined by a large number of activists from another local animal rights group. "We blocked the entrance to the auction yard so all the trucks coming in from the nearby ranches and farms with their calves and spent dairy cows could not enter," she says. "SPAR had determined that this would be a nonviolent protest, but pretty soon these other activists were climbing all over the trucks, spitting on the windows and frightening people. I found myself detaching protesters from these trucks, telling them that we're trying to be nonviolent. It was all very heated. These things can take on a life of their own. This is why communication among activists beforehand is so important." (This protest eventually led to some legal protection for animals at auction yards in California.)

With the ubiquity of smartphones and other video-capable mobile devices, many activists now record protests (as do the target's security personnel). While an outraged antagonist will often argue that you have no right to photograph or videotape them, if you're not on private property, the law is likely on your side. In the US, anyone in public should have no expectation of privacy, and provided your camera is not hidden, you are protected by the First Amendment. (Clearly there are some exceptions, such as a public restroom.) If you persist in recording someone against their will, however, even if you're in the right, be prepared for the situation to escalate.

Although physical danger at protest sites is extremely rare, it does occur. Perhaps the most infamous example of this occurred in England in 1995, when Jill Phipps, a 31-year-old activist, was killed beneath the wheels of a truck delivering calves for the veal industry to Coventry Airport. Jill was among 33 activists who had gathered to protest the export of calves to Amsterdam. It was common practice at the time to ship these calves in small crates to be distributed to farms across Europe. Jill and some of the other protesters had broken through a police barricade to sit in the road or chain themselves to the trucks. Soon after Jill's death, Coventry Airport vowed to never allow veal to be exported from its runways.

Protest Comebacks

There's a difference between avoiding an argument at a protest and responding to someone's question. Sometimes, passersby have a genuine question, and other times, they are trying to be rude. Whatever the case, these can be turned into opportunities to educate the public—provided you handle it properly. While it's tempting to respond to a cheeky comment with something offensive, don't. You won't win anyone over—or help animals—with rudeness. As Roger Yates observes, "Even if the person you are talking to is making ridiculous claims and is not really listening, other people who might be there will be."

Here are a few common comments or questions and suggested replies.

Why don't you get a job?
Actually, I have a job, but I choose to spend my free time out here raising awareness about animal agriculture. Do you know, for example, that most meat, eggs, and dairy products come from animals who have been denied nearly all their natural instincts and are forced to live in filthy, windowless sheds?

If God didn't want us to eat meat, why did he make animals delicious?
Ha! Good one! Fortunately, there are a lot of delicious foods we can eat that don't require killing animals.

Eating animals is a personal choice!
I hear what you're saying. But the choice to eat animals assumes that your actions have no consequences, when in fact it affects the animals, who have no say in the matter. It also contributes to environmental destruction, which impacts not only the planet but the health of other people.

Animals eat each other, so why shouldn't we eat them?
Animals do a lot of things in nature we wouldn't want to copy, such as eating their young or having sex in public. I think you'd agree we don't want to take our behavior cues from animals. But more importantly, carnivorous animals have no choice—they *have* to kill to survive. Humans, on the other hand, can survive without eating animals, and we have many delicious and nutritious foods made from plants.

I like the taste of animals too much to not eat them!
I know what you mean; I used to eat meat at least once a day. In fact, I didn't stop eating animals because I didn't like the taste—I stopped because I didn't want to support animal cruelty. Fortunately, there are so many plant-based "meat" products available now. Have you tried veggie burgers? You'll never miss the taste of meat. Or you can cook with foods like tempeh, tofu,

and jackfruit, which absorb the same seasonings used to make meat taste good.

I only buy humane meat, milk, and eggs!
Thank you for caring about animals and making an effort with your purchases. Unfortunately, though, labels like "humane," "free range," "organic," and "cage free" are virtually meaningless and are used by the industry to make caring people like you feel good about what they consume. Also, even farmed animals raised "humanely" are sent to the same slaughterhouses used to kill other farmed animals. There is no "humane" death awaiting them. If you really want to eat humanely, please try a vegan diet. Here's a brochure about it.

Plants feel pain!
A lot of people believe that, but plants have no sensory organs or a central nervous system, which they would need to feel pain. They also have no way of moving away from the source of pain, so from an evolutionary point of view, the argument for plants feeling pain makes no sense. But if you really want to believe that plants feel pain, you should be aware that 70 percent of crops go to feed farmed animals, so if you truly care about plants, not eating animals is the best way to ensure their safety.

More animals are killed by harvesting crops than in slaughterhouses!
Unfortunately, some small animals, such as mice and rabbits, *are* killed during industrialized crop harvesting. No one knows exactly how many. But with some 70 billion land animals butchered for human consumption worldwide every year, slaughterhouses remain the number-one place for killing animals—unless you consider the commercial fishing industry, which kills as many as 3 trillion fishes a year. Something to keep in mind is that most of the crops in the world are grown to feed farmed animals, not humans, so if you are truly concerned about

the deaths of field animals, you should go vegan.

> To be successful, we need a thousand small organizations addressing hundreds of thousands of issues. Strength is to be found in diversity of approaches and a diversity of ideas, tactics, actions and philosophies.
>
> **Paul Watson**
> *Satya* **magazine**, March 2004

Protecting Yourself at Protests

Participation in a protest may be your right, but it exposes you to certain risks. In addition to the physical danger, you could be arrested, even if you are not doing anything illegal. Activist Anita Krajnc, for instance, was arrested after giving water to thirsty pigs bound for slaughter during a demonstration on public property in Toronto, and it took two years for the legal system to declare she was within her rights. But there are other perils as well.

Physical Security

Help ensure your safety by planning ahead. Attorney and activist Judith Mirkinson of the National Lawyers Guild suggests you tell someone who is not attending the protest, such as a good friend or a roommate, where you will be. "Always go to a protest with a buddy, if you can, or at least be with other people," she says. "Take a pen and write the number of your attorney on your forearm." If you don't have an attorney, you can use the number for the nearest National Lawyers Guild office, she says. "If you are on medication, leave a list of your medications with somebody." (If you think you could be arrested at the protest, bring three days' worth of essential medication in the original bottle.)

Although almost all animal rights protests are peaceful, passions sometimes prevail and the tension can escalate, especially in the presence of opponents. Judith advises activists to stay alert and assess the environment for threats. "Ask yourself, 'What could happen at this protest, and what would be the best way to protect myself?' Don't try things you're not really prepared to do." Avoid getting so caught up in the moment that you ignore your fellow demonstrators, especially those who might be more exposed to dangers. "For women, we really need to build together, and we really need to be looking out for the most vulnerable in our communities, like women of color and queer and trans women," Judith says.

"Wear sensible clothes," she adds. That means no high heels, no expensive jewelry, and, if there's a chance the protest could get rowdy, no short pants (in case you fall). Judith also suggests carrying a little cash—and a snack. Bringing water is a good idea, too, as well as a hat.

Finally, keep in your pocket a bandana soaked in water and sealed in a plastic bag. You probably will never need it, but if police deploy tear gas, you can cover your nose and mouth with the water-soaked cloth.

Digital Security

It is not uncommon for police or security at a protest location to photograph demonstrators or make a video recording of them, sometimes using facial-recognition software to identify them (more about this in Chapter 10). While these measures are generally out in the open, law enforcement may also hack into your cell phone, which contains a treasure trove of personal data: your contacts, photos, texts, geolocation, web browser history, a record of your recent calls, and much more. Police might also seize your phone to find evidence of a crime. For these reasons, *do not bring your cell phone with you to a protest.* If you need a phone, buy an inexpensive phone that does not contain any of your personal information and with a phone number that is not associated with any of your accounts or online activity. Paying for it with cash or a gift card, rather than your credit card, adds another layer of security.

If you have only one phone and must bring it, enable full-disk encryption, which ensures that the files across your entire device are encrypted. Encryption scrambles information on your phone, making it unreadable by computers or people without the code. Protests can sometimes be chaotic and unpredictable, and losing your phone is always a possibility. Be prepared for law enforcement to seize your device if you're arrested. It's also wise to turn off text preview on your phone so that if your phone is locked and you get a message, the message will not appear on the screen.

Regardless of the phone or other device you're using, information created using third-party applications is stored on their servers, which may or may not be encrypted. So, for example, if you're at a protest and you use your phone to post photos to social media, you could be putting yourself at risk by making that information potentially accessible to law enforcement. In fact, says Judith, if you're doing anything even remotely illegal, don't take pictures of your fellow protesters and then share them online. "Black Lives Matter protesters did a march over the Brooklyn Bridge, and then they all took pictures and posted them. The New York City police came and arrested them [for shutting down the bridge]."

If You're Stopped by Police or Arrested
Public defender and social justice attorney Bina Ahmad says that if a police officer stops you, first ask them if you're free to leave. If the officer says yes, then they have no reasonable suspicion to detain you. Just walk away. "If they say no, ask, 'Are you detaining me?'"

If the police officer says you are *not* free to go—and they begin interrogating you—you do not have to answer all their questions. Some US states have "stop and identify" statutes, and you're required to give your name if an officer asks you to identify yourself. Wherever you live, it's good preparation to do a little research before your first protest to understand the local laws concerning what you're required to say if stopped by police.

Remain calm, and make sure to keep your hands where police can see them. If the law requires it, identify yourself; otherwise, tell the officer, "I wish to remain silent." Say nothing else. "Don't offer anything to them," says Judith. If you converse with a police officer and then they arrest you, anything you said prior to your arrest could be used as evidence later. In Australia, Canada, New Zealand, the UK, the US, and many other nations, you have the right to remain silent. Sometimes this right is explicitly stated by police, and sometimes it's not.

"If you are arrested," says Bina, "try not to resist, including not flailing your arms when the cops are cuffing you. The only thing you should say to the cops when you are arrested is, 'I'm not talking without my lawyer,' whether or not they read you your rights, and stay silent."

Judith warns: "Don't think you can fool the police, like, 'I know what to say.' Forget it. *Remain silent.*" She recounts a trick police in the Bay Area played on protesters to get them to talk. "The police were all over the place, and they arrested these people. They beat the shit out of some of them, and then internal affairs [a division of law enforcement that investigates police misconduct] came to them and said, 'We know that the police were violent. Can you tell us everything that happened?' And all these people talked—'I saw this person doing this, and that person doing that'—which was very bad for all the cases involved. It's not only about incriminating yourself, it's about what you say that could add to their picture. Later they said, 'We knew we weren't supposed to talk to the police, but this was internal affairs!'"

You never have to consent to a search of yourself or your belongings. Police may "pat down" your clothing if they suspect you have a weapon, and may search you after an arrest. You should not physically resist, but you have the right to refuse consent for any further search. "If searched, do not consent to any searches of you or your bags," says Bina. "Say loudly, 'I do not consent to a search!' while still physically complying and not resisting." If you do explicitly consent, it can affect your case in court. She also advises activists who are arrested not to sign anything (except if you are being released and they ask you to sign a form promising to return to court later to face your charges), not to discuss your arrest on the jail or precinct phone with anyone other than a lawyer you are calling for legal advice (because all calls except to your attorney are recorded), and not to speak to anyone other than your lawyer about your case—not even cell mates.

Sometimes, federal agents make house calls, often just to harass activists after a protest. "If the FBI comes to your house without a warrant, you do not have to answer their questions," says Judith. "Say, 'Give me your card. I will have my lawyer call you.'"

If Your Rights Are Violated
Remember: the street is not the place to challenge police misconduct. Do not resist officers or threaten to file a complaint. As soon as you can, write down everything you remember, including officers' badge and patrol car numbers and the law enforcement agency the officers were from. Get contact information for witnesses. If you are injured, take photographs of your injuries. Once you have this information, you can file a written complaint with the agency's internal affairs division or civilian complaint board; in many cases, you can file a complaint (anonymously, if you wish) with the officers' department or a

public complaint board. You can also seek the assistance of an attorney.

"If you witness an arrest or police brutality, and feel safe doing so," says Bina, "you may legally videotape the cops—but do not get too close or interfere, and if they tell you to move or threaten you, consider moving and saving the video in case your phone or camera is destroyed."

See "Appendix C—Know Your Rights" for more information.

Chapter 5

Animal Friendly: Food as Outreach

Now at last I can look at you in peace; I don't eat you anymore.
Franz Kafka

Thirty faces in the room suddenly look appalled. People who just a moment ago were laughing or whispering to the person seated beside them as they snacked on tempeh pâté appetizers have soberly fixed their gaze upon Colleen Patrick-Goudreau as she lets the attendees of her vegan cooking class in on the dairy industry's dirty little secret: Cows must be continually impregnated to give milk and their offspring are taken away immediately after birth. As Colleen sets up a row of a dozen non-dairy milk options for everyone to sample, she explains that female calves go back into the dairy industry system, to spend their lives either pregnant or lactating, while the male calves are raised and slaughtered for their flesh; many of these babies are sold to the veal industry, where they will live in tiny crates for four to six months before they are killed. The revelation is horrible and yet so obvious—how else could it be?—and it creates a communal *Aha!* moment. A veil of ignorance is uneasily lifted from a meat-eater in the last row and the color drains from his cheeks. He had said he came to the class to learn to eat healthier; perhaps he realizes it's equally important to eat more compassionately.

Food is an incredibly powerful component in the activist's toolkit, which is one reason Colleen has not only taught cooking classes but has written cookbooks and created other media in which food plays the central role. She understands that whether she's demonstrating how to make delicious vegan meals or talking about veganism in her podcast or at a public appearance, our universal passion for cuisine is a key to shifting people's attitudes. "With information and power, they will not only make changes in their behavior, but they will experience transformation in their heart, as well," she says. "I really believe positive reinforcement is better than anything that makes people feel bad."

When we speak of animal cruelty, the overwhelming majority of abuse is suffered by animals who are bred, raised, and eventually slaughtered because humans happen to enjoy eating them. Not because we *need* to eat them, but because they taste good to us (cooked and seasoned, that is). This does not mean that other forms of exploitation are less deserving of the activist's attention—vivisection, circuses, blood sports, and the fur industry, to name a few, all rightly attract the time and effort of countless animal advocates. But because most of the Earth's human inhabitants directly contribute to the needless cruelty suffered by so many billions of nonhuman animals each year simply by eating them, changing the hearts and minds of these people yields extraordinary benefits.

"There is no love sincerer than the love of food," wrote playwright (and animal advocate) George Bernard Shaw, who recognized that food is imbued with special meaning in the psyche of humanity. We need it to nourish our bodies, but we also look to food as the centerpiece of many of our rituals and ceremonies. For most people in the United States, Thanksgiving is synonymous with turkey flesh, as it is for Canadians at Christmas. Lamb "chops" are practically a point of national pride on Australia Day, while in Jewish households around the world the Passover Seder is celebrated with six specific foods, each symbolically linked to the Jews' Exodus from ancient Egypt. The birthday of Robert Burns, the bard of Scotland, is honored with a haggis supper by Scots at home and abroad. Eating is such an important aspect of culture that many religions proscribe certain foods and encourage fasting or not eating meat as a way of demonstrating devotion. Food or sources of food can even be an object of worship: the Mayans had a corn deity, for example, and Hindus revere Annapurna as the goddess of food and cooking. (And let's not forget Catholicism and its many "feast" days for saints.) Sitting across a table from each other, eating becomes an intimate act. We cook to demonstrate love, and we find comfort in certain foods.

Because of food's unique position in our lives, it also offers the promise of transformation, for what we place in our bellies can be the bridge to a higher level of compassion—a rich appreciation of life itself. The simple act of sharing a delicious plant-based meal with someone more accustomed to dining on dead animals may not inspire them to immediately embrace a vegan lifestyle, but it removes another brick from the massive edifice built upon the myths of ethical eating: that vegan food is strange, that it is hard to prepare, and, perhaps the biggest false premise, that a meat-based diet is ideal for optimum health.

Most of us were raised eating animals. Moreover, the meat, egg, and dairy industries spend considerable time and money promoting this lifestyle to keep consumers hooked. The meat industry has been at it so long that even producers of non-meat foods have tried getting into the act. A certain maker of ketchup and tomato sauce in the US, for example, once advertised its products as "Made from the *meat* of the tomato." So it's little wonder that most people cling to the primacy of animal flesh. We are creatures of habit, and like any habit, a person's preference for eating animals and their secretions (eggs and dairy products)

Food Fact: The Animals

The average meat-eater is responsible for the abuse and death of about 100 animals each year.

can be changed — sometimes gradually, sometimes quickly — and activists can play a critical role in making it happen.

The Herbivore's Dilemma

If you're new to veganism or vegetarianism, or you've just never used your love of plant-based food in your activism, getting started can seem a bit daunting. How does one begin? You needn't be a professional chef or cooking instructor to have an impact on another person. "Feeding people delicious vegan food is one of the easiest, most pleasant, and most effective ways to win people over," says Katie Cantrell of Factory Farming Awareness Coalition. "Vegan meats like Gardein and Field Roast don't require much preparation and always shock people with their authentic taste and texture. Or you can make your favorite meal to share with friends, families, and neighbors. Even if it's a simple dish, it can still impress people that there are options for quick vegan meals that are healthy, hearty, and tasty."

One crucial point about using vegan food in your outreach: Make sure the food is *delicious*. "I will happily eat good vegan food, but I will never offer good vegan food to non-vegans," says Erik Marcus, author of *Vegan: The New Ethics of Eating*. "Any food I offer to non-vegans has to be *outstanding*, or I won't offer it at all. We don't want non-vegans to try vegan food and decide it's only okay. We need them to think this is some of the tastiest food they've ever eaten." This attitude applies not only to the food Erik offers, but to the food products he recommends, the cookbooks he suggests, and the restaurants he takes his friends to. "Vegan food is indeed a powerful outreach tool, and that's why I make sure that non-vegetarians get only the very best of what the vegan world has to offer."

Whether you're bringing in treats to the office or having friends over for dinner, if you're hoping to encourage someone's own vegan culinary adventures, don't start them off with anything too complicated or that contains hard-to-find ingredients. "The food must be easy to make, so that those eating might actually make it at home," advises activist Monica Engebretson. Chilled Avocado, Tomatillo, and Cucumber Soup with Saffron-Lime Ice may be impressive and delicious, but any recipe that calls for saffron threads and toasted Hungarian paprika is not for beginners, and we want to emphasize that veganism is easy! Fortunately, one outreach effort that Monica and countless other activists have found particularly successful, food sampling, uses some of the easiest vegan foods you can find.

Colleen Patrick-Goudreau gets ready to teach a cooking class.
Credit: Joyful Vegan

Food Sampling

The idea is pretty simple: Hand out free vegan food to the public. After all, who doesn't like free food? This kind of edible activism helps dispel the myth that vegan foods are boring or tasteless. For a food sampling event—sometimes called a food tasting or a feed-in—activists prepare some vegan versions of popular meat-based foods, such as veggie burgers and "chicken" nuggets, and pass out samples at a location with lots of foot traffic—like the front of a fast-food restaurant. Passersby get to try some tasty vegan treats, have a non-confrontational encounter with an animal activist, and, we hope, walk away feeling that veganism isn't that strange after all.

Sarah's Maple Apple Dip

Sarah Kramer shares this simple recipe that can be used as a fruit dip or fruit salad topping. "It's high in protein because of the tofu and is one of those recipes that will convert any unsuspecting non-vegan into admitting that tofu can be yummy!"

1 cup soft silken tofu, drained

½ tsp cinnamon

½ tsp vanilla extract

¼ cup maple syrup

Blend all ingredients in a blender or food processor. Serve chilled with fruit slices.

Feed-ins can be as basic as one person with a platter of Tofurky sausage samples and some vegan literature, or several activists going all out with a table, veggie dogs with condiments and a banner declaring "FREE Vegan Food!" And the food doesn't even have to be cooked. "I have found that even just serving something unusual to people, such as a new-to-them fruit or vegetable, can get a conversation going," says culinary educator Jill Nussinow. "Many people fail to realize that they might already be eating many foods that are naturally vegan."

Robin Helfritch agrees that food sampling is an ideal way to get people talking, which is why it's one of her favorite forms of activism. "Even incorporating some type of free vegan food samples into an activity like tabling brings people in for conversation," she says. Robin suggests also asking vegan food companies to include any coupons they might have along with the free samples, giving potential customers even more incentive to purchase their product.

"The challenge with feed-ins is that the food has to be *really* good," says Nora Kramer. "Plus, you need to present it in a way that looks good *and* tastes good at that moment, like on a street corner. Vegan chicken nuggets, for instance, taste really good, if they're hot, with ketchup or barbecue sauce. If they're cold? Um, not so good. You're really not helping any chickens. Same thing with giving out vegan ice cream—you've got to keep it cold. If it's a hot day, no one's going to want your melted, liquidy ice cream. So, keeping things hot or cold and presenting it in a way that will make people want to try it is important."

Nora also notes that it's important people know why you're there. "It needs to be clear that you're not representing Soy Delicious or whatever," she says. "You're there volunteering your time because you care about animals and you want people to know that vegan food tastes really good."

You can host a food sampling virtually anywhere: outside concerts, grocery stores (ask the manager if it's okay), festivals, sports events, and even on campus—just get permission from the school's office and set up where there is plenty of student foot traffic. While any day is a good day for a food sampling (weather permitting), you can match your feed-in with a holiday or "national" day. Mother's Day, for example, would be a great opportunity to offer samples of plant-based milks and hand out literature explaining how cows are separated from their babies, and National Hot Dog Day is an ideal time to give your community a taste of vegan hot dogs.

Most of us don't have the resources to buy food for samplings. Fortunately, getting food companies to donate their products is not that difficult, according to Caroline McAleese, who has organized annual food fairs and monthly vegan food and information stalls in busy shopping areas. "If you do not already have a contact name at the company," she says, "I would send an email to the general address, then follow it up with a phone call and keep the contact name for next time. I normally write quite a detailed email about the event or stall. I would include how many people you would expect to come, the venue, and the aim of the event." Caroline also recommends giving the company an incentive, such as adding their name to a flier for the event, offering to give out their leaflets at the event, and posting a link on your website to theirs. "It's good to feed back to the companies afterwards, to show them photos and let them know how it went."

Vegan advocates can also apply for a grant from VegFund at least two weeks prior to their event and, if approved, they will be reimbursed for the cost of their food. (Visit vegfund.org for more details.) Indeed, VegFund has made feed-ins even easier with a website full of suggestions and advice.

Some food sampling tips from VegFund:

- Keep it simple! Give out samples of items that are readily available in local grocery stores and that are easy to make. Even if you serve the tastiest vegan food in the world, if people can't find it in grocery stores, or if it's a complicated recipe, chances are no one's going to buy it or make it on their own.
- No more than three, please! Serve no more than three types of items. Focus on the quality of each sample, as opposed to serving a large variety.
- Teach, teach, teach! Serving vegan samples is a great way to expose people to meat and dairy alternatives. So, use this opportunity to dish out some vegan veggie meats, vegan cheeses, and non-dairy milks. People are often pleasantly surprised by how delicious (and healthy) these products are.

- If you don't have a way to keep vegan cheeses hot and melted, we strongly advise against serving them. Cold vegan cheese normally isn't very appealing.
- If you serve vegan milks, you'll want to make sure they are chilled. One method is to keep the containers in a bowl of ice or in an ice chest.
- Another suggestion: wearing aprons and gloves (especially for those handing out food) will make your feed-in look more professional.

Menu Idea from VegFund: Vegan Veggie Meats on Toothpicks

Ingredients:
- Toothpicks
- Vegan veggie meat (for example, Gardein, Field Roast, Tofurky, or firm marinated tofu)
- Cherry tomatoes or olives (depending on which goes better with your chosen veggie meat)
- Mustard/Vegenaise for dipping

Instructions:
Cut veggie meat into bite-sized pieces. With the toothpick, skewer one piece of veggie meat and one cherry tomato or olive. Repeat until the desired number of samples are created. Make the mustard/Vegenaise available for dipping.

Dawn Moncrief of A Well-Fed World is another advocate of food sampling. "It's friendly, so it's appealing to most activists, especially those who don't like to protest," she says. "It gives us the opportunity to not just say something or someone is 'bad,' but to provide a superior alternative, saying 'Try this—it's better.' Food draws people in and gives activists an excuse to approach others. It's very easy to approach people when you have something they'll probably be interested in and actually like. Of course, then we can talk with them and provide veg literature." Dawn also likes feed-ins because they promote makers of vegan food products. "If we create more demand and make the veg food profitable, we'll have more to choose from and more stores offering them."

Vegan Potlucks

Potlucks are a fun and informal way to show the uninitiated that there is nothing "weird" about vegan food—that it can be delicious and satisfying. The idea here is that you organize a potluck with some of your friends, then invite a few omnivores, asking them to bring nothing more than their appetites and a desire to try vegan foods. If a guest insists on bringing *something*, you can suggest vegan drinks or ice cream they can provide.

In the meantime, discuss with your friends where the potluck will take place (don't forget that many apartment complexes have a recreational space with a kitchen that residents can often use for free) and who will prepare what—appetizers, main dishes, side dishes, and desserts. Make sure you address any dietary restrictions your friends or guests might have. If you know that any of the non-vegans have a special fondness for certain cuisines, you can tailor the food accordingly.

"Make it regular and start incorporating other things into it—maybe do screenings of vegan-leaning films to keep the conversation going," says Brenda Sanders, who hosts regular potlucks and other vegan food events in Baltimore. "Once you have some momentum, I would say move to the next step, which is finding a space to start holding these events, because the more people engage, the more people attend, it will probably outgrow your house or apartment. So, churches, community centers, and libraries are great places to start expanding. Churches and community centers already have a population you can engage with. Tell them, 'Come on out, have some delicious plant-based food you've never tasted before, see this film screening' — or whatever. Grow it from there. Find out what people are interested in."

Brenda also recommends keeping it fun. "You know, the world is serious enough," she says. "The world is hard enough. The reason so many come to our events is that we make sure people are going to have a good time. They're going to leave glowing. I know that food justice is serious business, I know that animal exploitation is serious business, but that doesn't mean that when you engage people, you have to come with the gloom and doom."

There's one ingredient that Brenda would suggest for a vegan potluck or any food event: macaroni and cheese. "People are super interested in mac and cheese," she says. She's been organizing an annual vegan mac and cheese cooking contest, and the response from the public has been overwhelming. Just how do people respond to delicious vegan mac and cheese? "Disbelief," Brenda says. "Amazement. Extreme surprise. Because they couldn't even fathom cheese without dairy. Even if you try to explain it to them—'It's cashews!'—they're like, 'I don't... I can't... this doesn't sound like it's going to be a good idea.' When they have it, they are always, always, always pleasantly surprised. We even had the mayor come out to the event last year, and she could not stop raving about the vegan cheese."

Food Fairs

Popular in the UK and catching on with activists elsewhere, food fairs (or "fayres") are a bit more elaborate than feed-ins or potlucks, but the opportunities for vegan and animal advocacy are exponentially greater. Food fairs create a social context for your activism, attracting many attendees while giving you the chance to make a presentation to promote compassionate living.

VegNews Mac and Cheese Recipe

Some would argue that macaroni and cheese is the ultimate comfort food. And given how attached many omnivores are to cheese, this dish is a delicious way to educate people about the joys of eating vegan.

What you need:

4 quarts water

1 tablespoon + 2 teaspoons salt, divided

8 ounces macaroni or rigatoni

4 slices of bread, torn into large pieces

2 tablespoons + ⅓ cup vegan butter, divided

2 tablespoons shallots, peeled and chopped

1 cup red or yellow potatoes, peeled and chopped

¼ cup carrots, peeled and chopped

⅓ cup onion, peeled and chopped

1 cup water

¼ cup raw cashews

2 teaspoons sea salt

¼ teaspoon garlic, minced

¼ teaspoon Dijon mustard

1 tablespoon lemon juice

¼ teaspoon black pepper

⅛ teaspoon cayenne

¼ teaspoon paprika

Instructions:

1. In a large pot, bring the water and 1 tablespoon salt to a boil. Add pasta and cook until al dente. In a colander, drain pasta and rinse with cold water. Set aside.

2. In a food processor, make breadcrumbs by pulverizing the bread and 2 tablespoons vegan butter to a medium-

fine texture. Set aside.

3. Preheat oven to 350 degrees F (180 degrees C). In a saucepan, add shallots, potatoes, carrots, onion, and water and bring to a boil. Cover the pan and simmer for 15 minutes or until vegetables are very soft.

4. In a blender, process the cashews, salt, garlic, ⅓ cup vegan butter, mustard, lemon juice, black pepper, and cayenne. Add softened vegetables and cooking water to the blender and process until perfectly smooth.

5. In a large bowl, toss the cooked pasta and blended cheese sauce until completely coated. Spread mixture into a 9 x 12-inch casserole dish, sprinkle with prepared breadcrumbs, and dust with paprika. Bake for 30 minutes or until the cheese sauce is bubbling and the top has turned golden brown.

Serves 6

(Courtesy of *VegNews*)

Not only do these events give attendees a better idea of what animal activists are like, but they showcase the amazing variety of plant-based food options and demonstrate that vegans do not live off iceberg lettuce.

"All the food fairs I have been involved in have attracted lots of meat-eaters, the majority of which have said they will reduce their meat consumption or go veggie or vegan," says activist Kelly Slade, co-owner of Vegan Tuck Box, an England-based subscription service that helps make vegan snacks more available. "All the feedback is positive and people always comment about how good the food tasted and how they were surprised at how much variety there is."

The more readily available vegan food is, the more the word vegan is out there and associated with something positive and yummy, the easier the transition will be. That is where culinary activism comes into play!

Isa Chandra Moskowitz

Satya **magazine**, June/July 2007

Tips for a Successful Food Fair

Location:

- Try to rent a large room in a busy area, such as a street with lots of shopping. This will increase the attendance.
- A room with a kitchen is ideal but not critical.
- Verify that the room will have tables and chairs; otherwise, you will have to rent them.
- Make sure you have a tablecloth for every table.

Promotion:

- Promote your fair with a press release to the local media and small posters around school campuses, health food stores, and any shops that will grant you permission.
- Include some details about your fair on social media—then direct people to the site in other promotion (posters, letters, etc.).
- Invite the media—newspapers, local radio, and television—to attend the food fair. Be sure to mention if you'll be giving a presentation, as that may entice the media outlet to send a reporter.
- Invite students from local schools to attend your fair via the post; don't email the invitation, as many schools' computer servers use filters that may block your message.

- Follow up with the media a couple of weeks prior to the fair. Try to speak with someone at the newspaper or television/ radio station to determine if a reporter might be covering your event. Suggest they also bring a photographer.
- Also, two weeks before your event, send letters to editors of local papers and mention your fair. Your letter will stand a better chance of being printed if you can tie it to a recent news event; there's so much happening in the world of veganism that this shouldn't be a problem (see Chapter 2).
- Ask animal groups to mail details of your fair to their members.

Food:

- Remember the importance of choosing delicious food for your event.
- Check with local vegan food companies to see if they might donate something. Some makers of vegan food products are happy to donate to pro-vegan or animal rights events.
- Ask VegFund for a grant!
- Book any bulk items of food with your local health food shop or local wholesalers at least two weeks before the event.
- Remember to have drinks on hand: water, soft drinks, etc.

Your fair:

- Ensure you have plenty of literature on hand and arrange it on a table off to the side but in plain view.
- Consider having a speaker make a presentation relative to animal rights. They might also speak about health or the environment.

If you're really ambitious, you might want to take it up a notch like Jessica Schoech did. Through her company Vegan Street Fair, Jessica emulates the street fairs of her native New York City and mixes it with the kind of "taste of" outdoor food festival you'd find in Chicago, but with a vegan spin. Here's Jessica's advice to anyone who wants to create a large vegan food event:

- Go in with a passionate mind, but a businessperson sensibility. In other words, know that money has to come in and go out, so be very mindful that you understand budgets and expenses so that you can pay your vendors and venues and you don't end up in the red. Losing money is not fun, but it can be avoided if one goes into it understanding the business side of things.
- Talk to the community! If you're not a part of the fabric of the vegan community there, take the time to really get to know the people, influencers, organizers, and businesses in the area so that they get to know you and trust you wholeheartedly.
- Do not step on the toes of other event organizers! Some people have very special events that they've crafted for years, and the last thing you want to do is make enemies out of the people on your side. So, get to know them well and make 100 percent sure you are setting yourself apart from everyone else by doing your own thing.
- The more different all of our events are, the better chance we all have of tapping into a market that one of us isn't into yet! Find a way to truly stand out and you'll have a winning combination.
- Social media is your best friend! You don't have to spend hundreds of dollars on traditional marketing when social media is already doing the work for you. Secure domains, social media handles, and pages, and assign someone to get to work on building your following. Use it every day

and never skimp! It's the wave of the future.

> ## Food Fact: Land Use
> A plant-based diet requires only half an acre of land—seven times less land than a meat-based diet.

Cooking Classes & Workshops

"Fervet olla, vivit amicitia," goes the Latin aphorism. "While the pot boils, friendship endures." In other words, knowing your way around the kitchen can feed your stomach *and* your heart. Being able to cook a delicious, nutritious meal is a valuable skill for anyone to have, but this becomes all the more important when you want to show meat-eaters the joys of ethical eating. There are many wonderful vegan cookbooks and cooking videos available, but if you're more comfortable with hands-on learning, a cooking class will certainly give you some culinary confidence. Typing "vegan cooking class" into your favorite search engine will point you to classes around the world.

The flip side for activists is, if you're good at cooking, consider sharing that talent by teaching a cooking class. And don't think you need to be a "professional" chef. "I'm not culinarily trained," says cooking instructor JL Fields, founder and culinary director of the Colorado Springs Vegan Cooking Academy. "I'm a home cook, so I approach my students as peers." Most of those students, it turns out, are not vegan or even plant-based, she says. "This is exactly why I teach vegan cooking classes! I want to show non-vegans how simple—and delicious—home-cooked vegan recipes are, and I certainly want to help the newbie along the way, too."

JL, who has also authored many vegan cookbooks, suggests those who really want to excel as cooking instructors should take classes themselves. "Just as good writers read, good culinary instructors need to take cooking classes."

But how does one go about teaching a vegan cooking class? If you feel you're ready to teach, you can begin by talking to a manager at your local health food store or someone in the activities department of your community college. Many markets and adult-learning centers will happily give you space in their facility to teach a veggie cooking course. Most will promote the class for you, and some natural-foods markets and co-ops will even donate the ingredients you'll need, since people will likely buy the ingredients from the store.

"My most successful free public cooking classes have been held in small cafés, family-owned markets, and out-of-the-box locations, such as a bar or a local 'co-working' space," says JL. "Fee-based classes can be tricky because you need to work in the potential cost for space. These days, in my cooking academy, I pay a rental fee for a kitchen and also pay for security. You'll want to assess the purpose of your class, how it will get funded and then brainstorm logical collaborators—stores, farmers' markets, nonprofit organizations, local businesses—who may be able to provide a free or low-cost venue."

Jill Nussinow agrees that there is a wide variety of possible locations for cooking classes. "I got my start at a cooking school," she says, "but often a better place to start is at your local community center—if you have one—your church or synagogue, a meet-up group, a community college, the library, your local vegetarian society, a natural food store, or cooking school. You want to get creative with where you might teach."

After finding a location, give a lot of thought to how you will publicize your class. "Promotion is the toughest part," says Jill. "It's all about networking and growing what you do. Connect with a meet-up group—or start one. Plan a lot of time for promotion and start at least a few months in advance. Get the word out with a news release to your local paper, local alternative paper, public radio stations, natural food store, and wherever you think that your audience might be. It might be parents at your children's school. One never knows. Put your creativity to work."

You can also have much the same impact with cooking workshops: you organize the menu, charge a fee for ingredients, and let the participants do the cooking while you monitor everyone's progress. Activist Alka Chandna conducted vegan food workshops for years right in her apartment in Canada. She created a booklet, placed classified advertisements in the local paper and promoted the classes to the university community. Alka says, "The idea was to use great food as a way to bring people along — to acknowledge that food is important, but to also acknowledge that there are serious issues, such as animals, the environment, and health, that we must consider when we make food choices. Although I didn't pull any punches or graphic details in painting the realities of factory farming, I also worked hard to keep the tone upbeat and non-judgmental." She says a number of people went vegan on the spot. "Most everyone else reduced their meat consumption, taking the recipes and incorporating them into their dietary rotations."

I find a lot of times that when we tell people about issues affecting animals, they instinctively want to know what they can do. On some issues, such as research, there may not be something they can do directly, other than writing a letter. But by changing their eating habits, they can do something immediately, and by encouraging them to spread the word, they can also change other people.

lauren Ornelas
Satya **magazine**, October 2003

Tips for a Successful Food Workshop
Preparation:

- Promote it. Post your workshop announcement with all the details on craigslist.org and other free websites, and post fliers in your neighborhood health food stores. Many newspapers will also print events and activities notices; check their websites.
- Charge a fee that covers your expenses. Asking for payment also helps motivate people to show up!
- Prepare a menu that demonstrates the wide variety of vegan eating. Alka recommends including a few entrées that are familiar to the Western palate like vegan shepherd's pie and vegan pot pie. She also suggests including some ethnic cuisine such as Indian and Chinese dishes. And don't forget dessert.
- Diversity is important, but don't attempt more entrées than your kitchen (oven, stove, countertops) can handle.
- Shop for ingredients the evening prior to your workshop.
- Set up your kitchen, tables, literature, and food just before attendees are due to arrive.

Execution:

- When all attendees have arrived, briefly introduce yourself and ask others to do the same.
- Divide everyone into small groups and give each group a good variety of three or four recipes to prepare.
- Let your workshop attendees prepare the meals while you observe, offer cooking guidance, and answer questions.
- Use questions about unfamiliar ingredients, such as why they're using soy milk instead of cow's milk, to emphasize both the nutritional value of the plant-based food and the cruelty involved in their animal-based counterparts.

- When it's time to eat, ask participants to critique the meals and their preparation.

Food Fact: Human Health

Whole-food vegan eating improves kidney function, reduces the risk of developing type 2 diabetes and heart disease, and may offer protection against prostate, breast, and colon cancers.

Vegan Starter Kits

As mentioned in Chapter 1, providing people with information about the source of meat, eggs, and dairy foods is one of the most effective ways to promote a vegan diet. Vegan starter kits— full-color guides available from many animal rights groups— explain where animal-based foods come from and demonstrate how easy it is to go vegan by offering simple recipes, nutritional information, and advice on where to find plant-based convenience foods.

Tips for Using Vegan Starter Kits

- Order a supply of kits from an organization such as Animals Australia, Animal Equality, Mercy For Animals, PETA, Vegan Outreach, and Viva! and hand them out in places with lots of foot traffic. See Chapter 1 for leafleting advice.
- Have a website? Post a link to one of the many vegan starter kits available for free from organizations.
- Ask your local library, veg restaurant, health club, co-op, or doctor's office if you can leave some vegan starter kits on the counter. Remember to re-stock frequently!

Tips for Using Food as Outreach

- Learn to prepare a variety of vegan foods: take a vegan cooking class, buy a vegan cookbook or video, or watch how-to videos online.
- Bring easy-to-prepare vegan dishes to potlucks and parties—and bring the recipe in case someone would like to prepare it at home.
- Offer to cook for holiday gatherings; make enough for everyone to sample it.
- Make sure you keep the wrappers of any product samples you want to recommend to people.
- Remember: taste buds are important—be sure the food is delicious!

Food Fact: Water Use

It takes 100 to 200 times more water to produce a pound of beef than it does to grow a pound of plant foods.

Insights from Vegan Chefs

Eric Tucker, executive chef at Millennium, a gourmet vegan restaurant in Oakland, does not necessarily see his work as activism, although he believes eating great animal-friendly food can lead to larger considerations. "Through what we do at the restaurant, the only thing we'd like to achieve through putting out some great vegetable-based chow is that people will eat more vegetables," he says. "Though through our support of local, sustainable produce—not just purchasing, but through cooking classes and demos, special events like our farmers' market dinners—we will pique our diners' curiosity on where their food comes from and how it is produced, both veg- and animal-based. From there they can make choices on whether and how much they want to support animal welfare. Education is the key."

Jo Stepaniak, author of *Vegan Vittles, The Ultimate Uncheese Cookbook, The Vegan Sourcebook* and many other related books, observes that most people in the West are stuck in a "food rut" and are often suspicious of foods that are the least bit different from their normal fare. "When someone reaches out and helps them over that hurdle," she says, "they are able to discover that their initial fears were unfounded. Then they are more willing to keep exploring and learn more about other new foods and alternative ways of eating." She finds that being friendly and approachable makes her a better vegan advocate. "This may be a subtler and more moderate approach compared to conventional views of activism, but I have found that it is as effective and has greater 'sticking power' than forceful or antagonistic methods."

Writer and chef Tony Bishop-Weston (*The Vegan Cookbook: Over 80 Plant-Based Recipes*) also runs Foods For Life, a nutrition and catering consultancy that emphasizes the health benefits vegans enjoy. "By pretending to be a mainstream health consultancy," he says, "we have managed to get vegan ideology into the mainstream media. We rarely tell people not to do things—we more often just focus on the solutions and the basic philosophy that eating more plant-based foods has positive repercussions to their health."

Vegan chef and author Beverly Lynn Bennett (*Vegan for One: Hot Tips and Inspired Recipes for Cooking Solo*) says she considers her writing and work as a chef to be animal activism. "The food choices that people make have a huge impact on animal suffering, and the bottom of the animal foods industry can fall out overnight if enough people wake up and go vegan. So those of us who advocate a plant-based diet, and try to show people how they can prepare plant-based foods in their own lives, are helping to strike a blow against the industries that are most directly responsible for most of the suffering that exists today."

Sarah Kramer, author of some of vegandom's most popular cookbooks, is another home-schooled cook. Her award-winning cookbook *How It All Vegan!* started life as a modest zine created for family and friends, and its bestseller status quickly inspired *The Garden of Vegan* and *La Dolce Vegan*. "In my experience," she says, "you can really open the mind of a meat-eater by starting with their stomach. Putting delicious, nutritious, and mouthwatering food in front of them speaks volumes to the kind of glorious food-filled life a vegan can live. I find it also helps to lighten the conversation to a level where you can really intelligently discuss your vegan lifestyle and choices without it being a back-and-forth argument where you're not making any headway."

Support Vegan Businesses

Help vegan restaurants stay in business by patronizing them—and bring a friend.

Chapter 6

Animal Pharm: Corporate Campaigning

Activism is the rent I pay for living on this planet.
Alice Walker

When activist Tina Clark noticed that Peelu Co. was marketing its gum as "cruelty free," she knew it wasn't true. The problem was, says Tina, the gum contained beeswax, an animal ingredient used in many other products, such as cosmetics, candles, and furniture polish. "I wrote them a letter asking that they either remove the beeswax or stop calling themselves cruelty free." She enclosed an article about how commercial beeswax production harms bees, including exposing them to pesticides and having their wings torn off by beekeepers. "I waited several months and didn't hear anything, which didn't surprise me," Tina says. "Then I received a letter from them saying that they had done some research and found a substitute for the beeswax and they would stop using the beeswax immediately. I hadn't actually expected anything, and this truly amazed me."

This is but one example of corporate campaigning, a strategy that, as implemented by animal advocates, encourages a business to adopt changes in the interest of animals. Although a protest can play an important role in this type of outreach, full-scale corporate campaigning relies on a broader approach that may mobilize the pressure of consumer buying power and/or public opinion to create an atmosphere in which companies realize that addressing the changes activists are seeking on behalf of animals makes good business sense. (For the purposes of this chapter, we will consider restaurant outreach as a form of corporate outreach.)

Some examples of campaign targets include:

- Pharmaceutical companies that test on animals
- Corporations and medical schools that support vivisection
- Manufacturers that subject animals to product safety tests
- Companies that sponsor events, such as rodeos, that abuse animals
- Agribusiness
- Retail shops that sell fur
- Restaurants (persuading them to offer vegan options)
- Corporate and college dining halls
- Local and national governments that support animal abuse
- The military, which often tests lethal weapons on animals.

The circumstances of each corporate campaign will dictate what tactics to use. Friendly persuasion and some face-time with a local business owner may be just the thing; persuading a multinational corporation to end an abusive business practice, on the other hand, may require more effort and creativity. The late Henry Spira used advertising campaigns and letters directly to corporate heads. Many of his successes were the result of companies not wanting the negative publicity Henry's tenacious tactics would surely generate: print ads exposing deceptive marketing, horrific cruelty, and corporate malfeasance aimed to shock the public and shame animal abusers.

His first campaign for animals targeted the American Museum of Natural History, which was researching the impact that castration and other mutilation had on the sexual behavior of cats. A full-page ad in *The New York Times*, funded by a local vegetarian group called the Millennium Guild, produced so much bad press that the museum was forced to stop the experiments in 1977. Animal activists praised Henry for spearheading the first campaign in more than 100 years of anti-vivisection outreach in the US and Europe to bring an end to any animal testing.

> Let's get out of the past and stop ignoring the vast majority of animal misery. We activists need to remember our objectives and why we're doing what we're doing. This involves a realistic recognition of the problems, a sense of what's possible, the ability to search out and seize opportunities as they appear and, whenever necessary, to switch gears.
> **Henry Spira**
> *Satya* **magazine**, June 1996

Starting Small, Thinking Big

An activist need not have the financial backing of sympathetic supporters like Henry Spira did or even be part of a large organization to engage in corporate campaigning. We can begin by going vegan and not supporting enterprises that exploit animals. We can also contact companies directly to encourage them to make improvements, such as insisting that animal welfare be included in the scope of their corporate social responsibility. But there's still room for some Henry Spira-style tactics today.

Although she campaigns against the battery egg industry and other animal exploiters, Wendy Parsons is passionate about rabbits. Armed with a ream of paper and a stack of images depicting bunny slaughter in China, Wendy uses her free time to wage a crusade against businesses throughout Australia that sell products using rabbit fur—and she's winning a number of important battles. "I write a letter enclosing the pictures," she says. "If it's a chain of shops, I send the letter to the head office with a copy to all their individual shops so that their staff knows how brutal the fur industry is. Australia's three largest department stores have stopped selling fur as a result of this, and Woolworths supermarkets and a swag of smaller shops and retail chains have stopped selling fur cat toys across

Australia."

Wendy often encloses a three-minute DVD showing the inhumane treatment of rabbits during handling and transport from fur farms to slaughterhouses, but she stresses that it's important to include evidence that cannot be avoided—no media files that can simply be thrown away without opening. "I enclose six pages of photos with only a small amount of text as a caption. When people open the letter they cannot avoid looking at the photos, which speak a thousand words. People always have a definite reaction—sometimes defensive, sometimes horrified— and on one occasion a sales assistant from a dress shop had to go home because she was so upset. After contacting a chain of more than 60 pharmacies that also sell gift items, they now invite me to check any 'suspect' stock [products possibly made of fur] they are thinking of buying." Wendy says the strategy is effective, but patience and tenacity are definitely keys to success.

"Animal abuse is often about corporate abuse," says Camilla Fox, an activist with many years of corporate outreach experience, "so we can't *not* conduct corporate campaigns." She believes it is crucial that activists know how to organize and run effective, politically savvy corporate campaigns. "That means doing the hardest thing for some activists, which is actually learning how to sit down and have conversations with corporate CEOs and figuring out how to appeal to them, generally from an economic standpoint." Camilla recommends that activists always have something to trade in exchange for what they want—something worthwhile. "We live in a capitalist society," she says, "so we have to think about the incentive we are going to offer to a corporation. If our position is 'Don't sell fur,' what are we going to advocate in place of that? What is going to appeal to a CEO?" She uses as one example the "leaping bunny" label for cruelty-free cosmetics. "That logo has become something that corporations and businesses and retailers *want* to have on their products because they saw that customers were seeking it. So, the incentive was that there is a demand for this."

While corporate campaigning has many challenges, lauren Ornelas says the hardest thing is not giving up. "I've been involved in corporate campaigns that lasted 10 years," she says. "Remember that you're just dealing with people." She adds that creativity is one of the keys to success. "Think of ways to approach your target. Finding out where their CEO is speaking and showing up there, for example."

One thing activists who have engaged in corporate campaigning all seem to agree on is that it works. "It takes many types of activism to propel a social justice movement," says Jaya Bhumitra, "but corporate outreach is one of the most efficient ways to effect change for a significant number of animals who suffer in the most egregious conditions."

Grassroots Activism

To underscore the profound role individual activism can play in convincing businesses to stop carrying fur, Fiona Pereira of Animal Aid explains that UK-based activists have been voicing their objection to department stores across the country, forcing these companies to confront some callous realities. Fiona reports that such stores as Liberty, Harvey Nichols, and the Zara clothing chain have all stopped selling fur. And while many businesses are reluctant to admit the power activists can have in influencing corporate policy, "Selfridges cited this as the primary reason they adopted a fur-free policy," she says.

Other UK businesses are also feeling the pressure from corporate campaigns. Although foie gras production is essentially banned in Britain, the country still imports more than 4,000 tons a year, making it one of the world's largest consumers of this "fatty liver." Grassroots activists have helped Viva! halt the sale of foie gras in supermarkets, and they're working hard to eliminate this cruel delicacy—what they call "torture in a tin"— from restaurants as well. "With foie gras and so-called 'exotic' meats, such as kangaroo, crocodile, and ostrich, Viva! initially presumes that businesses may not be aware of all the cruelty inherent in its production," says campaigns manager Justin Kerswell. "In the case of foie gras, each business receives an information pack, which details how the meat is produced and the major welfare implications resulting from force feeding."

Justin says that local activists are critical to the success of such campaigns, since they can fill out customer feedback cards and ask restaurants to remove foie gras. Viva! will also send activists foie gras leaflets, stickers, and large posters to help educate restaurant owners and patrons. "If these measures do not work, Viva! contacts local media—to put pressure on the business and to raise awareness of the issue with the public at large—and we step up local actions such as protests and leafleting. These campaigns have received widespread media coverage at both the local and national level."

On the importance of working with small activist groups, Juliet Gellatley, the founder and director of Viva!, adds: "We need local groups to provide numbers, and local groups need us as big corporations are unlikely to react to a solitary local demo."

Longtime campaigner Jake Conroy believes animal activists have an enormous task. "We have to convince the world to rethink and reshape its ideas and actions around the treatment of the environment, as well as human and nonhuman animals," he says. "To succeed we must reconfigure almost every fabric of our societies, communities, and cultures. It's an almost insurmountable mission to even think about. So, it's imperative that we spend our time being as effective as we possibly can be. When it comes to activism, I think nothing beats strong, strategic, grassroots corporate campaigning."

As part of the group Stop Huntingdon Animal Cruelty USA (SHAC USA), Jake helped encourage more than 100 companies—including some of the world's largest financial and

pharmaceutical companies, corporate insurers, and auditors—
to cut their ties with the infamous animal testing laboratory
Huntingdon Life Sciences, which kills an average of 500 animals
per day. "We utilized every tool in the toolbox to do so," he
says, "ranging from petitions, letters, emails, and faxes, to
demonstrations at offices and homes. Others engaged in acts of
civil disobedience, and while we didn't participate, organize, or
fund it, there was an underground element that utilized property
destruction and the liberation of animals to get their point
across." (Make no mistake: big corporations have deep pockets
and wield lots of power, even over the government. Ultimately,
Jake paid a heavy price for his SHAC campaigning, which we'll
explore in Chapter 10.)

Organizations like SHAC can make a tremendous impact, but
they needn't be large, says lauren, who encourages activists to
start their own grassroots group. "It's not about numbers. It's
about what two people can achieve. One person can achieve a
lot; two people can double that. Look at James DeAlto and his
Vegan Chalk Challenge. It's a campaign to get people out there
doing something and sharing a message of veganism for the
animals. He started that on his own." She adds that the number
of people at an event or the media coverage you get is not a true
measure of success. "I am more impressed by actual changes
that have been made than by media."

Campaigning Against a Government

Yes, you can target a government with your activism. Since
almost every nation earns a percentage of its income from
foreign visitors, the animal abuses they will most likely be
swayed to ban are tourist-related, such as trophy and canned
hunting, swim-with-dolphin experiences, the ivory trade,
gorilla visits, lion walks, tiger temples, and elephant rides and
elephant-back safaris. As an activist, you can also encourage a
government to:

- Increase protections for wild animals
- Declare a species to be legal persons
- Ban the use of animals in circuses
- Ban animal testing
- Criminalize types of animal abuse, such as dog fighting.

Convincing a government to protect the country's wildlife is a vast campaign that any concerned individual can engage in. It involves more than communicating with legislators; it requires outreach to community leaders, companies, and the general public. Here are some suggestions for taking action:

Do's:

- Educate yourself on the issues.
- Contact the country's tourism department and voice your concerns about animal exploitation there, such as the ivory trade, hunting, the export of live animals, etc.
- Write to provincial and national conservation authorities and object to the opening of conservation areas to hunters.
- Write letters to editors of newspapers and magazines expressing your views.
- Let hunters know that you are opposed to their violent pastime.
- Support campaigns to end hunting, elephant-back safaris, the ivory trade, etc.
- Write to or speak with travel agents and tour operators asking them not to support elephant-back safaris. Also ask them to approach the government through their tourism bodies to identify reserves and resorts where hunting is allowed so that ethical tourists may choose to avoid such facilities.
- Only support tour operators and destinations that do not

support elephant-back safaris.

Don'ts:

- Don't visit reserves, resorts, or conservation areas that allow hunting.
- Don't purchase ivory or products made from ivory.
- Don't purchase the byproducts of hunting, such as deer meat ("venison"), biltong, animal skins, or curios from hunted animals.
- Don't patronize stores or companies that sell hunting equipment and promote hunting.
- Don't join or support conservation organizations that promote or tolerate hunting as an acceptable component of "sustainable use."
- Don't patronize zoos or circuses that use animals.

Animal Testing

Among the most egregious abusers outside agribusiness are those who test on animals: vivisectionists and manufacturers of pharmaceutical and consumer products. Despite studies that show that the physiological differences between humans and other animal species cause our bodies to react differently to drugs and diseases, millions of animals suffer and die in the name of "medical progress." Moreover, modern humane, non-animal research is more accurate and less expensive than its cruel counterpart. Still more animals are subjected to torture in the course of testing beauty and household products such as cosmetics, soaps, shampoos, lotions, cleaners, and, ironically, food for companion animals. Fortunately, many companies understand that animal testing is unnecessary and inhumane — and they even engage in their own corporate campaigning.

Andrew Butler is the campaigns manager for Lush, a natural-cosmetics company based in the UK. The mostly vegan company is working to make all its products animal-friendly and hired Andrew, a longtime activist, to advise Lush on animal-related issues. The company has launched its Supplier Specific Boycott Policy, which means it refuses to do business with any supplier still carrying out chemical testing on animals. "However," Andrew says, "as soon as a manufacturer commits to stopping *all* animal testing, they immediately become eligible to supply Lush, regardless of when they were last engaged in animal testing." This gives an incentive to ingredients manufacturers to stop all testing in order to get more business. "And the more companies that adopt this policy, the more pressure there is on manufacturers to divest themselves of animal testing."

Andrew observes that financial incentives are a key ingredient to successful campaigns. "I think the thing people should remember—and thankfully most activists do—is to not only put pressure on those companies that are involved in bad practices, but also to congratulate and reward companies that are doing good."

What You Can Do to Combat Animal Testing

- Educate yourself. Few people, activists included, realize the massive scale of animal testing; read the literature available from groups working to eliminate this abuse, such as the American Anti-Vivisection Society, Animal Aid, Cruelty Free International, and PETA.
- Educate others. Armed with what you know, talk to family, friends, and co-workers about the suffering animals endure in testing labs.
- Write letters—to editors, legislators, and the companies that test on animals—expressing your position against this form of senseless abuse. It's crucial that your opinions are heard and that offending companies know you are boycotting their products because they test them on

animals.

- Contact medical schools that still abuse animals in the name of education and ask them to eliminate live-animal labs from their curricula.
- Make ethical choices when you shop: purchase products that have not been tested on animals.
- Call or send an email to companies *not* testing on animals: tell them their no-animal-testing policy is why you buy their products.
- If you're a student, give a presentation to your class that makes a compelling argument against animal testing.
- If you're a biology student, don't dissect animals—and let your teacher, fellow students, and school administrators know why you refuse to participate in this callous and archaic practice.
- Contact an animal rights organization that campaigns against animal testing; volunteer to table for them or participate in demonstrations.
- Go undercover. Photographic and video documentation, usually obtained covertly, is incredibly powerful evidence against those who test on animals. Large animal rights groups like Mercy For Animals are always looking for people to engage in undercover investigations. (See Chapter 9.)

Restaurant Outreach

Vegan eating is becoming more mainstream every day, so asking a local eatery—or your campus cafeteria—to carry more vegan options is not the challenge it might have been even a couple of years ago. Independent restaurants are likely to be more receptive to meeting with you, as they have much more freedom to alter their menus than a franchisee or a national restaurant operated by a large company like McDonald's. Your local, family-owned restaurant is also able to make changes rapidly,

---

The Buck Stops Here

If a rodeo comes to your town:

- Call and write letters to sponsors; explain the cruelty and ask them to end their support.
- Voice your concerns to local authorities: the rodeo could be violating anti-cruelty laws in your area.
- Send letters to the editors of your local papers.
- Leaflet at the gate.
- Hold a protest.

Contact CompassionWorks International, the European Anti-Rodeo Coalition, or SHARK for leaflets and video footage documenting rodeo cruelty.

---

while large companies spend time with market research. The Denny's restaurant chain, for instance, took years to switch from a vegetarian patty, which contained eggs and dairy, to a vegan patty (and bun) for the veggie burgers at all its locations in the US.

Clearly, convincing a restaurant to adopt a vegan-friendly menu calls for a one-on-one meeting with a decision-maker. If this is a new model of activism for you, start off with an eatery you've been to at least a few times: you're a familiar, friendly face, and they want to keep their customers happy. (If your favorite restaurants are all vegan or vegetarian, pick a place you go to with non-vegetarian friends or family.) Ask to speak with the owner or manager and then schedule a brief meeting. Tell them that you would like to come back during off-peak hours and bring some samples of delicious, vegan foods for them to try. Assuming they are receptive to your suggestion, there are two things you will need to bring:

1. Food. Well, not just food—*delicious* food free of animal ingredients. Mock meats (also called "meat analogs") are becoming more popular every day, making it easy to turn common meat-based entrées like spaghetti with meatballs or a turkey club sandwich into a vegan meal. The common mock meats we enjoy today have their origins in centuries-old recipes for seitan (wheat gluten), tempeh (fermented whole soy beans), tofu, rice, mushrooms, legumes, and other plants seasoned and prepared to make the meat analog taste (and often look) like a wide variety of animal-based foods. More recent mock meats use a soy-based textured vegetable protein (TVP).

The owner has probably already heard of veggie burgers or veggie hot dogs, but these analogs may come as a surprise:

- "Chicken" made from soy
- "Beef" made from seitan
- Tempeh "bacon"
- Meatless pepperoni and sausages in many flavors
- "Chicken" nuggets made from soy
- Ground "beef" made from soy (delicious in tacos and burritos)
- Pulled "pork" made from jackfruit
- Ice cream made from almond-, soy-, cashew-, or other nondairy milks
- Dairy-free cheeses and yoghurts
- Vegan cookies
- Soyrizo
- Vegan margarine
- Egg- and dairy-free mayo (such as Vegenaise)

You'll find these items in just about any health- or natural-food store, and even the larger grocery chains are carrying them now. Choose the foods that will be most appropriate for the business. A Thai restaurant with lots of chicken dishes on its menu may be interested in trying soy-based foods, for example, while veggie deli slices will be right at home in a sandwich shop. Also, remind the restaurant owner or manager that they can promote these items as not just vegan, but cholesterol-free and usually lower in fat than their animal-based counterparts. The Physicians Committee for Responsible Medicine recommends that restaurants adapt their existing menu items to offer familiar dishes, such as pancakes with veggie sausage, scrambled tofu, vegetable lasagna, Thai burritos, fruit smoothies, and fresh fruit salad.

2. Information. An important part of this outreach effort will be to educate your audience. Take the soft-sell approach: you're not necessarily trying to make the owner go vegan (though that could be a consequence of your efforts), so bring literature that helps decision-makers understand the health benefits of a vegan diet and the increasing desire for these foods among restaurant patrons.

Tips for Successful Restaurant Outreach
Here are some suggestions to help make the most of your meeting:

- Don't arrive during peak business hours. Choose a time when the restaurant is not busy serving patrons, such as after the lunch rush but before dinner seatings begin.
- Dress professionally. First impressions are extremely important, especially when you are presenting an unfamiliar concept to someone. Dressing as you would at a job interview helps boost your credibility enormously. Remember, you are not just endorsing vegan products, you are also representing the vegan movement.
- Be organized. Having all of your literature and food samples ready to be displayed furthers your professional approach.

- Be appreciative and friendly. As soon as you meet the owner, introduce yourself and thank them for allowing you the opportunity to meet. And throughout the course of the meeting, don't forget to smile!
- Start at the beginning. Before offering the food samples, show the literature you brought so the owner has some background information on vegan eating.
- Appeal to the owner's taste buds. Following up with the food samples brings home the appeal of adding more animal-friendly fare to answer customer demand.
- Be honest. Chances are, the owner will have a string of questions (see below). Answer truthfully. If you aren't sure of a response, simply tell the owner you will research the question and provide an answer within a specified time period.
- Explain the appeal of vegan items. For many people, there is no difference between "vegetarian" and "vegan" fare. Explain that vegans opt not to consume any animal products, including whey and casein, and that adding completely animal-free items to menus will appeal to vegetarians, those with lactose intolerance or health concerns, as well as vegans, whereas dishes with eggs or dairy products won't.
- Be helpful. Even if the restaurant owner is enthusiastic about adding more animal-friendly menu items, the next step in actually doing so may be daunting. Offering your help in any capacity—from developing menu ideas to taste testing to promoting its new vegan options—shows your commitment to the campaign and your follow-through proves your professionalism.
- Be appreciative. At the meeting's end, thank the owner again for taking the time in a busy day to meet with you.
- Schedule a follow-up date. Giving the restaurant owner time to mull over ideas and talk with the chef is helpful,

so suggest that you'll check back in—via phone or a meeting—to see if you can do anything to help with the process.

Change from Within

One animal advocate, who wishes to remain anonymous, told me they keep their veganism secret at work—because they're employed by one of the largest zoos in the United States. "It was about two years after starting this job that I went vegan," they say. "I feel like trying to influence my own employer is a big part of what I can do at work. The primary thing of importance to me is maybe not what a lot of animal rights activists think about in terms of zoos." Rather than focusing on captivity issues, they are trying to get co-workers to make the connection between animals and what is served in the zoo's restaurants, and there has been some progress. "Suddenly, there appeared two vegan options at one of the restaurants in the last few months. Prior to that, vegan options were practically non-existent. I'm on the internal conservation committee and keep the vegan stuff on the table there, too, although, as with the rest of the world, it's a tough nut to crack."

Frequently Asked Questions

In general, try to keep your conversation and any responses to questions focused on the growing popularity and appeal of vegan eating, rather than the ethical reasons you are vegan. You're there to encourage a restaurant owner to offer more animal-friendly items, not to explain your philosophical beliefs. If the owner feels judged or lectured to, chances are good the meeting will not be productive and, of course, not in the animals' best interest.

Some frequently-asked questions and possible responses include:

Q: Why are you doing this?
A: For a variety of reasons, more and more people are choosing to eat vegan foods than ever before. I'm just helping to make it more convenient for them.

Q: Why are you vegan?
A: Like so many people, I chose to be vegan for many reasons: to avoid supporting cruelty to animals, to improve my health, and to help the environment.

Q: I offer salads and vegetable sandwiches. Isn't that enough?
A: The majority of people who are now vegan or vegetarian didn't give up meat and other animal products because they didn't like the taste. They gave them up because of health, ethical, or ecological reasons. And many people who do eat meat are interested in cholesterol-free foods, which all vegan fare is, or lighter dishes that are commonly found in vegetarian options. So, offering pure vegetarian items—or going even further with mock meat and mock dairy items—will definitely diversify your menu while attracting new customers.

Once you've had success with one restaurant owner, ask for recommendations of other establishments that would be interested in creating or expanding their vegan options. Many times, owners associate with others in the restaurant business, and their connections and suggestions can be valuable to your outreach efforts.

Dining Halls

If you eat at a school cafeteria or corporate dining hall, you can engage in a variation of the restaurant outreach strategy and meet with your food services representative and ask that they carry more vegan entrées. Here are a few tips from Ken Botts, who created the first all-vegan dining hall in the US at the University of North Texas in 2009.

Tips for Successful Dining Hall Outreach

- Know who the boss is. Go to your campus dining webpage and find out who is the director of dining services. The director of dining is the person who typically makes the decisions and is the person you will want to speak with. Always start at the top because you will accomplish your goal much faster. In most cases the director of dining will report to a higher authority within the university hierarchy like the vice president of auxiliary services. It is a good idea to know who that person is too, just in case the director isn't as responsive as you'd like.

- Organize your voice. Odds are, you're not the only one on campus who wants vegan options added to the menu. Find out if there is a vegan, animal protection, or environmental club on campus. Attend the meetings of these campus groups and get to know others who are willing to add their voice to your cause. If there's not a club on campus, now would be a good time to start one. If there are many students (especially meal plan holders) asking for vegan options, the administration is more likely to listen.

- Request a meeting. Send the director a polite email asking for a meeting or, even better, walk into the dining office with a note asking for a meeting. Your email/note should be professional, respectful, and to the point. It should include a brief introduction of who your group is, what you are asking for (more vegan options) and your request for a meeting on or before a certain date... within the week is usually realistic. Close the email/note with a sincere thank-you and include your contact info. If you don't hear back from the director by the date you requested, then your group should visit his/her office or call him/her on the phone and follow up until the meeting is scheduled. Patience, yet persistence, is key.

- Congratulations! You have your meeting scheduled. Have two or three students from your group go with you, select someone to be your spokesperson, dress professionally, and show up 15 minutes early. Ensure that all parties meeting with the director know to stay on message with the main reason you're there. Once you're in the director's office, introduce yourselves, thank him or her for meeting with you, tell him/her why you are there, and ask for the changes you want to see. Be reasonable in what you're asking for. If your campus only has one dining hall, ask for more vegan options or a vegan station. If your campus has four or five dining halls, ask for all the halls to have more vegan options or ask if one entire dining hall can go vegan, similar to the one at the University of North Texas. Before you leave the office schedule a follow-up meeting and thank the director again for taking time to meet with you.

"If you get what you ask for on the first try, make sure you thank the director in person, send a thank-you card signed by everyone in your group, and celebrate the change with your fellow students through social media," says Ken. "Of course, there's a chance that you may not get all you ask for in the beginning, so be prepared to work with the director towards an acceptable solution. Be persistent, speak with the director frequently, and don't give up. Set a deadline and if you feel that you're not getting anywhere, then you may need to schedule a meeting with the director's boss, but most of the time that's not necessary."

We can't begin to imagine what it's like to be a battery hen or a pig in a gestation crate; the suffering of animals on factory farms and in slaughterhouses is beyond our worst nightmares. So yes, there is ample reason to become dispirited, misanthropic and generally unhappy. But that won't help animals, and really, we have come a remarkably long way in, historically speaking, almost no time at all.
Bruce Friedrich
Satya **magazine**, January/February 2004

Targeting the Food Industry

As the largest abusers of animals, the corporations that produce meat, eggs, and dairy foods are a prime target for campaigning. Recent improvements in the lives of confined animals are clear indications that such outreach is working. "I think a lot of the campaigns that are currently being done to put pressure on the big corporate players with deep pockets — and actually sitting down around negotiating tables with the executives behind multi-billion-dollar organizations like McDonald's to discuss animal welfare initiatives — have proven to be extremely effective," says activist Lisa Franzetta. "Take the example of Smithfield Foods agreeing to phase out gestation crates as an admitted result of their consumers leaning on them to provide improved welfare standards — and by 'consumers,' they mean massive corporate purchasers like McDonald's and Wal-Mart. In order to achieve small improvements in the treatment of animals raised in abusive industries, especially factory farms, I think this model is proving extremely effective. Money talks, so if we can make compelling arguments to the people behind the paychecks, I think we're using our time very effectively."

Lisa raises an important point. When lobbying a company to make changes, think not only in terms of what's best for animals, keep in mind that a financial return (and the bigger the better) is what motivates corporations. That's why boycotts are effective: they impact buying habits and thus a company's bottom line.

"A corporate policymaker is, for the most part, concerned with the profits of the company and its shareholders," says activist Michael Hayward. "If you, as an animal advocate, are able to illustrate to these companies and policymakers that improved animal welfare, or whatever, will profitably improve their perceived image in the public eye or their corporate efficiency, they may be motivated to pursue your ideas strictly for monetary reasons."

And the impact of a shift in corporate policy can have enormous ramifications for animals who are raised for food. Although we realize the ideal solution for everyone would be the total liberation of animals, improvements that can be implemented before that happens will help alleviate suffering.

Even small outreach efforts to the food industry can have an impact, as Joyce D'Silva of Compassion in World Farming has discovered. Because of the growth of the European Union, it has become more difficult for animal advocates to get reforms passed in the EU. So Joyce and other activists have started lobbying the food industry, in particular the grocery stores and retail outlets that buy from agribusiness. She's quickly learned the value of media coverage in these efforts.

Joyce's group tried to get Tesco (which she calls "the Wal-Mart of the UK") to label their battery eggs as being from hens confined to cages, but the chain's executives told them their focus-group studies showed Tesco customers did not want to feel guilty when buying battery eggs (Tesco needed market research for that?). "We organized a tour of 18 major Tesco supermarkets in good media centers throughout the country—where there would be regional television and radio," Joyce says. "We had a big model of a de-feathered battery hen. On the morning we started the tour, my colleague was on one of the big radio programs with someone from Tesco. The Tesco representative repeated that people don't want to know where their eggs come from. At 10:30, Tesco faxed us to say they were considering our position. At 11:30, another fax came through saying 'We've decided to label all our battery eggs as being from caged hens.' It just shows the power of the media. So we called off the rest of the tour and celebrated."

Joyce advises other activists who want to go after grocery stores to first speak with the manager, explain the issue you want addressed and suggest how it might be rectified. "If that fails, you might have a little demo outside the store, call the local press, hand out leaflets, talk to shoppers, and ask them to sign petitions." And making it easier for the public to participate always helps. "One thing we did once was to print customer-comment cards that looked quite like the cards the stores use, only we printed ours with information about battery eggs and left room for customers to write their own bit," she says. "It helped build awareness at the top levels."

Whether it's doing food industry outreach or any campaign, remember your audience, advises Charles Stahler, cofounder of the Vegetarian Resource Group. "When working with the mainstream, you may have to change your tactics somewhat," he says. "You can't always say what you would say when talking to other activists." Charles recommends that activists trust their own voice. "People should appreciate and understand each other's role, not feel they have to replicate what others are doing or that everyone has to be like you. Each activist should work in a way they feel comfortable without feeling other activists have to be like them."

Advice from a Pro

Leah Garces, executive director of Compassion in World Farming USA, has spent two decades protecting farmed animals, and she's compiled a list of lessons for changing the hearts and minds of even the most hostile stakeholders. "While it's not always easy to face opponents in good faith," she says, "it is often the most effective way to build the better world we seek." If you find yourself sitting across the table from an opponent, remember these tips on finding common ground and engaging in meaningful dialogue:

- **Recognize that the reason your opponents aren't doing what you want might be that they simply don't know how.** Take heart in the fact that you've made it to the table at all. If you were able to secure a meeting, your opponents have likely realized that they have a problem and that they lack the expertise to solve it. So many times, I've sat at a table with high-level executives from Fortune 500 companies—people who have ample resources at their disposal and are forced to acknowledge that they are out of their depth. Be confident. You're not there to reprimand them; you're there to help them.

- **If they aren't under pressure, they won't care.** Another thought that should give you confidence: If they weren't feeling the pressure to do better, they would have no need to build bridges. In the case of my organization's work with food companies, pressure to improve animal welfare standards is coming from all directions: from consumers, investors, and animal advocates. It's important to be clear about what they need to do to alleviate that pressure and provide a path to getting it done.

- **Your opponent will welcome you doing the job for them.** Don't forget: You're dealing with executives who are overwhelmed and don't have your knowledge regarding veganism or animal rights. If, after laying out goals, you can also provide the resources to get the job done, the chances of reaching an agreement rise exponentially. Whether it's technical expertise or policy templates, offering opponents the tools for success can seal the deal.

More Tips for Effective Corporate Campaigning

- Before beginning any campaign, clearly understand what it is you want to achieve for animals—and what compromises you're willing to accept from the target company.
- Do your corporate research: Find out what your target's corporate strategy is, profile the people who you will be contacting, and frame your message to your audience and to their corporate culture.
- If you get a face-to-face meeting, dress appropriately. Your target will look for ways to dismiss you and your message—don't give them one.
- Before any communication, write out your talking points or draft an agenda so that you are organized and able to convey your message.
- Frame dialogue as a joint problem-solving session where you are looking for mutually advantageous solutions, rather than: "You have to do what I say because I say so!"
- Find support from other activists and groups. These need not be animal rights groups, either; indeed, expanding your efforts to include people and businesses outside the movement demonstrates your issue is important to the entire community—or beyond—and not just "animal people." For example, if you're targeting a local government that plans to use a toxic poison to kill predators, you could enlist support from environmental and conservation groups.

- Boycott companies that are not animal-friendly, but don't keep it to yourself: Write letters, send emails, and make phone calls to the target companies telling them why you are boycotting them. Stage protests outside their stores and offices, too.
- Contact the media—they can be a powerful ally. Send press releases to local and, if applicable, national news outlets telling them about your campaign.
- Don't forget to be positive: Always let target companies know that you will patronize them again once they make the animal-friendly change you're asking of them. (Without an economic incentive, most companies will not acquiesce.)
- Collect petition signatures to demonstrate support for your viewpoint.
- Don't be intimidated by big talk. Companies or other entities may say you haven't the support—or the right—to stand against them.
- Use the Internet: Add details about your corporate campaign on your social media pages and any other websites you can. If there's a video available that addresses your position, post it on video-sharing sites like YouTube and Google Video.
- Add an action item to your email signature, asking recipients to take action in support of your campaign. Be specific: Tell them what you want them to do and provide links, if any.
- Ask an animal rights group in your country for advice on contacting businesses. Animal Aid, Animals Australia, CompassionWorks International, and SAFE, for example, all have experience with corporate campaigns.

"Long story short," says Andrew Butler, "pick your corporate targets with care, go after the companies that can make the biggest influence in their field, and don't let up until they do the right thing. When they do, *reward* them. Also make sure that the companies you support are the ones really doing something positive, not simply using it as a marketing tool."

Chapter 7

Animal House: Sanctuaries, Shelters, & Rescue Centers

I am no longer accepting the things I cannot change. I am changing the things I cannot accept.

Angela Davis

Pam Ahern remembers the moment volunteer Sue Werrett became a hero. Pam, founder of Edgar's Mission animal sanctuary in Australia, says an epic drought had left livestock paddocks dry on farms across the country. "Sadly, another sight that was becoming all too familiar to us was of pathetically thin sheep stuck in the quagmire of mud that was once a dam," she says. One particular farm with a muddy dam (reservoir) and negligent farmer had been the scene of many tragedies as animals, drawn to the last vestiges of water, perished in the deep sludge. But luckily for one trapped sheep, Sue happened to drive by.

"I did a double take when I spotted what appeared to be a large rock in the mud," says Sue. Her heart sank when she realized the "rock" was a full-grown ewe. She immediately called Pam, who started off for the farm as quickly as she could—but Sue was not about to let the sheep languish. "She was wedged up to her shoulders in muddy water infested with mozzies [mosquitoes] and other flying things," says Sue. "I cleaned the mud out of her eyes as best I could and talked to her; I wanted her to know I was not going to let her die."

Sinking into the mud herself, Sue slipped her arms beneath the ewe's chest and pulled. Nothing. She pulled once more, straining against both gravity and the turbid suction. The sheep would not budge from her mucky trap. "I pulled again and again and again," Sue says. At last she felt movement—just an inch or two, but it was something. Bolstered by compassion for the ewe and anger at the farmer for his neglect, Sue at last pulled the animal free. "I lost one boot and my mobile phone, and my jeans were very low slung by this stage!"

The ewe, exhausted and unable to stand, lay on firm ground beside her liberator. "I will never forget the look in her eye as she gazed towards me, just lying there," says Sue. "I sat beside her and started to gather my thoughts as well as my jeans." The farmer, alerted by Pam, was now racing over the hill, and Sue, assuming he'd press trespassing charges, primed herself for a confrontation. "I was ready for a showdown. Yes, I was trespassing, but I trespassed to save one of his sheep! What could he say? Would he have a go at me, a member of the community, for caring? I was doing his job!"

Sue knew the sheep would not survive without proper medical attention. "I offered to take the ewe off his hands as he obviously had a lot on his plate," she says. Eyeing the dam bank, and clearly struggling to keep his animals watered during drought conditions, the farmer agreed; he even helped maneuver the mud-encrusted sheep into Sue's car.

"This is your lucky day," Sue said, patting her new friend, now christened Whoopi, on the head and driving them to her new home at Edgar's Mission.

Sue is just one example of countless people who volunteer at sanctuaries, rescue centers, and shelters around the world. Whether you're kept busy with such important tasks as walking dogs, doing hands-on care, or giving tours to visitors, there are lots of great reasons to volunteer, including:

- To gain experience working with animals (who knows — you may run your own sanctuary one day)
- To learn more about animal issues
- To surround yourself with like-minded people

- To become active in your community
- To be part of the solution.

It's also important to remember that as activists—especially activists who spend a lot of time online—we need to walk away from social media, at least once in a while, and reengage with animals face to face. We need to access our off buttons and interact with others and our community in the real world.

Sue Werrett with Whoopi, whom she rescued from certain death. Credit: Edgar's Mission

Sanctuaries

Animal sanctuaries around the world rely on volunteers. The work may not be glamorous, but it is among the most rewarding work you will ever do as an activist. There's just nothing quite like seeing hens, pigs, cows, and other animals able to indulge in their natural behaviors, or whistling to turkeys and having them gobble in reply.

Photojournalist Jo-Anne McArthur interned at Farm Sanctuary and remembers what an impact it had on her. "The Farm has really shaped and changed my life," she says. "I really would not be who I am today if it hadn't been for Farm Sanctuary. In 2003 I applied to do an internship. I'd only been there 24 hours and my life was already irrevocably changed. I had been vegetarian until that internship, but became vegan at the Farm and never looked back. The Farm is a place of refuge not just for animals but for compassionate people and activists, and there's also a lot to learn from the Farm and its staff and its inhabitants. It's my favorite place on the planet."

Many activists share Jo-Anne's feelings about sanctuaries. Gary Loewenthal sees spending time at a sanctuary as important for his activism. "It's beyond restorative to me," he says, "it's practically sacred. The animals are wondrous, beautiful, and amazing. It's not just therapeutic—but that alone is powerful—it's inspiring. A huge side benefit is that the more you go or volunteer, the more you know about these animals firsthand. I find that ranchers can no longer pull the 'Have you ever worked on a farm?' line with me. I can tell them I've gotten to know and understand animals from volunteering at a sanctuary in ways that are impossible when one simply breeds them, takes them from their families, fattens them, and slaughters them at a fraction of their lifespans. One also amasses lots of touching and profound stories about animals' experiences, terror, recovery, abilities, emotions, and personalities from spending time with them and learning their backgrounds."

Reputable sanctuaries that allow visitors also provide an opportunity for activists to spend time with animals they might otherwise only see being abused. As Farm Sanctuary's national shelter director, Susie Coston witnesses countless people—meat-eaters as well as animal advocates—engage with cows, pigs, chickens, ducks, turkeys, goats, sheep, and geese. She believes visiting an animal sanctuary can provide activists with critical emotional support, because they can see the happiness of animals that they are fighting for every day. "Seeing an animal even at a small farm is so different than seeing animals who are thriving and feel secure at a sanctuary," says Susie. "It gives some semblance of hope and also shows that even after the abuse, these animals can recover mentally and physically. I find it makes me stronger knowing that they can live through some of the most egregious acts, and come from the most horrific conditions, and forgive and live life fully and happily."

To give you some idea of what sanctuaries do and the opportunities they offer volunteers and, in some cases, interns, following is just a sampling of the organizations that might be a good fit for someone interested in a career in animal protection or simply looking to enhance their effectiveness as activists.

Edgar's Mission (Australia)
Pam Ahern founded Edgar's Mission in 2003, naming the sanctuary after a piglet who'd entered her life that year. She's a firm believer in the power of "meeting your meat" face to face. Once people understand that farmed animals have personalities, needs, and desires—and that they feel emotions like happiness, sorrow, and fear—they can make more informed and compassionate lifestyle choices. Indeed, among the many quotes you'll see around the sanctuary is one from Pam herself: "If we could live happy and healthy lives without harming others, why wouldn't we?"

Volunteers can assist with work around the 153-acre sanctuary, outreach programs such as leafleting, and administrative tasks. "I also manage to rope in a few people now and then when I drive the van around Melbourne showing video footage of a particular animal issue such as live export," says Pam. The sanctuary has more than 400 residents in their care, many with special needs.

Farm Sanctuary (US)

With humble beginnings in the backyard of a Wilmington, Delaware, row house, Farm Sanctuary opened the first shelter in the United States for victims of food animal production in 1986. Today they operate sanctuaries in New York and California. In addition to their animal rescue work, Farm Sanctuary engages in legislation, advocacy, and educational efforts, and Gene Baur, the organization's president and cofounder, is one of the most visible farmed animal advocates in the world. "We have events around the country," says Gene. "We work to empower people to make a positive difference in their daily lives and in their own communities."

Activists interested in becoming a Farm Sanctuary intern are advised to be prepared for hard and sometimes mundane work: interns may be shoveling manure one day and stuffing envelopes the next, but they gain the knowledge and skills that make them better advocates for animals when they leave.

"Being able to spend time with the animals was really valuable," says former intern Nora Kramer. "I don't think I'd ever seen a chicken in person before I went to Farm Sanctuary. But the most important thing is that for the first time I was spending time with other people who felt exactly the same way I did. And I became such a better cook just by living with people who had also been experimenting with vegan cooking."

Greyton Farm Animal Sanctuary (South Africa)

Volunteering at this picturesque sanctuary for pigs, geese, ducks, chickens, and sheep outside Cape Town is a bit different. Here the volunteers live on-site and trade their labor—seven hours a day, six days a week—for room and board. Or they can opt to work just four hours a day, feed themselves, and pay R75 a day (about US$5.50) for their living quarters. "We suggest a one-week maximum commitment at first, but this can be extended if it is working out," says founder Nicola Vernon, who adds that volunteers must adhere to a strict vegan policy while living on the property.

Volunteers can expect to help with such chores as morning feedings and putting out fresh straw for the animals. "At weekends," adds Nicola, "a bit of mucking out—during the week our three men workers do it—letting the pigs out into the full 40 hectares and making sure they don't run into neighboring fields; helping with fencing, putting up shelters, if basic do-it-yourself skills are there; caring for our two special needs pigs, Iris and Munchkin: turning them, physio, bed bath, mucking out, feeding, watering. Also, taking photos and posting on our social media."

Hillside Animal Sanctuary (UK)

As with any sanctuary, each of Hillside's residents comes with a story. There's Matilda, for example, a "breeding sow" who attacked a farmer as he handled one of her screaming piglets. Rather than slaughter her, the farmer released Matilda—and her piglet, Sugar Plum—to Hillside. Alice the camel was likely destined for a circus when a Hillside supporter donated the money to buy her at auction. A duck named Lucky escaped a processing plant and was discovered wandering outside by a Hillside investigator. And national publicity helped win the life of Spot, a wild baby rabbit who had journeyed across the sea from Holland amid a delivery of chrysanthemums. When the media announced that authorities planned to euthanize Spot because her six-month quarantine would cost £700 (about US$950), a public appeal quickly raised the funds and this long-eared stowaway found a home with Hillside's other rescued rabbits.

"The only volunteers we have at the sanctuary are those who help with the animals," says Pauline Lynch. "Because of health and safety regulations, anyone coming to work at the sanctuary has to undergo training and therefore we prefer to take on volunteers who are able to work with us on a fairly long-term basis, even though it may only be for a couple of days a week." In addition to its rescue work, Hillside, located in Norwich, England, engages in undercover investigations and public outreach.

Leilani Farm Sanctuary (US)
Comprising eight lush acres on the Hawaiian island of Maui, there are few sanctuaries as beautiful as Leilani Farm Sanctuary. Luckily for volunteers here in paradise, there are plenty of projects to be done, such as cleaning the barn, gardening, carpentry, animal grooming, deck cleaning, tree trimming, manure collection, weed whacking, mulching, window washing, grass cutting, chain sawing, chipping, painting, carpentry, concrete work, trail maintenance, invasive plant removal, and fence installation/repair. Founded by Laurelee Blanchard in 1999, Leilani is now home to some 300 rescued animals, including cows, pigs, goats, chickens, geese, rabbits, donkeys, and deer.

Paws Awhile Animal Sanctuary (New Zealand)
Located near the coast on New Zealand's North Island, Paws Awhile Sanctuary cares for cows, chickens, pigs, miniature ponies, dogs, and cats who have been abused or abandoned. The sanctuary is on a large parcel of land, and there are many animals, so volunteers can definitely lend a hand. "Most of the work is not glamorous or petting animals," says Anna Dahlberg, who founded Paws Awhile in 2014. "It's mainly things like building new shelters, gardening, spraying gorse and grubbing weeds from the paddocks, cleaning out the animal feed bins and troughs, helping me worm the animals, cleaning out the chicken coops and mucking out the stables, helping me clip the dogs and wash the donkeys in summer, picking up poo from the paddocks, planting trees for shelter, and reorganizing the tack room." If that all sounds like fun to you, Anna recommends that you coordinate your visit with the Auckland University Animal

Rights Group, which arranges weekend volunteering trips to the sanctuary four or five times a year.

Performing Animal Welfare Society (US)
Circuses, zoos, traveling shows, safari parks, and other places of "entertainment" are anything but amusing to the elephants, monkeys, bears, tigers, and lions who are often taken from the wild, cruelly trained to perform tricks, and forced to live in lonely, unnatural conditions. The Performing Animal Welfare Society (PAWS) is home to many of these animals, as well as victims of the exotic animal trade, who have been rescued and can now live in peace and contentment. PAWS operates three sanctuaries in California (they occasionally have open house; otherwise, it's closed to the public), and they need many volunteers to assist with special events, grounds keeping, clerical support, supply transport, fundraising, fence building, and many other jobs. "We have an enriching, learning environment, and we encourage new volunteers and interns," says Kim Gardner of PAWS, who adds that some volunteers have been with them for 20 years.

Pigs Peace Sanctuary (US)
About 50 miles north of Seattle, on a 34-acre plot of land, this sanctuary is home to some 200 pigs. There's Albert, who was found tied to a post and has a fondness for spaghetti. And Bunny, who as a small piglet had been dropped by an eagle along a highway and rescued by a couple who bottle-fed her for a week. Another couple bought Oliver at six weeks old with plans to butcher him, but his personality won them over and they stopped eating pigs. (Well, it's a start.)

Judy Woods founded Pigs Peace Sanctuary in 1994 and credits the book *Charlotte's Web* with inspiring her fondness for these animals. Because of the time and effort it takes to train people to work safely around large animals and sanctuary equipment, Pigs Peace requires that volunteers commit to help for a reasonable amount of time. "To be perfectly honest," says Judy, "the one-time or occasional volunteer does not really help us because of the learning curve. It's the regular volunteer who 'knows the drill' who provides the most effective help."

Because 200 pigs produce a large amount of waste, one of the biggest jobs for volunteers is cleaning up poop. But there are plenty of other things to be done here, including moving hay bales, weeding, repairing fences, and painting barns. Volunteers are also needed to work at Vegan Haven, a grocery store in Seattle that Judy bought in 2006 to help fund the sanctuary.

VINE Sanctuary (US)
Anyone who questions the sentience of birds would do well to spend some time at VINE Sanctuary (formerly Eastern Shore Sanctuary), where chickens, ducks, turkeys, geese, pigeons, and doves—as well as cows, emus, and alpacas—have the freedom to indulge their natural behaviors and display rich emotional lives. (Many of the roosters at VINE are cockfighting survivors or are the unwanted results of backyard egg-keeping.) Watch the hens preen and dust bathe and forage. Notice how the birds interact with one another—and with you. Ask pattrice jones, the sanctuary's cofounder, about a certain rooster named Viktor.

Discovered in a ditch on the side of the road, Viktor had probably jumped or fallen from a truck taking him to one of the many nearby slaughterhouses. He was the first bird pattrice and sanctuary cofounder Miriam Jones brought home. Because the early months of his life were spent in the alien environment of a factory farm, Viktor was unsure how to socialize as more chickens arrived at what would become VINE Sanctuary. A pair of young chickens, Violet and Chickweed, perplexed him. Viktor didn't know if he should be a father to them or a peer; or perhaps he should court the hen and mentor the younger rooster. He tried each role, says pattrice, finally deciding everyone was happiest with him as a very devoted single parent. Viktor also fell in love. When Rosa, his first love, died, Viktor spent months mourning her. He eventually found love again, courting a new arrival named Ellie Mae. As the sanctuary's elder rooster, Viktor was vigilant and protective, even at the risk of his own safety: When he spotted two hawks circling overhead one day, Viktor stood in front of two chicks who hadn't taken cover. But it was agribusiness that would take Viktor's life. He died of a heart attack at about 18 months of age, his body unable to cope with the rapid growth that "broiler" chickens are bred for by the billions each year.

Located in Vermont, VINE Sanctuary is an LGBTQ-run and explicitly ecofeminist organization. They would love to have volunteers assist with campaigns, fundraising, and social media. "People who live nearby can come and help out on a regular basis," says pattrice. "And some people who live a few hours away come for a work day every now and then to help out with big projects in the barns or yards."

Volunteer Jocelyn York takes a break with Lois the turkey.
Credit: Meg York and VINE Sanctuary

Wishing Well Sanctuary (Canada)

Not many sanctuaries make international headlines, but when Wishing Well Sanctuary took in a piglet who had escaped a transport truck bound for a "fattening facility," they immediately gained worldwide attention. Named Yoda, the pig has become one of the better-known stories of farmed animals demonstrating their will to live and not be exploited. He even has a Twitter account.

Brenda Bronfman founded the sanctuary, located just outside Toronto, in 2011 as a home for rescued horses, cows, goats, sheep, llamas, ducks, roosters, donkeys, and, of course, pigs. Wishing Well needs help not only with the usual cleaning and grooming chores related to a sanctuary, but also with fundraising, graphic design, construction, and marketing.

You'll find a more comprehensive list of international sanctuaries at www.vegan.com/farm-sanctuaries.

Wildlife Rescue

No matter where you call home, living in harmony with wildlife is crucial to sustaining the delicate balance of nature. But if you live near an urban area, you probably know that the encroachment of humanity can kill or injure animals and threaten habitats. Even animals far from civilization may suffer the consequences of pollution, oil spills, hunters, motor vehicles, climate change, predatory animals, and much more. Helping to educate the public and protect animals, wildlife centers around the world rescue and rehabilitate animals in need, releasing them back into the wild. Many wildlife centers also serve as advocacy groups, doing outreach and humane education. Although a wildlife rescue organization may have a paid staff, they rely on volunteers to assist with the thousands of animals they may help throughout the year. Here are just a few.

Center for Animal Rehabilitation and Education (South Africa)
On the banks of the Olifants River, along the western edge of Kruger National Park, the Center for Animal Rehabilitation and Education (CARE) began in 1989 as a facility to treat small mammals, reptiles, and birds who had been injured or orphaned. But as CARE grew, founder Rita Miljo welcomed larger animals, and now baboons are the center's main focus. Most of the baboons CARE rescues have been orphaned by hunting, road accidents, poaching, or fire, or they are the traumatized victims of medical experimentation, habitat destruction, or other abuses at the hands of humans. Once integrated into new troops, the animals are successfully released back into the wild.

Volunteers are needed to care for and socialize orphaned baby baboons, as well as to assist in CARE's daily operation. The Center appreciates compassionate, patient volunteers who have experience working with animals, a positive attitude, a love of nature, a sense of humor, and a desire to ensure the survival of South Africa's natural heritage.

The Fox Project (UK)
The fox has certainly had a rough time in the UK. Characterized in folklore as one of nature's tricksters and hunted for thousands of years throughout Great Britain, the fox is also revered by many. Trevor Williams is among those working to aid these animals through his organization. Based in Kent, the Fox Project rescues sick and injured foxes and abandoned fox cubs, providing for their care, treatment and rehabilitation back into the wild. Because some householders still regard the fox as a villain, the Fox Project offers a humane fox deterrence and advice service.

"We operate with around 75 volunteers," says Trevor, a former hunt saboteur. "There are rescuers, fosterers, rehabbers, cleaners, and fundraisers. Rescuers are simply folk who we call when an incident occurs near to them so that they can get hold of the animal more quickly than our duty wildlife ambulance.

Fosterers look after healthy cubs, post-weaning, or convalescent adults prior to release, in cages on their own properties, thereby alleviating pressure on our central treatment facilities. The rehabbers' job is to release a group of five hand-raised cubs from a rehab cage on their property at end of summer when natural dispersal would be taking place. Cleaners speaks for itself, really. Their job is to keep cage areas on main facilities clean and tidy and to administer medication. Fundraisers carry out all the usual can shaking, sponsored events, raffles, and such on our behalf."

(Though fox hunting with hounds is now officially banned in England and Wales, enthusiasts of this blood sport are working to overturn the law and, as Trevor observes, "It was never carried out by a particularly law-abiding section of society, so it still continues in most areas of the country with no real policing to curb it.")

Friends of Free Wildlife (South Africa)
Founded in 2015 by wildlife rehabilitators, this rescue center in Johannesburg is where the public can bring injured animals such as doves, owls, egrets, tortoises, jackals, and bats from urban communities to be cared for and released. Volunteers must be at least 18 years of age and attend an orientation. They begin by preparing food for the animals and cleaning and enriching enclosures, all while observing the rehabilitation process. Volunteers can then advance to higher levels of work by taking required courses, eventually becoming a full voting member of the center.

Kingbilli Wildlife Rescue (Australia)
Georgina Beach was 23 feet (7 meters) up a tree, face to face with an injured koala, when she lost her footing. Fortunately for Georgina, who runs Kingbilli Wildlife Rescue, and for the elderly marsupial, who also became dislodged from the tree, a Dutch couple volunteering for Kingbilli were waiting below.

"This was the best advertisement for having two volunteers present on a wildlife rescue," she says. "One volunteer to catch the koala—and the other to catch me!"

Most volunteers at this busy wildlife refuge and rehabilitation center in the central highlands of Victoria, however, don't have direct contact with the animals. It's a matter of not having proper training, Georgina explains. "The biology, ecology, and behavior of native wildlife are a world apart from those animals with whom most humans are familiar, and at least a basic understanding of these areas is required before people can work hands-on with them." Volunteers are more likely to be helping with manual labor at the refuge or crowd control during rescues.

In addition to koalas, Kingbilli rescues a veritable roll call of outback critters, including kangaroos, wallabies, wombats, possums, phascogales, and agile antechinus. "Wildlife rehabilitation is not all cute and cuddly," says Georgina. "It involves considerable hard work—and much more than its fair share of heartache." Although she says the work is difficult, "the most mundane, boring, or back-breaking tasks are just as important as bottle-feeding a cute and cuddly baby."

Proyecto Asis (Costa Rica)
Costa Rica is well known for its wide variety of animals. What is less known is the impact that human activities have had on those animals: encroaching development, habitat destruction, and hunting have led to a precipitous decline in wildlife populations. This rescue center rehabilitates wild animals and releases them back into nature; animals who cannot be released have a permanent home at Proyecto Asis. Here you're likely to see toucans, sloths, spider monkeys, parrots, coatis (members of the raccoon family), and peccaries—wild pigs. "Costa Ricans see on TV and movies how people bring potbellied pigs into their homes," staff member Carlos Barrantes told me during a visit in 2017. "But Costa Rica does not have potbelly pigs, so people go

out into the rainforest and take baby wild pigs home." Peccaries emit a pungent, musky odor, so it's only a matter of time before neighbors complain and the animal is confiscated. Many of them end up at Proyecto Asis.

The sanctuary offers a number of volunteering opportunities—with tasks that include cleaning enclosures, feeding the animals, and general maintenance of the facility—but be prepared to pay for the privilege. Unlike many other sanctuaries, Proyecto Asis counts on tourists to fund their own one-day "volunteer adventures" that in turn support the rescue center.

Southern Cross Wildlife Care (Australia)
Founded by veterinarian Howard Ralph, Southern Cross Wildlife Care (SCWC) treats and cares for injured, sick, and orphaned wildlife. It was after a brushfire that Dr. Ralph noticed the lack of volunteer assistance for Australia's injured native species. "The wildlife were getting so little help and I thought, 'Well, I have only got one life and I should put it to the best use I can, and the wildlife need it the most,'" he says.

Dr. Ralph is not just a vet—his remarkably diverse medical background includes work as a surgeon, aesthetician, and emergency care worker. He and his fellow volunteers at SCWC treat more than 2,000 native animals every year. When lauren and I visited Sydney in 2011, he humbly showed us a photo album full of examples demonstrating the patience with which he cares for even the smallest animals.

"Howard never gives up on even the most sad and hopeless-looking situation," says volunteer Lindy Stacker. "If you were a sick animal, trust me, you would want to look up and see the eyes of this most kind man looking over you. It is very difficult getting vets to care for wildlife. They just won't afford our precious but often desperate wildlife the time and attention they need. It really breaks our hearts."

WildCare (US)

WildCare is one of the few truly urban wildlife rehabilitation centers, located near a thriving downtown area in Marin County, California. The organization pursues its advocacy through nature education, wildlife rehabilitation and community outreach, and it relies heavily on volunteers.

"Each year our incredibly dedicated volunteers reach and teach more than 40,000 Bay Area children and adults, encouraging an awareness of the need for sustainability and a love of nature," says Alison Hermance, WildCare's director of communications. "Our wildlife hospital is 95 percent run by volunteers, so we couldn't treat the more than 3,000 animals we take in every year without their help. Volunteers handle the majority of the feeding, medicating, cleaning and caring for our patients. Our goal is to rehabilitate animals and then release them back into the wild, and we absolutely could not provide such quality care for the more than 200 different species of animals we treat without our volunteers."

WildCare also welcomes people to work on their wildlife hotline, fielding calls from the public regarding the many issues involved in sharing the region with wild animals, and for the foster care of baby wild patients and to represent WildCare at fairs and other outreach events.

"WildCare's volunteers come from all walks of life and all ages," says Alison. "Volunteering has given them the opportunity to come face to face with amazing wild animals, participate in their healing, and share a love and respect for the natural world with the next generation."

Wildlife Rescue Association (Canada)

Located in British Columbia, Wildlife Rescue Association (WRA) cares for thousands of injured, orphaned, and pollution-damaged wild animals every year. Upon completing a hands-on training program, volunteers work directly with animals, returning them to their natural habitats as soon as they are healthy and able to live independently in the wild.

"WRA volunteers begin with the pigeon cages, as pigeons are the gentlest birds to work with," says Liberty Mulkani, a former volunteer. "To clean a bird's habitat you first have to carefully wrap the bird in a towel and transfer him or her to a cardboard cat carrier. This can be quite intimidating as you want to be as gentle as possible without letting them escape, which could lead to further injury." Liberty says one of the most challenging aspects of the job is not speaking to the animals. "As the patients at WRA are all wild animals, the staff is very strict about the importance of not allowing them to imprint on humans, as this would detract from their survival chances once re-released." As volunteers become more comfortable with pigeons, they're moved to other birds such as gulls, crows, ducks, geese, swans, starlings, and hawks. WRA also assists the occasional chipmunk, beaver, raccoon, deer, and bat.

Shelters

Unlike most animal sanctuaries at which animals spend the rest of their lives, shelters offer animals for adoption to members of the public. Overpopulation of dogs, cats, rabbits, and other domesticated animals forces shelters to euthanize about half of the millions of animals who end up in shelters each year. Although "no kill" shelters may seem like a wonderful solution, the reality

How often do we take the time to look at ourselves? Can we even allow ourselves a moment to put ourselves first? Or would that be selfish—are we too busy, can't say no to helping out, who else is going to take care of my critters, the homeless, the environment?

Kymberlie Adams Matthews
Satya **magazine**, April 2005

is these facilities only accept the most "adoptable" animals (who may spend years in a cage), while the animals turned away likely end up in an open-admission shelter down the road—or simply abandoned to fend for themselves on the street.

Shelters need activists willing to donate their time and energy, and such volunteer work might include:

- Exercising, grooming, and socializing animals while they wait for loving homes
- Cleaning cages, the backyard, or the shelter's office
- Helping to reunite animal guardians with their lost companions
- Participating in community outreach activities to educate the public about the need for humane treatment of all animals
- Helping with shelter events and fundraising.

Don't be afraid to suggest your own ways to help. For example, if you're computer literate, you could offer to maintain a shelter's website or their social media accounts for them and keep them current with information on the animals available for adoption.

Because most cities have an animal shelter, all of which need volunteers, a list of suggested places to start is not necessary. You will need to contact each shelter directly to learn about volunteer needs and opportunities. Look online for an "animal shelter" or "humane society" location near you.

Improving a Shelter
No shelter is perfect, of course, but poor conditions may indicate a shortage of staff or financial resources, rather than a lack of compassion. According to the Animal Legal Defense Fund (ALDF), as a baseline, a humane shelter should be a safe haven for all animals in its custody and provide humane care for all stray and relinquished animals.

If you find yourself volunteering at a shelter that needs real reform—or you witness neglect or abuse—ALDF recommends that you document your findings, noting dates, locations, and specific problems in a detailed journal. Photographs, video, and other evidence of the abusive conditions are helpful and persuasive.

Ideally, you would work with the shelter staff and management to facilitate the needed changes; however, if they refuse to engage in a conversation about improving the conditions for the animals in their care, contact the people or agencies who oversee the shelter and provide them with your documentation of the abusive conditions. This is often the sheriff's department, city council, mayor, or city manager. Also, check with your state

---

Roadside Animal Emergencies

- Because you never know when you may come upon an animal who needs your assistance, keep a small box with air holes (like the cardboard carriers found at shelters) in your car, along with a towel, heavy gloves, and a leash.
- Know the locations and phone numbers of your local pet hospital and wildlife-rescue center.
- When approaching an injured animal, move slowly and quietly; resist the urge to speak to them.
- Wearing gloves, gently lift the animal into the towel and place him or her into the box and close the lid. If they won't fit into the box, wrap them in the towel and cover their eyes.
- Back in your vehicle, keep the radio off. If it's cold outside, leave the heater on. Don't speak to the animal.
- Note the location where you found them. If they can be rehabilitated and released, this will help rehabilitators return them to their home territory.

Department of Agriculture to inquire about oversight of the agencies in question. It is imperative that local authorities fully investigate the case.

Another major issue: many shelters don't understand that serving meat and other animal products at fundraising events is hypocritical. If your local animal shelter serves meat, eggs, or dairy foods at events, ask them to set a compassionate example by taking these foods off the menu. Remind them that by doing so they are not only being consistent in their ethic, but they are helping to make all supporters feel welcome. They also won't be faced with the embarrassment of trying to explain why they are helping some animals but eating others. (Such a request will likely be better received coming from a volunteer, since you'd already be in a position to engage in meaningful discussion and shelter staff recognize your commitment to helping animals.)

Rabbit Rescue

As the third most popular companion animal in the UK, US, and other countries, rabbits have a devout following. Humans who live with them are usually amazed by the rabbit's intelligence, beguiled by their gentle natures, and captivated by their lively personalities. Sadly, domestic bunnies are also some of the most abused creatures in the world. They are slaughtered for their flesh, skinned for their fur, used in entertainment, blinded to test cosmetics, bred for show, drugged in the name of science, exhibited in zoos, clipped for wool products, killed in vivisection labs, sold as food for pet snakes, shipped by breeders, and imprisoned in small cages by guardians who haven't learned about proper bunny care. To add insult to all this injury, we chop off their paws and tout the rabbit's foot as a "good luck" charm.

Too often people give little thought before bringing home a rabbit, impulsively buying them at pet stores (especially during Easter season) and then, when the novelty has worn off, discarding the bunnies at shelters or dumping them in a park, where they are usually unable to survive. Responsible rabbit guardians take the time to learn about bunnies before rescuing one (or two!) from a shelter and then spaying or neutering their new companions.

Because of the rabbit's unique position as perhaps the only companion animal humans abuse to such a vast extent, I wanted to provide information on a few organizations that shelter bunnies and find new homes for them. This is by no means a comprehensive list, and I have tried to include only organizations that do not support any rabbit exploitation, such as breeding and rabbit shows, and that advocate rabbits living indoors as part of the family, not in backyard hutches. All of these organizations count on volunteers.

House Rabbit Society (US)
With chapters across the United States, the House Rabbit Society (HRS) rescues thousands of rabbits every year. The majority of these rabbits come from shelters where they have yet to find a permanent home and are thus facing euthanasia. HRS also takes in bunnies saved from neglect and abuse cases.

"Activists can help most easily by downloading HRS materials off of our website and educating the public at veterinary offices, pet stores, special events, and at other places by handing out or putting up materials," says Margo DeMello, president of HRS. Margo encourages activists to also get involved at their local shelters by socializing and grooming the rabbits, bringing in hay or toys, and helping with adoptions. HRS is always looking for responsible people to foster one or more rabbits as well. "If they really want to be involved as an HRS volunteer," she says, "they can apply to be an educator, or, if they already are fostering and educating and have a nonprofit group formed, they can apply to be a chapter." As part of their ongoing outreach, HRS also invites activists to help with tabling at events.

Rabbit Rescue (Canada)

For as long as she can remember, Haviva Lush has been devoted to animals. She went vegetarian at age five and has pursued animal rights and environmental issues ever since, attending and organizing protests, doing outreach, and rescuing animals. As the founder of Rabbit Rescue, she now finds loving homes for domestic rabbits who have been abandoned, abused, or neglected.

Rabbit Rescue works with shelters across the province of Ontario, taking in about 300 animals a year who would otherwise be euthanized and helping those organizations in adopting rabbits. Rabbit Rescue spays and neuters every rabbit who comes into their care, and they are dedicated to special-needs rabbits who require ongoing medical treatment.

"The biggest way to help us is by becoming a foster parent," Haviva says. "We work with the highest-kill shelters in Ontario, and as soon as we have another foster home, it's another bunny saved."

SaveABunny (US)

SaveABunny is a volunteer-run organization where people can bring their passion, commitment, creativity, and talent to directly help save the lives of animals. "We genuinely believe that anything people enjoy doing—whether it be cleaning bunny pens, designing a T-shirt, transporting animals and supplies, creating artwork, or whatever—they can apply these interests in a fun and meaningful way to help animals in need," says Marcy Berman, who founded SaveABunny in 1999. The organization assists northern California shelters in finding loving homes for more than 300 domestic rabbits every year, including many special-needs bunnies who were abused, neglected, or have health issues.

"SaveABunny is a proactive and progressive group that deeply values our members and supporters," says Marcy. "Many long-lasting friendships have been made while caring for the rabbits, and our events are notoriously fun." In addition to disseminating informative educational materials, conducting community outreach, and providing hands-on grassroots rescue work, SaveABunny has a sense of humor. "Our merchandise and organizational activities tend to have an urban sophisticate feel mixed with professionalism and the right touch of 'rabbitude.'"

The organization opposes the production, sale, or use of rabbit fur, rabbit skin, and rabbit meat; these campaigns are run by volunteers. "We welcome compassionate, responsible people to help us advocate and care for these special little companions who deserve protection, respect, and love," says Marcy.

Vancouver Rabbit Rescue and Advocacy (Canada)
Their name pretty much says it all. VRRA founder Olga Betts says her organization does quite a bit of outreach, educating the public about rabbits, and they have plenty of opportunities for activists who would like to get involved. "We will train people to help with rabbits, but there are a lot of other things we need," she says. "Education help, event help, fundraising, marketing, promotion, graphic design, web design—the list is endless. Quite frankly, there is so much we would like to do and we talk about but it never can get done because we need people to do it."

Chapter 8

Animal Planet: The Global Reach of Multimedia

Unless someone like you cares a whole awful lot, nothing is going to get better. It's not.
Dr. Seuss

Karl Losken and Lindsay Bickford enjoyed talk radio, but they found little sympathy whenever they'd phone in to their favorite radio shows to discuss animal rights. "Basically we became tired of calling in on other hosts' talk shows and then being cut off when raising the animal issues," says Karl. "So we started our own radio program." They found a home for their show, *Animal Voices*, on Vancouver's community-based Co-op Radio in 2001, and it's still going strong. The weekly program explores a wide variety of animal-related concerns and is heard throughout much of British Columbia and northern Washington State over the air and around the world as a podcast. Perhaps best of all, no one interrupts when *Animal Voices* is addressing such topics as vivisection, endangered species, or animal activism.

Karl twice attempted to submit films to the Vancouver International Film Festival: *The Witness*, which explores how Eddie Lama embarked on his street-level animal activism, and *Peaceable Kingdom*, the groundbreaking film about animal agriculture. Karl's application was flatly rejected both times. "Instead of accepting *Peaceable Kingdom*, they played a movie on how to skin a cat," he says. Buoyed by his success on the air, he created the Animal Voices Film Festival, devoted to, as Karl describes, "celebrating the glory of the animal kingdom." The event plays to a full house every year.

Welcome to the modern age of animal activism.

While their success may seem like an anomaly—how many of us could hope to have our own radio show or launch a film festival?—Karl and Lindsay simply put their talents to use for animals in the best way they could. And their story is really not that uncommon; as we'll see, the emergence of the digital realm has created a truly universal activist community, with one person's outreach message received and shared by a global audience. Some of the tactics now being implemented include:

- Social networks—Facebook, Twitter, Tumblr, Periscope, LinkedIn, and so many more
- Personal websites
- Videos—posted to YouTube, Vimeo, and more
- Podcasting
- Blogging
- Digital images—Instagram, Flickr, Snapchat, Pinterest, etc.

There are so many platforms, in fact, that it might be difficult to decide which one to use. "I think they all serve a unique and specific purpose," says Aph Ko, a Black vegan feminist theorist and independent digital media producer who uses a variety of media platforms in her activism. "Your strengths will dictate which medium you use, so if you're better at articulating your thoughts and making connections through speaking, for example, you might want to make a video. If you are better at organizing your thoughts through writing, you might want to write a post."

Social Media Activism

Can social media make a difference? Or is it more like "slacktivism"—online actions taking only a moment while having little, if any, impact? Well, let's consider the 2011 revolts and political change that took place in Egypt and Tunisia. Popularly

> Consciousness is a gift. And even consciousness about suffering is a gift. We experience the suffering but we are also given the gift of the consciousness about it, and it's better to be awake than asleep most of the time. We're committed to living life with integrity, and integrity means not being split off from who we ourselves are.
> **Carol J. Adams**
> *Satya* **magazine**, July/August 2001

known as the Arab Spring, the uprisings were organized and publicized by activists using social media. While it's been widely reported that the protesters used Facebook to plan demonstrations and share horrifying images of state violence, they actually used several social media platforms, including Twitter, Skype, and YouTube. Another example is Black Lives Matter, which was born as an online phrase to identify messages among the Black community and display solidarity and has grown into an international social movement.

"Social media plays a critical role in my ability to help animals," says Carrie LeBlanc, executive director of CompassionWorks International (CWI), which campaigns against animal cruelty and also helps activists take action in their own communities. "CWI would simply not exist without the opportunities for connection that social media offers. From building awareness of animal issues, to finding animal advocates to work alongside, to sharing productive actions that people can take to get involved, to generating organizational name recognition, social media has revolutionized the way that advocacy is conducted and advanced, as well as how new nonprofits are grown."

One common mistake that animal advocates make is to oversaturate their personal social media outlets with animal rights messaging, says Carrie. "Staggering posts dedicated to helping animals with personal items like family photos helps to prevent attrition in the number of people who follow you. For instance, if you invest a lot of time in building a network of vegans and posting multiple times a day with every new piece of vegan-related news that comes up, you'll soon find you've lost the attention of your family and friends and are just posting to your echo chamber." While building community and networks is important because animal advocacy can be a lonely journey, Carrie suggests that activists consider segmenting their social media so they aren't posting too often and potentially losing the attention of people who haven't yet opened their eyes to the realities of institutionalized animal cruelties. "Another possibility is to dedicate one of your social media channels solely to advocacy — Twitter works well for this — and then another, like Facebook, for gently peppering in messages related to advocacy alongside posts that do not address animal issues regularly. That way, you will keep friends and family engaged with your messages and they're not prone to unfollow you."

Social media is also an excellent tool for finding activism opportunities. When Dana Portnoy relocated from Boston to the San Francisco Bay Area, she was a busy activist. "Whether we were protesting the circus or foie gras or volunteering at a farmed animal sanctuary, there was always something to do to help the animals," she says. "But when I moved back to Boston, that same animal rights community didn't seem to exist. I became an armchair activist, which never really felt right to me." That changed after she saw that the Pet Express store in her local mall was selling dogs from a puppy mill. "Outraged, I immediately pulled out my smartphone to Google it, and the first thing that came up was the Boycott Pet Express Facebook page. Ah, the power of social media! I sent the group a message, indicating I was standing outside the shop furious and would love to get involved in their campaign. The woman who led the organization sent me an invite to their next protest. And just like that, I was an activist again."

Dana became involved with the Mass Coalition to End Puppy Mills, fighting puppy mills in Massachusetts. "Throughout the last few years," she says, "I have attended protests with them throughout the state and helped in their efforts to obtain a ban on the retail sale of puppies, kittens, and rabbits in the City of Boston. Many of the members of the coalition have even gone vegan, thanks to a little nudging from their local vegan, sharing recipes and news articles on Facebook." Dana has since gotten involved in other forms of activism, and social media even led her to the Strong Hearts Vegan Power running team, which has been an integral part of her life since 2015. "I'm now one of the lead organizers of the team," she says. "And it all began with a message on Instagram, saying, 'Hey, would you like to join the vegan running team, running a relay race on Cape Cod?'"

Although social media is a wonderful tool, Mariann Sullivan, cofounder of the indie media powerhouse Our Hen House, cautions activists not to assume that posting something our friends will see has the same effect as personal engagement. "I think all social media runs the risk of allowing us to think we are having more of an impact than we are since it's easy to reach a circle of supporters and get a lot of positive feedback and not really be accomplishing much in the way of reaching non-choir folks," she says. "This is not to say that social media isn't important—it's the most important tool most of us have for spreading information and ideas, and creates opportunities that simply didn't exist 20 years ago. I remember when I first got started in animal rights how difficult it was to find out what was happening to animals, who the various groups were, what they were doing, what information sources were available, and what information I could rely on. It was a huge struggle that can largely be resolved nowadays with a few clicks from your Facebook feed. So social media is absolutely crucial and has changed everything, even though it requires rigorous self-monitoring for effectiveness."

Widening the Circle

While digital communication may be fast and cost-effective, it's important for us to remember that not every animal advocate is comfortable with new technologies. Animals Australia, for instance, produces videos, maintains a strong online presence through social and video-sharing sites, and keeps most members updated via email. But they also produce a printed magazine and advertise in publications and on radio and TV. "We do need to keep a variety of communication methods going because some of our supporters are older and do not have access to the Internet," says Glenys Oogjes, the group's executive director.

Using Social Networks

If we have the ability to show up for real-life encounters, nothing can replace face-to-face activism. But social media can still serve as a powerful tool for:

- Organizing protests, campaigns, and other events
- Sharing educational articles, images, and videos
- Posting comments on the pages of companies we wish to influence
- Sharing stories, links, and vegan recipes
- Showing solidarity with other social justice movements
- Following the work of groups you support.

Some other tips to consider:

- Think critically before you post an article or information.

Are you sure it's accurate? If it seems more like propaganda than news, don't share it.

- Keep in mind that social media offers no privacy, so even when you believe you are part of a "private group," be careful not to discuss strategy online. "Know that whatever you post to social media is no longer yours alone and can be used against you or your campaign at any time," warns Tara Baxter.

- Don't post graphic images. "It's traumatic and upsetting and will shut down many people," says Martina Bernstein. "I personally unfriend everybody who posts especially distressing photographs because I cannot handle the images. There are ways to inform and request action without graphic depictions of gut-wrenching cruelty."

- Learn how to work the Facebook algorithm effectively. "It's constantly evolving, but Facebook has a very detailed algorithm to determine who sees your posts and in what frequency," says Jake Conroy. "If you don't work it, it doesn't matter what you post or how much you post it, because people won't see it. Most people bang their heads against the wall when it comes to social media and are convinced they are being censored, but really they just aren't working the system." (Jake says this isn't difficult, but it takes a decent amount of time and dedication.)

- Be personal. "My following is mainly on Instagram, and I've used it for both business and activism," says Jessica Schlueter. "The most popular posts I have are always about my own life. Especially as your following grows, people look up to you more, so they feel special to have access to your daily life. If you just post general stuff about animal exploitation, they don't pay attention to the source, so they don't develop a trusting relationship with you and therefore don't engage as much with your content."

- Don't overwhelm people with one issue. "Be very selective

in what you choose to post and how often," says Andy Tabar. "People are much more likely to perk up and take notice about, for instance, a vegan post if you don't post about it too often—as opposed to the folks who flood their daily feed with only vegan links and rants."

Different social networks are popular among different demographics—millennials, for example, are not necessarily going to use the same platform favored by baby boomers or the Gen Xer. So, to ensure your message reaches a wide audience, it makes sense to participate in a wide number of online spaces.

Using a social media management tool can help you schedule your messages and reach a wider audience at the optimum time.

Desktop Outreach

Activist Samantha Smith has a clever method for spreading the word: she's created a "Go Vegan" folder that she saves onto the desktop of computers at her school, the University of Cape Town. The folder contains articles, studies, images (many of which highlight cognitive dissonance), video links, recipes, guides on going vegan, and book and documentary recommendations. "The purpose is to appeal to as many people as possible," she says. "Some will be swayed by poignant imagery and documentaries like *Earthlings* and *Cowspiracy*, while others will be persuaded by compelling health reasons. It is also valuable to include factual pieces which debunk misinformed arguments against veganism."

Blogging

With the advent of blogs, just about anyone can publish organized content online. And as more people turn to the

Internet as a source for information on everything from fashion and entertainment to health and nutrition, blogging has become a state-of-the-art model for animal activism.

Starting a blog is simple, and it's a great way to reach a wide audience. Shortly after the first edition of *Striking at the Roots* came out, for example, I launched a blog with the same name, in which I publish my interviews with activists and general articles about animal activism around the world. It seemed like a natural adjunct to this book, and it's proven to be pretty popular.

"Blogs can be very important and useful to animal advocacy, whether they be newsy, recipe or cooking blogs, or focused more on activism—though there are not many of these around," says Gary Smith, who produces a blog called The Thinking Vegan with his wife, Kezia. "Non-vegans and new vegans are looking for information and inspiration, and blogs are a great space for both. A well-written and credible blog can sometimes get as much attention as a traditional news outlet. Our issues are often outside the mainstream, and we sometimes must depend on blogs in the absence of other press coverage. That said, the line between a blog and an online news site is very, very blurry today."

Laura Beck, who blogs for Vegansaurus, advises activists interested in blogging to jump right in. "Just do it," she says. "And stick with it! Vegansaurus didn't have, like, any readers or followers for maybe almost a year. It takes time to build a community—or become part of a community—and most people just quit, so if you stick with it, you will find your place at the table."

Gary agrees. "Do it, if you can either find an angle that isn't already being done out there, or if you feel like you can attract an audience that is underrepresented. If your voice goes against the stream or you have something to add to the community that doesn't currently exist, then by all means, jump into the fray." But Gary warns against copying the work of others. "Because our movement is so small in comparison to others, what I don't like seeing—whether it's nonprofits, vegan food businesses, cookbooks, blogs, or even T-shirts—is a duplication of our efforts or too much overlap. We can't cannibalize each other at this point. There aren't enough of us yet."

In fact, assuming the purpose of your blog is to increase awareness about animal suffering, consider a blog site that is *not* focused on animal rights. Take one of your other interests— travel, running, cooking, or whatever—and create a blog around that, occasionally weaving in discussion about veganism or animal rights issues. In the same way that an op-ed critical of animal testing will likely affect more hearts and minds by being published in your local newspaper than in an anti-vivisection publication, a smattering of blog entries on veganism or a link to a powerful video could result in helping more animals than spending all your activist time preaching to the choir.

But try to post strategically, rather than emotionally. "If you are using social media as a tool for your activism, then you really should think through what you would like to achieve," says Gary. "Think about who your audience is, who reads your posts, and what type of results you are hoping to get from your posts. One really heartfelt and thought-provoking post every week or two is probably more effective than posting a new meme or 'sign this petition, please' every few hours."

One of the beauties of writing a blog is you don't need to know HTML, CSS, or any other fancy coding languages—the sort of script that on the screen looks like a mash-up between an unceasing line of typos and the periodic table of elements. It's basically as simple as using a word processing program. There are so many free how-to guides online to walk you through the process of launching and maintaining a blog site that I need not go into detail, but here are some highlights:

- Pick a blog name... something memorable that reflects

you and what you'll be blogging about. Once you've got it, search online to see if anyone else is already using it.

- Decide who will host your blog site. Will it be a free platform like WordPress, or do you want to buy your own domain (i.e., www.yourblogname.com)? Some online research will help you here.
- Register your site. Again, read up on this.
- Write your first blog post! Proofread your blog posts carefully before publishing them, but don't worry if you find a mistake later: you can always make edits.
- Promote your blog posts on social media sites.

In fact, promoting your blog may be your biggest but most important step. "Share it on your social media, send it to your friends, send it to vegans online who you like and identify with," says Laura.

"Remember that for self-produced blogs," says Jasmin Singer, "it's important to try to get readers from various other circles to read our words, as opposed to just the 'vegan choir.' So try to write your blog in a way that will have some opportunities for coalition-building, retweeting, and sharing."

Not all blogging experiences are positive, nor is it always a safe space for everyone, especially groups that are already oppressed. Aph Ko says she's learned this the hard way. "I've had my ideas stolen, re-packaged, and I've seen others get financially compensated for basically saying exactly what I have written—even activists of color have taken my work. It's made me much more cautious about writing online. When you're saying something new or interesting, people have a tendency to gravitate towards you and then literally take what you've written. This has made me rethink blogging as a whole, to be quite honest." Such experiences have made Aph distrustful of the online world as a vessel for social change. "This is why I'm starting to explore more opportunities when it comes to print.

I think minoritized activists should invest energy into writing books, or creating zines—something tangible that they can own rather than using white digital land to cultivate their intellectual thoughts." (Aph's first book, *Aphro-ism: Essays on Pop Culture, Feminism, and Black Veganism from Two Sisters*, co-written with her sister Syl, was published in 2017.)

Podcasting

With the democratization of technology, audio media capabilities that were once only available to broadcasting corporations can now be accessed by anyone with a computer, a microphone, and access to the Internet. As a result, you can find podcasts on virtually any subject, from veganism and animal rights to animal law and activist burnout. Behind each of them is at least one person—and often two—with a passion for the topic.

"I love that podcasts allow incredibly niche subjects to find their audience for a relatively low cost," says Andy Tabar, who teamed up with his fellow hirsute friend Paul Stellar to create "The Bearded Vegans" podcast. "We didn't really start the podcast with any grand plans in mind. At the time, I hadn't found many vegan podcasts that really spoke to my specific sensibilities. So when Paul invited me to be his co-host, I thought it would be a fun opportunity to create that very content. As things progressed, we realized that we wanted to carve out a place where it's okay to be excited about new vegan products while also taking issues within the vegan community very seriously."

Another pair of friends with a successful podcast, Callie Coker and Nichole Dinato, take a holistic approach to animal rights with their show "Vegan Warrior Princesses Attack!" You're as likely to hear them discuss feminism or human rights as you are veganism, and they find podcasting the ideal format for expressing their views. "The platform lends itself well to deep discussions and the breaking down of complex ideas, so it's an ideal space to introduce people to new or different points of view and get to really thoroughly make your case," says Callie, who adds that listeners seem to have more patience for podcasts than for other forms of social media. "When we launched our show, we assumed most people would already be on the same page as us, but we've been surprised by the countless messages from people that have gone vegan after listening to the show, or from people that already were vegan but have learned about a social justice issue they weren't fully aware of and have expanded their views or activism dramatically."

To create "Our Hen House," the podcast she co-hosts with Mariann Sullivan, Jasmin Singer read *Podcasting for Dummies*. "I learned how to podcast from reading that book front to back," she says. "I would also strongly suggest listening to a variety of podcasts and taking notes on what works and doesn't work. For instance, nobody wants to hear a podcast with only one person represented the entire time, especially when that one person is screaming at you. When you hear podcasts you like, what is it about them that resonates with you? And what are the things you need to do better? Is it your interview skills? Your time-keeping and pacing? Your content ideas?"

Jasmin advises activists to get a friend to work with you — either on-air or on a production level — because podcasts can be a lot of work, and frequently require a second opinion and an extra hand.

That's something Andy agrees with, and he says podcasting takes much more time and discipline than he thought it would. "Even a show like ours, which is a relatively unpolished long-form conversation, requires a lot of time to prepare and edit. If you're down for the heavy workload, then make sure you actually have something unique and interesting to say, or make sure you can do it better than someone that's already doing what you want to do. From there, just go for it. You're never going to be fully ready. But that's the beauty of podcasts — they evolve along with you as you grow."

"Just take it step by step," says Jasmin. "If I had gone into podcasting overthinking how to do it, there is no way I would have ever started. People frequently ask me for advice on how to get started at something—be it working in animal rights or speaking up for animals in their communities or podcasting. The answer, at the end of the day, is that you *just start*."

Virtual Reality

Although it's going to be a while before the average grassroots activist is using virtual reality (VR), technology has a way of becoming more accessible with time. After all, the first commercially available cell phone was a 1983 Motorola that cost US$4,000, weighed about 2 pounds, and had all the ergonomic elegance of a concrete brick. I'm willing to wager that it won't be too long before having VR in our homes is nearly as common as having a blender.

In the meantime, more and more animal rights groups are adopting VR, so it's important to understand its advantages and limitations. VR is a step between undercover images and actually being inside a slaughterhouse or factory farm. I was able to sample the technology when Animal Equality, one of the first groups to begin using VR, previewed their original iAnimal project at an animal rights conference in Washington, DC. After Animal Equality cofounder Jose Valle placed an oversized pair of goggles and headphones on my head, I felt as if I were standing in the middle of a factory farm for pigs with a 360-degree, three-dimensional view from the animals' perspective. Everywhere I turned my head, I was bearing witness to cruelty. As you might imagine, the sights and sounds of rows of pigs unable to move are heartbreaking. Jose had warned me that there would be scenes of pigs being slaughtered, so I turned the device off early. Still, it was a very emotional, you-are-there experience.

"You can actually look an animal in the eye moments before

they are slaughtered, or see everything from the perspective of an animal confined in a cage," says Jose, explaining that Animal Equality had been given access to animal factories and slaughterhouses, and that his team used a custom rig built with six special cameras to film the footage, which was later stitched together to create an immersive, vivid sense of reality. Viewers have full control over where they want to direct their attention and are able to behold their grim surroundings, from floor to ceiling and all around, in full, stereoscopic 3D. Animal Equality has gone on to create an entire series of virtual reality films, including those focused on dairies and chicken farms. It's a major tool in helping consumers realize empathy for others, transforming them from passive meat-eater to someone with a more informed and engaged point of view.

"There has been a significant number of people who, even though they already knew about the horrors of factory farming, have only decided to stop eating meat after watching our iAnimal films," says Jose. "For example, the study *Effect of Immersive (360°) Video on Attitude and Behavior Change* carried out by Diana Fonseca from the Aalborg University of Denmark indicates that people who have experienced virtual reality tend to eat less animal products than those who have watched the same film in standard screens or those in the control group."

It's not an exact reproduction of being behind the scenes, of course. For one thing, anyone who has been inside a facility where farmed animals are intensively confined remembers the smell, and that's yet to be replicated with VR. The next step could be augmented reality, in which the viewer is able to interact with the animals, not just watch them. "Given the current state of this technology, achieving a high-quality interactive experience would require an immense amount of resources," says Jose. "It is simply too early for that, but as the processors become more powerful and augmented reality viewers improve and increase their field of view and capabilities, we will start to see more cost-effective applications to augmented reality." He adds that given the increased interest of consumers to learn more about the origin of their food and the practices involved in producing it, VR could also be used to provide that information in a visually compelling way. "The current cost of the equipment and the cost per viewer is higher than using other offline interventions such as leafleting, or online interventions such as using Facebook ads," he says. "However, it has a higher emotional impact on the viewer than these other methods of outreach."

Email Security

The activist-oriented merits of email are clear: communicating quickly with companies, sending letters to editors, staying in touch with other activists, organizing events, etc. In fact, the benefits and uses of email are so obvious in the 21st century that there's no reason to explore this as a tool. What *does* need to be mentioned, however, is the potential for emails to be used against you. The sad reality is governments routinely spy on their own citizens, and even the content of innocuous emails can be used to build a profile on you and your fellow activists.

I don't mean to scare you. If the only activist-oriented uses of your email are to send letters to editors or occasionally contact a company about their use of animal testing, for example, you're probably of little interest to the government or an investigator. On the other hand, if you think you have any reason to worry about surveillance, I have two words for you: email encryption.

Email is an easy target for hacktivists and officials who want to sabotage your work or gather information on you, so protect the emails you're sending using a program like PGP (which stands for Pretty Good Privacy) to encrypt them. While such programs won't absolutely guarantee your emails will never be hacked and read without your consent—technology allowing such breaches gets better every day—it's an added layer of security. Advances in email encryption are also improving, so do a little research online to determine what works best for you.

The Power of the Press

Be sure to tell investigative reporters in your local media outlets about animal-abuse issues. Reporters sympathetic to animal rights can have a real impact. For example, when activists in the San Francisco Bay Area launched a campaign to get Whole Foods Markets to stop selling bunny meat, rabbit advocate Tara Baxter contacted reporter and news anchor Vicky Nguyen of NBC Bay Area. As part of an investigative report for the television show, Vicky met rabbits rescued from meat farms and was shown cuddling one in the story. It helped lead to an end in sales of bunny meat at Whole Foods just four months later.

Video & Film

Video is an extremely effective outreach tool. In terms of activism, using video can be as simple as posting an animal rights documentary online or it can be an integral part of a campaign. "I utilize social media channels on a daily basis to engage the public with animal issues," says Carrie LeBlanc. "We focus especially on creating engaging, visually compelling content in the form of graphical images and short videos that can stand up and be noticed in our media-saturated society." Carrie says that through trial and error she and her team have concluded that a 30-second video focused on one aspect of one issue is more effective than crafting a 3–5-minute video packed with more information. "By learning the strengths and weaknesses of each social media channel and coming to understand your audience, you can tailor your messaging in order to gain the widest possible audience on each channel. And the wider the audience, the more hearts and minds you are reaching and, hopefully, changing."

Other activists, however, embrace the longer form of this technology and use to it give audiences a deeper understanding of what animals experience under the yoke of human exploitation. Three vegan filmmakers—Keegan Kuhn, co-writer, co-director, and co-editor of *Cowspiracy*; Liz Marshall, writer and director of *The Ghosts in Our Machine*; and Marisa Miller Wolfson, writer, director, and editor of *Vegucated*—shared their insights about what makes an effective documentary, and they offered advice to future animal rights documentarians.

"I think that being able to show the general public the sights and sounds of what is happening behind closed doors has the ability to pass through all of the barriers we build and go straight to our hearts," says Keegan. "Many people intellectualize injustice, violence, suffering, and pain to the point that they become almost abstract ideas, but film and video have a way of bringing these issues back into stark reality. We are all heavily influenced by films and television, whether we realize it or not, and as activists we should be capitalizing on that and using the tools to bring about real change."

Keegan observes that with technology now allowing people to create a video with their phones and post it directly online, virtually anyone can be an activist-filmmaker. The key to success, however, is making your video go viral. "I think the best way to get people to share a video online is to have something that really tugs on people's heartstrings," says Keegan. "Videos depicting cute animals or friendships among different species that showcase their array of emotions and individuality are vital. Just as important are the emotionally troubling videos of violence against animals. Though most people want to ignore these images, these types of videos can be extremely life-changing. Both videos are important for dramatic social change toward compassion and justice for animals."

That said, Keegan suggests that the most effective way to use film as a tool for activism is to take the time to learn how to use filmmaking equipment. "If we want people to watch our films and videos, we need to make them watchable. No one wants to watch poorly filmed, shaky, grainy, bad-audio videos and films that are edited with little consideration of the viewer in mind. We are up against a massive cultural resistance to the messages and images we want to share with people, and so the least we can do is make sure that our videos are at the very least audio and visually engaging."

But documentary filmmakers are not simply activists with cameras, cautions Keegan. "We should strive to be filmmakers who are also activists. If we invest the time, money, and energy into making a video or film, we should make sure that it is the absolute best we can make it. Study other films, documentaries, and videos and figure out why they are effective and then do the same. Invest in the highest-quality cameras and equipment that you can and make filmmaking a passion."

Liz agrees there's much to be learned from other media. "Watch and study other films out there on the subject and other subjects; read books, literature, and online media about issues you care about; and consider how your film can be different and inspired by something that resonates for you. Use filmmaking techniques to elevate the issue for a broader audience, so that lots of people are watching and considering the issues. You will need to find your way with it." It's important to remain partially removed, she says, but that doesn't mean you are not passionately invested. "Include non-vegans and people who do not share your awareness or beliefs in your process. Listen to their opinions, invite them to your rough-cut screening. As an example, *Ghosts* is an open-ended yet personal film that poses questions and doesn't preach. We achieved this, but critics often think documentaries need to conform to rules of journalism, which I don't agree with."

(L to R) Jason Milligan, Susie Coston, Liz Marshall, John Price, and Jo-Anne McArthur on location at Farm Sanctuary in New York during the making of *The Ghosts in Our Machine*. Credit: Jo-Anne McArthur

"I think I made every single mistake in the book, which could be expected of someone who made a film without ever having taken a film class before," says Marisa. She says she could write a book on how *not* to make a film, but instead distilled her advice into a list of do's and don'ts for potential filmmakers:

DO pick a subject that you are so passionate about that you spring out of bed every morning, eager to tackle the next challenge.

DON'T expect filmmaking to be sexy and glamorous. Meaningful and rewarding—yes. Sexy and glamorous—no.

DO estimate the worst-case scenario for how long you think it will take you to make the film, then consider multiplying it by about five. I think it was the amazing filmmakers at Tribe of Heart who told me that, and I brushed it off. In the process, I realized that's how long it will take you to make it if you want to make it well.

DO go the extra mile to find compelling film subjects. Feature those whom you care about and focus on their stories, not just on information you want to convey.

DON'T make a talking-head movie where you "travel around the world talking to experts," which has been done a million and one times, and festival curators (and viewers) are sick of it. You need a story with plot tension and an emotional arc if you expect your viewers to stay awake and engaged.

DO hire a good crew with great references/experience. If you have to spend a year or two raising money and finding a good crew to shoot the film, do it. I learned the hard way that there are no retakes in documentary film, and you'll just make it harder in post-production if you rely on volunteers, who tend to flake out or don't have the necessary skills.

DON'T start shooting without a basic understanding of legal issues pertaining to film: crew contracts, location and personal release forms, music use, etc. I learned the hard way that it's like pulling teeth to track down people to sign contracts later, which distribution companies do require. It's best to hire an entertainment lawyer before you start shooting.

DO expect to be affected by the soul-wrenching footage of animal abuse you have to wade through and DO practice really good self-care, whether it's working through your feelings regularly with a sympathetic friend or mental health professional, visiting a farmed animal sanctuary to spend time with animals who've been saved from the awful fate, or taking the time to stretch and exercise. Sitting at the editing dock for hours on end can really do a number on your back. I have the herniated disk and acupuncture bills to prove it.

DON'T think you're finished editing when only your film team has seen it. *Mad Cowboy* author/filmmaker Howard Lyman told me that the true editing begins when you start screening it. He's so right.

DON'T just screen it for your friends or fellow activists. They will be nice. You don't need nice; you need honest.

DO reach out to other filmmakers in your community for help and feedback. Joining the FilmShop filmmakers' collective was the single smartest choice I made. These peers reviewed and critiqued the film at various stages in production and helped me discover that I hadn't actually told the story I was meaning to tell, that I was not being clear, or that my tone or approach were off-putting. I revised and refined it for years, and I owe so much of the film's success to that group. I also screened the film for fellow vegans/vegan activists, who gave super-helpful critiques as well.

DO engage your audience in your process. Marketing starts when you start working on the film, not when you finish it. Kickstarter and IndieGoGo are great ways to raise not just funds but also a fan base.

DON'T expect to be done when the film is finished. Making the film is half the time and money; releasing it is the other half. The era of making a film and passing it on to a distribution company, then sitting back and relaxing as they do all the work, is over. Because cheap digital filmmaking tools have democratized the filmmaking process, there is a glut of films out there and the big distributors can't/won't wade through them all and find a place for them all. *You* have to do so much more of the work now.

DO consider "four-walling," or renting theaters, for premieres around the country if you don't get a traditional theatrical release.

DON'T stop at theatrical, given the many ways to connect

with your audience, whether it's through community screenings or digitally.

DO know that, if you feel stuck in the muck during the long process, there will be a moment someday when you're sitting in your premiere watching the film you made, with audiences laughing and crying and being moved by the film. And then people will start telling you how your film has changed their lives and their perspectives or their world view, and there will be no feeling like it in the world.

Public Screenings

Screening a film or video at your library or on your college campus is a great way to help people see animals as more than just things to be exploited. Documentaries like *Cowspiracy*, *The Ghosts in Our Machine*, or *Vegucated*—or commercial films like *Babe* or even *Star Wars: The Last Jedi*—can inspire lively discussion. Check with your public library, community center, or student activities office about arranging a screening. "Screening films at libraries is your best bet," says Brenda Sanders, "because they all have a room that they make available to the public. Usually for free, although sometimes you have to pay. If you are part of a community center or a church community, then those would be good." You can also show films at home, she says, and projectors are getting more and more affordable. "Connect your laptop to the projector and project it right onto the wall." Brenda recommends serving vegan food at film screenings, too. "Everything I do, I make sure there is food. It's just a rule, because we've got to be exposing people to plant food."

You might also screen the film for students. Activist Jim Corcoran has found that instructors of environmental courses seem most open to it, especially films like *Cowspiracy* that show the impact animal agriculture has on our planet. "Almost every higher-learning institution has at least one environmental course, and the trick is finding a sympathetic or open-minded instructor," he says. Jim begins with a search of the campus website to locate the instructors' contact information, then he offers to bring the film to their class. "I send them a link to the trailer and several environmental quotes to back up the assertion that animal agriculture is seriously threatening life on the planet. I give them a few days to read and respond, and if I don't hear from them, I try again. I will also follow up with a phone call if necessary. I'm not beyond visiting an instructor to push the point in person."

Once he has agreement from an instructor, he schedules the screening and decides what literature he'll bring. "I always have something attendees can take away and contemplate later," says Jim, who sometimes offers to answer questions after the film. "Each time I have shown *Cowspiracy* there has been spontaneous applause at the conclusion. That tells me that most of the students got the message and are now open to changing lifestyles. I have to tell you, that is a good feeling—well worth the effort it took to get it shown in the classroom! People just need to get out of their comfort zone and keep their eye on the prize. It is gratifying to know that you have, at the very least, planted seeds of compassion, sustainability, and health in the minds of students and instructors alike."

Wherever you host your screening, set up a table with plenty of animal rights information, and let people know that the purpose of the event is to promote compassion for animals.

Photography & Beyond

Imagery has become so ubiquitous in our meme-happy world that it's easy to forget how much work (and risk) can go into creating a compelling photograph. An image captured by an undercover activist, for example, has the potential to convey some of the pain and suffering endured by animals used for food, fashion, research, and entertainment and thus give the public a better understanding of these forms of exploitation. The photos of few animal rights photographers are as beautiful and heartrending as those of Toronto-based photojournalist Jo-Anne McArthur, who has directed her lens toward animal cruelties around the world. She is also the founder of We Animals, a project that makes her extensive archive of images available to activists and nonprofits for free.

"Photos are windows into what's hidden," says Jo-Anne, "and when it comes to animal industries, from fur farming to 'food animal' farming to bear bile farming, all of these things happen behind closed doors. Those who run these industries know that people may not want to support the cruelty that goes on there, if they knew, so it's important to have good documentation of what these facilities are like, so that consumers can learn and make more compassionate decisions. As we all know, images can instantly draw attention to an issue in a way that text can't. They can make people feel instantly, be it empathy or revulsion or anger or happiness. Images are a key part of the animal rights movement."

To anyone interested in using their photography skills to advocate for animals, Jo-Anne says you don't need to travel and you don't need to own expensive photo gear. "Start close to home. Unfortunately, animal cruelty is all around us. It's at the local meat markets. It's at the pet stores, where exotic animals and dogs from puppy mills are sold for profit. It's at the local zoo or circus or rodeo or fishing hole. There is much to document. Just go out and document it, and share those images via social media, local media, and wherever you can."

She emphasizes the importance of creative, high-quality photos—photos that will grab the viewer's attention. "People turn away from cruelty," she says. "No one wants to see it, so it's important that the images are engaging, which will draw people in, make them wonder, make them ask questions." In other words, don't just take photos—tell a story.

"If you *are* a traveler, a great way to document animal issues is to volunteer for organizations who are helping animals," Jo-Anne says. "Be it at an oil spill, where groups are helping save lives, or at sanctuaries that are constantly bringing animals into their care. You can document their work, and so not only do they benefit from your donated photography, but it helps promote their work and expose the issues at hand. I've done this for many groups, from Farm Sanctuary to Sea Shepherd, for groups helping birds at the Gulf oil spill to groups helping end the bush meat trade across Africa. Whatever you want to or can photograph, begin it now. The animals need you."

Sharing your work is key, especially when you're just starting out. Jo-Anne acknowledges that social media has made it easier than ever for people to see a photographer's work, but if you want to use your skills frequently, your work must be consistent. "Creating an audience will get people sharing your work on a regular basis as well. Tight, ruthless editing is key, and getting editing help—by editors or photographers whom you respect, for example—is important in your learning process as well. It's also helpful to reach beyond the choir. Your friends and animal-loving folk are going to like your work, but reach farther, so that people who need to know about animal issues can see the work. Send your images to local publications on a regular basis, offer to do a column or supply images regularly, so that you can broaden your reach and your audience."

Note: In the US, law enforcement officers routinely command people to stop taking photographs while in public spaces, even though it is their constitutional right to do so. See "Appendix C—Know Your Rights" for more information.

Chalktivism

Few forms of personal expression are as basic as drawing on concrete, and activists have been chalking messages on sidewalks and other public spaces for years (this was a popular tactic among suffragists, for example). But it's hard to match the passion and creativity of James DeAlto, who launched the Vegan Chalk Challenge in 2015 and took it worldwide. He started off with brightly colored messages of peace and compassion—sometimes enlivened with depictions of animals—at locations near his home in Raleigh, North Carolina, and posted photos of his creations on social media. It went global from there, with activists in Australia, Germany, India, South Africa, and elsewhere sharing their hand-crafted messages online.

"This is not about creating a masterpiece," James says. "It's about fostering a sense of empowerment for activists who, like myself, are still apprehensive about wearing a vegan T-shirt for fear of ridicule or rejection." There are a number of reasons he thinks drawing these messages is so effective:

- It's simple. "It requires so little time," he says. "I can literally write a message like 'Vegan Is Love' in 15 seconds inside a busy parking deck and it will be seen by hundreds of people."
- It's unexpected. "Just seeing the word 'vegan' in a public space, written as a personal, artistic expression of one's beliefs, is unexpected and makes people curious. When people see these messages in nature, especially in parks or greenways, they're in a headspace to actually contemplate the message, to discuss its merits with their walking partner or to reflect on a time when they may have previously been vegetarian or vegan. In parks and on greenways, the distractions are much fewer, and because my messages are appearing in spaces where political expression is unexpected, the messages are memorable."
- It's emotional. "People who read my messages intuitively understand there's an emotional element that inspired me to take action. People are interested not only in the

message, but in the person behind the message. The mystery for those who haven't yet figured out it's me has become a very interesting aspect of this story, which keeps people's attention and leaves them interested to see what I'm going to write next."

- Since it's not an in-person solicitation, viewers are less likely to be defensive. "Chalk is usually associated with childhood, and people are naturally curious. My neighbors, when they find out it's been me leaving the messages, have often told me they thought it was a little girl! Because I'm usually absent when people read the message, the focus is squarely on the words themselves, removing any negative bias the recipient may have otherwise had, based on my appearance or body language."

- Chalk messages lead to conversations. "People have told me they're thinking more about their food choices because of my actions. Knowing my audience is already concerned with health and environmental issues, I like to leave messages that will encourage them to talk about these particular issues. I'll often use statistics from *Cowspiracy* with the message 'Watch *Cowspiracy* on Netflix.'"

- Effective activism strengthens the vegan community. "Public chalk messages offer other vegans a sense of validation. I have a vegan therapist who runs on the greenway where I leave my messages. She told me that the first time she saw one, she threw her arms up in the air and yelled, 'Yes!' What we're doing provokes a sense of excitement in 'closet vegans,' offering the assurance there are others out there like themselves. This can go a long way toward normalizing veganism, which I think is one of our main tasks as a movement."

- The afterlife of a chalk message is much longer than what we leave on the pavement. "When people post their pictures on Facebook, the love and appreciation that pours out in the comments fuels my desire to go out and do more. When others post pictures of their own chalk messages and share their personal experiences, it makes my entire day. What's most exciting is the growing community of activists who are starting to see the potential in what we're doing. The Vegan Chalk Challenge has become an unfolding story, which makes it very exciting for me personally."

James has gotten positive reactions with such messages as "Nothing humane happens in a slaughterhouse," "Vote for peace 3 times a day. Go vegan," and "In a world where you can choose to be anything, choose to be kind. Be vegan." Some other examples of messages he and others have chalked include:

- "Peace is just around the bend—Choose vegan." (Just before the turn on a footpath.)
- "There's no such thing as a Happy Meal. Go vegan." (In front of a McDonald's.)
- "Exercise unlimited compassion. Choose vegan." (Near some public outdoor fitness equipment.)
- "This landfill is the permanent resting place of over 25,000 unwanted shelter dogs. If that bothers you, please adopt one today. #AdoptDontShop." (On a footpath in North Wake Landfill District Park in Raleigh, North Carolina, which was once used to bury dogs euthanized in shelters.)
- "Help build a bridge to a kinder world—Choose vegan!" (Just before a bridge on a footpath.)
- "Vegan Parking" (A parking space.)

The good news is that creating chalk messages is easy, inexpensive, and potentially powerful. The bad news is it's not always legal. Although the drawings are only temporary— even if no one touches them they'll be erased with the next

James DeAlto demonstrates that you can chalk a vegan message almost anywhere. Credit: Kathy Martin

rain shower—some jurisdictions consider them vandalism, not protected free speech, so consult with local government offices if you're unsure about the legality. Some cities even require a permit to draw on sidewalks.

Personalized Checks

There are many printing companies from which you can order personal checks online. Have your checks printed with a pro-vegan message, such as "Choose Kindness— Choose Vegan." Every time you write a check you'll be promoting compassion.

Some Thoughts on Using Imagery
Social justice activist and author Aph Ko spends a lot of time

working with different forms of media, including the site she founded, BlackVegansRock.com. I asked her to expand on an observation she once made: that the animal rights/vegan movement relies too much on imagery and not enough on critical thinking. Here's what she told me:

I'm known for saying: *People weren't shocked into eating meat and they won't be shocked out of it.*

Let's back up a little: The biggest issue the white animal rights movement has is that they can't properly locate *why* animal oppression is happening. They see the aftermath of oppression—they see the victims—but most of these activists have no conceptual clue as to why animals are systemically being hurt. Sometimes it's painful to watch activists from the dominant class try to create campaigns to stop animal oppression—without realizing how they are perpetuating it—and other times, it's comical.

White folks don't seem to realize that white supremacy systemically harms animals. White folks don't want to move out of their leadership positions, but they want to stop animal oppression, which basically means they don't want to change behaviors that are discursively hurting animals.

Because a lot of uncritical people are the leaders of the movements, they rely on really basic, surface-level tactics to "shock" people into a political lifestyle. That's why veganism gets such a bad name—it's surface-level and sensationalist. Imagery can work, especially if it's attached to a new framework, but creating new conceptual frameworks is usually the part that's overlooked.

Imagery tactics remind me of the ways some feminists rely on sexualized imagery of women to shock people into caring about sexism. It's like, if you don't provide a new framework for people to understand problematic behaviors through, then all they're looking at is more imagery of objects being objectified.

I'm not suggesting that people can't change their behaviors when they see imagery like that; I'm saying that I don't necessarily think long-term change will happen. In our movements, we focus way too much on the victims without understanding why these bodies are victims in the first place. They didn't become victimized overnight, and we have to do the work conceptually to solve this problem as well. So many people don't realize that thinking is actually part of our activism. For too long, thinking has been co-opted by academia, so we assume that theory and thought is for "those" elitist people, when in reality, this should be a part of the public domain.

In large part, animal oppression isn't so much a story just about animals, it's a story about white human supremacy, so we have to uproot that part of it and examine it before we hyper-focus on the victims with no context. That's what ends up happening, though: we are supposed to examine animal oppression imagery without any context for who the real oppressor is, which produces so much confusion about strategies to end animal oppression.

I hope that if you are a white activist (especially a white, privileged, male activist), you will take Aph's words to heart and really think critically about the role we have historically played in perpetuating the oppression of animals and other nondominant groups. Keep in mind, for example, that the system of industrialized animal agriculture was created and propagated by capitalist whites, who have spread the model to the Global South.

Public Service Announcements

A public service announcement (PSA) is a short video or audio message, usually played on television or radio, that is intended to inform the public about a specific issue or event. PSAs can also be published in newspapers and magazines. In all these cases, the media time or space is made available for free to advocate groups, nonprofits, community associations, and for-profit organizations that are promoting a nonprofit event.

PSAs generally run for 10 to 60 seconds and must contain information that will benefit the community. Ask the program director at your local radio and TV stations for their guidelines about content and formatting.

Standard lengths for PSAs:

- 10 seconds (25–30 words)
- 20 seconds (45–50 words)
- 30 seconds (60–75 words)
- 60 seconds (120–150 words)

According to Aubrie Kavanaugh, who founded the group Paws4Change to educate people about companion animal issues and has produced many PSAs, activists should not be intimidated by public service announcements. "Creating a PSA is as easy as developing a concept, creating some content—using images, short video clips, and perhaps an audio track—and connecting with local television and radio stations to determine their requirements for PSAs. There are a host of software options available to edit together images and video clips with sound." Aubrie warns that you must not use *any* copyright-protected content, however, and suggests that a station is more likely to broadcast a PSA that is empowering and creative, rather than dark and depressing.

Television stations receive many PSAs from various nonprofit organizations on the local and national level, and they can pick and choose what they will play. Because stations will require a high-quality production, you may want to rely on a large animal rights organization to supply you with a professional videotape or digital file. Send a thank-you letter or card to the contact person at the station once they have aired the PSA.

"Most television stations will accept a PSA as a movie file," adds Aubrie, "which you can transmit to them using a file-sharing website like Dropbox. You may also be asked to provide proof of nonprofit status by providing a copy of your IRS determination letter. Radio stations are a little different. Some will allow you to record a short PSA that you share with them to broadcast, while others will invite you to the station to record your PSA using station equipment."

Steps to Getting a PSA on the Radio

- Contact an animal rights group in your area and ask if they are eligible for PSAs. If they are, ask if they have a recorded PSA they can send you and explain you want to get it on the air. Or...
- Call or visit your local radio station or college station and ask to speak to the person who handles public service announcements. This person's title is often "community service director" or "public service director." At college radio stations, this may simply be the DJ.
- Explain the PSA you have and ask if they will play it. If they can't or won't meet with you, download the files from the site and email your pitch to them with the PSA files attached.
- Call the radio station a few days after delivering or sending the materials to see if they plan to air the PSA. If so, find out when it will play.
- If they have not yet reviewed the PSA, ask when you should follow up to determine their interest. Don't be afraid to be a little pushy.

Steps to Getting a PSA into Print Media

- Contact an animal rights group in your area and ask if they are eligible for PSAs. If they are, offer to help them place a PSA into a local publication. They should be able to provide you with a finished file.
- Compile a list of the newspapers and magazines in your area.
- Contact each publication and ask who handles donated space.
- Send an email to the appropriate person, asking them to run the PSA and explain why it is beneficial to animals and the community; make sure to include your name, affiliation, and a telephone number with the best times to reach you.
- If you are with a large organization or are working with several groups, consider having other representatives sign on to the letter to show support.
- Follow up. Call your contacts at each publication a few hours after sending the email. Ask if they are willing to consider running the public service announcement. Remember to be brief and polite.
- If the publication has space, ask for the space size, their spec sheet (which includes the publication's production information), whether the PSA will be in color or black and white, what format it should be submitted in (PDF, jpg, etc.), whom to send it to, the deadline, and if there is anything else you need to know before submitting it.
- Make sure to thank the outlets that run the PSA with a letter or card.

Television

Viewers of commercial television generally see animals the way multinational corporations want animals to be seen: as

> I think anybody who cares about animals should be so thankful that anybody does anything to help animals, even if they don't do everything we think they should. If they are out doing trap-neuter-release work or working to bring about a no-kill shelter or protesting rodeo, how can we not be thankful? We are all imperfect creatures, in an imperfect world.
>
> **Tom Regan**
> *Satya* **magazine**, August 2004

a source of food, fiber, or fun. So, the major networks mostly present programs featuring animals trained to do tricks—which parallel the advertisements filled with dogs, chimpanzees, and other animals exploited in the name of capitalism. If there's a farmed animal on the show, chances are they are the centerpiece of a holiday dinner. Rarely are animals depicted as having a full range of emotions or engaging in their natural behaviors. For that, viewers must turn to cable networks or documentaries.

If you have a cable television station in your area, you probably have access to a virtually untapped resource for advancing the interests of animals. Public access television stations around the world permit members of their community to submit documentaries for broadcast on a wide range of topics. This is a very effective tactic, and animal rights organizations report that many people tell them they ordered a vegan starter kit or other information because of a documentary they saw on cable television.

You can request high-quality documentaries in various formats from GourmetCruelty.com, Mercy For Animals, PETA, and many other organizations. To get the most out of the broadcast, promote each program the station airs for you. If you're part of a group that the documentary might interest, ask the email manager to send a notice to all members. You can also ask local vegan, vegetarian, and humane societies to post a notice of the broadcast on their websites. Finally, ask your local paper if they'll print a program listing in their television schedule.

More ambitious activists may follow the example of Helen Marston, who was looking to increase coverage of animal rights and animal-welfare issues in the mainstream media. Helen created a program for Australia's public television called *Animals Matter*, which offered information on vegan and compassionate living but didn't shy away from featuring video of animals in confinement or discussing animal rescues.

"This is definitely something others can try in their country," says Helen, executive director of Humane Research Australia. "I think the most important thing is to find a good production company that understands your motives for wanting to do this." In Helen's case, it was the production company that approached her with the idea. "They had already been doing a lot of work with community television and so had the contacts there. I originally thought it was an impossible dream, but they knew how passionate I was about animal rights issues and convinced me that I could really do it—and we did!"

Your (Free) Ad Here!

Newspapers that sell advertising space frequently run short of paid advertisers to fill the allotted display ad area. This shortfall is called "remnant space," "remainder advertising," or "last-minute advertising." Although media often sell this remnant space to businesses at steep discounts, they frequently give the space away for free to worthy causes. Because newspapers publish daily or weekly editions, they offer many opportunities to get your message seen by their readership.

What to advertise: Vegan starter kits, food fairs, animal shelter adoptions, and fundraising events are all a great fit for remnant ad space.

Creating the ad: Your ad doesn't have to be fancy, though it will need to look professional and be submitted in the publisher's required format (this generally means a digital file). One indispensable resource is a desktop publishing program that will allow you to turn a standard text document such as Microsoft Word into a portable document format (PDF). You can also download PDF-style writing software for free online: just type "create free pdfs" into your favorite search engine for a selection.

Create a few designs that include the contact information and website address, if appropriate, and then ask friends what they think of the ad. Remember that the ad must fit the paper's width and height specifications.

Steps to Getting a Remnant Ad Placed

- Create a list of the print publications in your area (this is easy to do online), as well as those you read regularly.
- Don't forget local TV and radio stations—especially the ones you enjoy most.
- Determine who handles the advertising at each publication (this is generally the advertising sales manager).
- Send an email or place a phone call to introduce yourself and ask if they have any remnant space in their next issue; explain what it is you'll be advertising.
- If they do have space, a typical response may be, "Yes, I have a one-column spot that's two inches high. Can you email me your ad as a PDF by three o'clock Thursday?"
- Ask if they have any special requirements—some publications, for example, want you to insert their logo in your ad.
- Check the page on their website that shows the display ad

dimensions, or ask them to email the ad specs to you.

- Be sure to get your ad file to them by the deadline!
- A publication will usually not know until the last minute if they have any remnant space available, so be prepared with an ad in all the publication's ad sizes.
- After the ad has run, send a thank-you note (not an email) to the ad manager or person who helped place your ad.
- In my experience, newspapers don't mind if you keep asking, even if they have published an ad for you already — so ask again!

The Medium Is the Message

Media can sometimes transform an advocate's efforts into something beyond their wildest activist dreams — all the more now that so much is archived online, to be downloaded and emailed in seconds. Just ask Karen Davis. Karen runs United Poultry Concerns and didn't like that National Public Radio was characterizing domestic fowl as unlovable. For several years in the 1990s, an NPR program called *This American Life* did an annual show that ridiculed turkeys, ducks, and especially chickens. So, Karen started a letter-writing campaign to the program, and the show's host, Ira Glass, heard from animal advocates throughout the United States. Surprised by this outpouring of support for animals he considered to be "a pain in the ass," Ira ended up visiting Karen's sanctuary and interviewing her for his radio program. She introduced him to many chickens that day — birds like Ella and Henry and Dolores — and you can hear the seeds of a new attitude being planted as Ira gets to know these "refugees from the commercial poultry industry," as he calls them. His voiceover, recorded sometime later, belies his earlier criticisms as he tells listeners about the poultry industry's practice of using selective breeding and specially formulated feed to make a "meat" chicken grow to full size in just six weeks, rather than the six months nature intended. Karen explains this is just one reason all the chickens at her sanctuary suffer illness and will die prematurely. When Ira defends his NPR show as harmless, Karen is adamant that it perpetuates the myth that chickens are stupid. "You're one of the many components of the abuse," she says. "You're part of the problem!"

Fast forward six years. Ira Glass is a guest on a different NPR program and he recounts his tale of visiting Karen and the chickens, admitting it had an impact on him. Then, in April of 2007, Ira appears on television's *Late Show with David Letterman* and shares his story with Dave, the studio audience, and four and a half million viewers at home, explaining that chickens have real personalities. Many in the audience laugh as Ira speaks of Karen's activism, and even Dave chuckles at the term "chicken advocates." But no one laughs when Ira says he became a vegetarian because of what he had learned from Henry and Elise and Lois and Lambrusco and Karen Davis. "She got the last laugh on me," he says. (You can view the interview clip on YouTube.)

The scope of multimedia is so broad that it may seem daunting to some activists. Yet fueled by new technologies, animal advocates are using different media to create everything from simple chalked messages to elaborate video productions and radio shows. Perhaps the best way to sum up the use of multimedia to advance the interests of animals is to give a few of its proponents the final word.

"To optimize success on the Web, it's important to be passionate about the Web, as well as passionate about the interests of animals," says Jason Das, who founded SuperVegan. com. "The methods and techniques for reaching people on the Web are constantly changing. It helps to be something of a Web nerd, and enjoy shaping and following these trends." Jason also advises activists to think outside the cause. "Too many activists live in a bubble of their scene. To change the real world, you need to live up to real-world standards. A writer has to write on a level that would get them hired outside the movement; a podcaster has to have radio skills and presence that would impress in any context."

Sarah Von Alt oversees the creation of blogs and social media content for the nonprofit Mercy For Animals. She says she had no idea what she was getting herself into, but has grown to feel inspired by giving people valuable information every day. "If you want to be successful at social media," Sarah says, "it's important to make your audience feel something. Eliciting an emotional response—positive or negative—can help increase the engagement on your posts. And make sure you have a strong call to action!"

Lauren Corman, who produced and hosted the *Animal Voices* radio program out of Toronto, suggests that activists with an interest in starting their own show should first volunteer at their community or campus radio station. "Not only will this demonstrate that you're dedicated and reliable, but it will also give you a chance to familiarize yourself with the technology, political climate, and culture of the place," she says. Lauren adds that in her experience, you'll need to show how your program will involve some level of balance. "As an animal rights show, you will likely be seen as having a clear agenda, which may or may not be acceptable for the station. Depending on their political perspective, you might be asked how you intend to represent 'the other side.' Talk about the diversity of programming you'd like to offer, including the diversity of perspectives you'll feature, and demonstrate how you're interested in initiating dialogue rather than pushing propaganda."

Finally, Karl Losken offers this simple advice: "Follow your intuition. Enjoy what you do and fill a need that you feel exists."

Chapter 9

Animal Liberation: Direct Action

You have not lived today until you have done something for someone who can never repay you.
John Bunyan

The rescue was as quick as it was brazen. As the Ka Shing Chinese restaurant in Dublin, Ireland, was bustling with the Friday-night dinner crowd, a group of animal activists stepped inside. While some distracted the restaurant staff, others removed all nine lobsters from an aquarium tank near the front door, placing them in plastic bags. They then rushed back outside with the animals in hand—pursued by a few Ka Shing workers. "It was quite a wet night," one worker said, "but they were wearing runners [sneakers] and we were wearing proper shoes so we couldn't catch them."

The activists—made up of members from the Alliance for Animal Rights, Direct Action for Animals, and the National Animal Rights Association—made their way to the coastal suburb of Clontarf, about a mile away, and released the crustaceans into the sea. They recorded everything on video, and made no effort to disguise themselves.

Laura Broxson, spokesperson for the activists, told news media that they had voiced their concerns to the restaurant about them serving lobsters, explaining that the animals feel pain and fear, but received no response. "For us it was an act of compassion," she said, "and we are willing to face any legal consequences brought to us because now these lobsters have a chance of living instead of being boiled alive and eaten."

Not only was the action announced in headlines around the world, making consumers think about the lives of lobsters, but

Laura says the charges filed against them were dropped—and the lobster tank was permanently removed from the restaurant.

While different people will have different definitions of direct action, this chapter will address actions that bring the activist into closer contact with businesses responsible for animal abuse: animal factories, research labs, slaughterhouses, et al.

It is important you understand that many direct actions against animal exploiters are considered illegal and should be undertaken with the knowledge that you could be arrested and go to jail, even if you are acting on ethical grounds, such as offering your home to a hen rescued from a battery shed. Other direct actions, including investigative work to document abusive practices, though legal, are likely to prove both upsetting and nerve-racking. Primatologist Sarah Baeckler, for example, spent more than a year working undercover at a Hollywood "training" compound for exotic animals where she witnessed staff members beating chimpanzees used in movies and television. The good news is the owner of this concentration camp for animals is no longer allowed to own or work with primates, and the rescued chimps are now safe in sanctuaries. "My small part in saving them is absolutely my finest accomplishment," says Sarah.

Rattling Cages

Pioneered in the 1990s by Patty Mark of Animal Liberation Victoria, open rescue is one of many tactics that fall under the general heading of direct action. It's a popular model that has been used for many decades: Mohandas Gandhi's direct-action campaigns in India are among the most famous examples, and his passive resistance inspired activists such as Martin Luther King, Jr., Cesar Chavez, the Dalai Lama, Nelson Mandela, and Aung San Suu Kyi to use nonviolent activism as a means to achieving social change.

Framed in the tradition of these advocates, open rescuers

are activists who have grown frustrated by what they see as a lack of interest on the part of government officials to make improvements in the lives of animals used for food, entertainment, clothing, and research. Armed with cameras and a passionate determination, they record the conditions inside an animal enterprise and the treatment of animals, often removing some to provide them with veterinary care and place them in loving homes. This can be grueling work, since activists witness and document immense abuse and suffering. And unlike the other models of activism presented in this book, open rescues generally involve unlawful activity, which means there is also the threat of being caught and prosecuted for a variety of crimes, including trespassing. But every activist who engages in this tactic of direct action agrees that it's worth the risk and that the danger they face in exposing inhumane treatment is nothing compared to the cruelties animals must endure. It is vital, they say, to report their findings to authorities and the public.

As the world's hunger for cheap animal protein continues to grow, factory farmers in the poultry industry have succeeded in making the chicken the most exploited animal in meat production: according to United Poultry Concerns, worldwide more than 50 billion chickens are raised and slaughtered every year. And the egg industry only compounds the abuse these intelligent creatures suffer, with hens forced to produce an unnatural number of eggs before they too, their bodies exhausted, are slaughtered. Their male counterparts, who are of no economic value to egg producers, are killed immediately after hatching: suffocated, buried, or macerated (ground up) while still alive.

With such egregious abuse considered business as usual, it is little wonder animal activists have focused on the "broiler" chicken and egg industries, rescuing these animals from some of the worst industrial-farming conditions imaginable.

"Open rescue is a great model of activism because others can see that ordinary people like themselves are so outraged by what is happening to animals on factory farms that they are driven to take the law into their own hands," says Deirdre Sims of Direct Animal Action, a group of animal rights activists from cities all over New Zealand. Deirdre became involved in open rescues because she wanted to do more to directly help animals raised for food. "I wanted to see for myself the conditions and the suffering. I wanted to get animals out of these places and to give them a chance at a decent life," she says. "And I realized that I could do exactly that, simply by getting over my fear of the

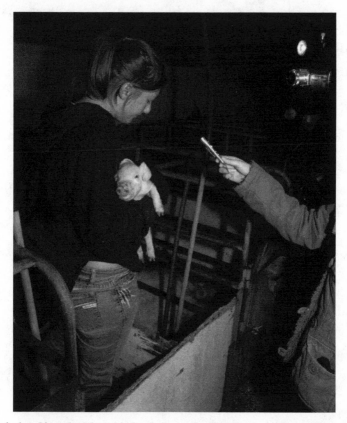

Deirdre Sims holds a piglet being rescued from a farrowing crate. Because piglets require very special care, rescues of pigs are not common. This little guy was placed in a happy home. (Note that the activists document the rescue.) Credit: NZ Open Rescue Collective

possible consequences and taking action."

Deirdre says that police raided the house of one of their team members shortly after their first battery-hen rescue. "However, despite an investigation called 'Operation Chicken,' no charges have been laid," she adds. "Since then, we've openly rescued many more animals from factory farms and have had no apparent interest from the authorities." Why don't authorities press criminal charges? "We believe that the factory farm industries are unwilling to prosecute as they know this will simply lead to more media coverage. This means more images of suffering animals on TV that they don't want their customers to see. If we ever do end up in court, our argument will be that we were not 'stealing property' — we were saving lives."

Breaking In Down Under

The modest woman credited with launching the open rescue model in the 1990s would much rather be out helping animals than discussing her exploits; nonetheless, Patty Mark paused long enough to recall the first rescue she organized. "It wasn't a matter of me saying or thinking, 'Well now, let's start doing open rescues and see how we go with them' at all," she says. "Nor did I think at the time, or even wonder, if open rescues had happened anywhere else; I really don't know if they had. I was very aware of the ALF [Animal Liberation Front] with their balaclavas, bravely breaking into the animal prisons to save as many suffering animals as they could, and I understood their anger at destroying the equipment used to torture animals, but for whatever reasons I didn't have this ability in my nature. Perhaps it was my strict religious upbringing and the implicit allegiance to authority that religion instills. All I know is when I saw the look on the faces of the animals the ALF rescued, I was happy."

Whatever latent reluctance held Patty back would be overcome by a force familiar to many activists: vivid images of animals suffering. "In 1992 I received a call from an employee inside a huge battery-hen farm [north of Melbourne]. She told me horror stories of how the hens were packed so tightly in the back cages of the shed they couldn't move at all. Some of the hens pushed their way out of the old cages or escaped when dead birds were removed and fell down into the manure pit below." The caller described farm workers shooting these hens for fun. "It all sounded too weird to believe," recalls Patty.

So, she sent a volunteer from her organization to work undercover at the battery farm for three days. "We talked every day on the phone, and he was teary at what he saw and what the birds suffered," Patty says. "He verified everything and more of what the worker told me. The birds were brutally ripped out of the cages, carried four or five in each hand by one leg, and slammed into plastic crates. Some fell to the ground and were run over by the transport trucks below. The hens were placed in row after row of cages up on the first floor, and the ground floor was an enclosed area under their cages where all their droppings piled up, sometimes six feet [1.8 meters] high. There was no care taken whatsoever during the removal of the hens from their cages, and he could hear their bones pop from the rough handling. Some of the workers kicked the birds who had fallen to the floor."

A video, taken undercover by another volunteer on a follow-up visit to the same farm, pushed Patty to take direct action. "Everything in my mind, body, and heart screamed out at me, 'Just go up there and get them out of that manure pit ASAP!'" By this time, Patty had spent 15 years campaigning against battery cages, using every legal means at her disposal. She'd had enough. "I knew too well about the cover-ups, the clean-ups, the 'Don't worry, she'll be right, mate' attitude. But what I saw totally disgusted and haunted me. It was vital and overwhelming, in my mind, to get to those birds as quickly as possible and get them out of there. I contacted a few brave people around me who did undercover work at the time and told them I wanted to contact a leading current affairs program and take them onto the property to film this obscene cruelty and suffering and rescue these animals openly; that is, we will go in undercover to gain entry to film and rescue, but then not hide our identity, as it was the owners of this property who should hide their faces!"

Hinch at Seven, at the time one of Australia's top-rated current affairs programs, accompanied Patty and her confederates on their uninvited visit to the battery farm. The segment the production team put together, titled "The Dungeons of Alpine Poultry," aired nationally on November 9, 1993. "The suffering of battery hens was on TV screens around Australia," says Patty, "and open rescue was born."

In 1999, Karen Davis brought Patty to the United States to speak at United Poultry Concerns' Forum on Direct Action, the first conference of its kind to discuss direct action for animals. Participants in the forum also included Bruce Friedrich of PETA, Miyun Park and Paul Shapiro of Compassion Over Killing (COK) and Freeman Wicklund of Compassionate Action for Animals (CAA). US activists were familiar with the covert rescue method used by the ALF, but Patty's open rescue approach was a revelation. "The response to Patty's presentation was absolutely awesome," says Bruce. "People were *blown away* by the simplicity and beauty of the personal, political, powerful witness that also had real results."

Freeman and members of CAA carried out the first open rescue in the US, removing 11 hens from a battery egg farm in Minnesota in 2001. A few months later, activists from COK openly rescued eight hens from a factory farm in Maryland, sent out a press release, and held a press conference at which they showed the media compelling, high-quality video footage taken inside a battery shed. Soon activists across the country were learning about—and engaging in—the open rescue model.

I've had countless hours in lock-up cells, but only two short times in prison, one for five days and one for 10 days. It's not a good place to be, and I have the utmost respect and regard for those animal rights prisoners who are incarcerated for the long haul. If anything, those times I've been denied my own personal freedom have only strengthened my resolve to do open rescues.

Patty Mark

Satya **magazine**, March 2004

Gaining Traction

As we've seen, authorities may not press charges against activists engaging in open rescue, but that's not always the case. The US animal rights organization Compassionate Consumers made headlines in 2006 when three members of their group were arrested after they made public the results of an investigation and rescue of chickens from a factory farm in New York State. The group's president, Adam Durand, was eventually sentenced to six months in jail. We will explore Adam's experience a bit in Chapter 10, but his encounter with authorities is symptomatic of the general post-9/11 climate, coupled with an increase in animal activism, that has resulted in US courts growing less tolerant of anything they believe smacks of "domestic terrorism."

Activists in other countries, notably Australia and New Zealand, have not experienced such legal woes, however, and have if anything increased their open rescues. There's even an activist in the Czech Republic who is doing this full time. Michal Kolesár has been liberating hens — as well as the occasional lamb, goose, and fox — since 2006, placing them into permanent homes. He even holds workshops for would-be open rescuers. He advises them to learn as much as they can about the sites from which the animals will be liberated. "Get to know them in the daytime and in the night," he says. "The better you know [the site] and the better you adapt, the less evidence you will leave behind."

For Deirdre Sims, rescuing animals is the ultimate activism. "To me, open rescue is about three crucial things: saving lives, documenting abuse, and raising awareness by exposing what is hidden behind closed doors to as wide an audience as possible," she says. "Activists wanting to participate in open rescues need to accept the possible consequences of their actions. You need to know that your house might get raided and you might end up in court. If you can handle that, then get started!"

Following is Deirdre's advice on becoming involved in open rescues:

- Organize a group of like-minded people and start planning.
- First, you'll need to locate a safe place to bring the animals you rescue. You can't take them back to your house because that places the animals at risk if the authorities should happen to turn up. The animals will need to be placed with people who know how to care for ex-factory farmed animals, as they have special needs.
- Use the Internet or phone book to locate factory farms, or go out for some drives in the country. You'll also need video and photographic equipment to document the conditions. Safe and comfortable transport boxes or cages for the animals are another essential.
- Get familiar with your animal welfare laws so you can point out breaches of them on camera. Know your facts about the animals you are rescuing so that you can talk about this to the camera. For example: you've found a "broiler" chick with splayed legs, but why are they splayed? Because these birds are bred for maximum growth rate in a minimum timeframe to increase poultry

industry profits.

- Your job isn't done after saving some lives: Now you've got to get that footage on TV and those photos in the papers and on the Internet. Get your message on the radio. Hold workshops, film screenings and stalls (tables) and talk to people about what you've seen and why you did it. Raising public awareness and keeping the debate alive is one of the crucial aims of open rescue and probably one of the most important elements that will create change for these animals.

Freeman Wicklund advises activists not to use violence during rescues. "Our nonviolent code included not causing any property damage, or minimizing damage if it was necessary to gain access or to offer immediate help to an animal," he says. "Thankfully,

Jamie Yew (left) and Patty Mark of Animal Liberation Victoria rescue a hen from a battery shed. The hen was placed in a sanctuary. Credit: Noah Hannibal / openrescue.org

the factory farms were never locked and we never needed to cause any property damage. Still, if we had to cut a lock to gain entry, we were willing to replace it with a new one or reimburse them for the damage."

"I believe that open rescue is a very public-friendly form of direct action," adds Deirdre. "When we get media coverage of a rescue or show footage at a film screening, people can see that we are just like them in a lot of ways. We are just ordinary people who feel so strongly that our legislation is failing animals that we can no longer sit by and do nothing."

Other Rescue Models

Another, some say more pragmatic, form of direct action is the covert rescue model exemplified by an international confederation of underground activists called the Animal Liberation Front. ALF members work in small, autonomous groups. They don masks to remain anonymous as they carry out the liberation of animals from animal factories, research labs, and fur farms, often inflicting financial losses by damaging or destroying property. Sites of economic sabotage may include actual places of animal exploitation (e.g., laboratories and fast food restaurants) as well as vehicles, boats, or other property owned by animal abusers.

An additional difference between open rescue and the model embodied by the ALF is that the open rescuer generally takes animals like chickens and pigs who can easily be placed into a safe home, while the covert teams also liberate animals, such as mink and deer, into the wild. ALF members do document their activities on video, but they keep their identities hidden. Whatever their reputation (the FBI calls them "domestic terrorists"), the ALF has never physically attacked a human being.*

Some animal activists who engage in rescue work do so without taking direct responsibility for their actions, thus avoiding both the ski masks and their 15 minutes of fame. These liberators have gone into factory farms, documented conditions on videotape, removed animals and then leaked the video anonymously to authorities. No one but the exploited chickens, pigs, or ducks (from foie gras farms) need appear on camera.

Lobster Liberation

While actions of activists who rescue animals directly from the enterprises that exploit them exemplify a person's willingness to lose their own liberty to gain the freedom of an animal, not all activists run the risk of prison while rescuing "food" animals. There was the famous case of Homer the lobster, for instance, who was the featured prize in a contest to guess his weight. At nearly 10 pounds (4.5 kilograms), Homer sat in a tank of sea water in a Halifax, Nova Scotia, grocery store as people passed by, marveling at his size. The person who guessed the crustacean's exact weight would be able to take him home, presumably to boil him alive in their kitchen.

But local activists had a kinder idea. They mobilized members to submit their own guesses to the Atlantic Superstore contest, and in the end, compassion won.

These activists transformed the victory into an animal rights event. On the Saturday afternoon when they picked up the lobster, activists distributed "Being Boiled Hurts" leaflets outside the store and spoke to customers about animal cruelty. They emphasized that lobsters have nerve endings and pain receptors and experience physical suffering just like any other animal.

Later that evening, a few activists, accompanied by a marine biologist, set Homer free at an undisclosed location somewhere along Nova Scotia's South Shore. The only concern was that Homer, whom local biologists estimated to be between 20 and 30 years old, may have been weak from living for days in the grocery tank with no food and rubber bands on his claws. But the last time activists saw Homer, he was moving on his own and undoubtedly happier to be back in the ocean.

And the media covered the entire event.

Lesson: Direct action, including animal liberation, can take many forms.

Investigations

Kate Turlington had just graduated from college when she landed a job as a laboratory animal technician at the University of North Carolina (UNC). Kate worked in a research lab with rats and mice, providing the animals with food, water, and clean cages. She also notified the vet staff of any signs of illness she noticed in the animals. A keen observer, Kate kept complete notes on the animals' care—or lack thereof: At one point, she witnessed an experimenter using household scissors to cut the heads off of fully conscious baby rats. He admitted that the approved research protocol called for him to numb the babies with ice first, but he told Kate he chose his method because it saved time. She found live mice shivering and distressed in the dead-animal cooler, forced to eat the remains of other animals to survive; she discovered cages so severely overcrowded that animals died from being trampled and from suffocation; and she routinely encountered animals who were undergoing painful, lingering deaths, yet were denied veterinary care and euthanasia.

Perhaps to the surprise of her colleagues, after six months of working at the UNC lab, Kate quit her job. The next day, it was revealed that she had been even more thorough in her observations than anyone had expected: Kate was an undercover investigator with PETA, and in addition to making notes about the treatment of the rodents in the lab, she had documented the abuses with hidden cameras. The front page of the local paper carried the story, and PETA submitted a formal complaint to the National Institutes of Health (NIH), which supports UNC with hundreds of millions of dollars in federal grant money every year.

"We learned that as a result of our investigation, several experimenters were placed on probation and my building supervisor resigned and was replaced," says Kate. "In response to the numerous cruel killing methods I documented at UNC, the NIH issued a directive to every research facility in the nation regarding approved rodent killing methods."

Although regulations do exist to enforce certain areas of animal welfare, it often takes a covert investigation like this one to discover how enterprises are actually treating the animals used for medical research, food, breeding, and the like. This form of direct action is extremely useful in collecting evidence against animal abusers, because most of the businesses exploiting animals are generally off limits to the public. But what does it take to make a good investigator?

"Contrary to what most people might think," says Kate, "investigators must be—and remain—sensitive, compassionate, and empathetic. I assumed that the only way that a caring person could function in such a job would be to emotionally numb themselves out in an attempt to not internalize the animals' suffering." But she learned that the worst thing she could do as an investigator would be to harden herself to the suffering she witnessed every day. "After all, if we do not maintain our keen sensitivity to what the animals are going through when we infiltrate the industries that use and abuse animals, then we are no better than the ordinary employees who cause the animals to suffer." Kate also points out that investigators who become desensitized lose the ability to be critical observers, and therefore run the risk of accepting a cruel practice as the norm.

Because investigative work is so emotionally loaded, it's critical that activists engaged in this model have realistic expectations and deal with their feelings as they arise. "Don't expect a lab or slaughterhouse to be shut down as a result of your efforts," Kate warns. "Every investigator handles stress differently but, in general, I believe it is incredibly important for investigators to be emotionally mature and honest with themselves about their feelings. As tempting as it is, we cannot push down or otherwise avoid or deny our feelings; otherwise, we will go insane and will not be able to help the animals!"

One of the feelings Kate and many others experience while being undercover is fear. "For me, working undercover was *very* scary," she says. "In addition to the difficulty of being a witness to animal suffering, investigators live with the fear of being caught. They must always be on their toes, not only to follow up on animal concerns and document them to the fullest, but also to make sure they don't accidentally slip up and say something to give themselves away, get caught with a camera, or be seen associating with known animal activists."

My attitude is not "If I didn't think we'd win, I'd quit," to which I would say, "Then quit." Working for animal rights isn't a football game or a beauty contest. It's working to modify our species' attitudes and behavior at a deep level, to develop a different set of genes—fundamental elements of human nature that have largely been ignored, overridden by other elements thus far.

Karen Davis
Satya **magazine**, July/August 2001

Is It for You?

While not for every activist, undercover investigations generate the most compelling evidence of animal suffering and have resulted in many victories for animals; moreover, because these cases generate lots of media attention, they help educate the public and encourage discourse on animal rights. To help activists decide whether they have what it takes, Kate and her team put together this list of the qualities shared by PETA's effective undercover investigators helping animals around the world:

- **Unshakable work ethic.** Investigators essentially work two full-time jobs, as their days are spent laboring at a job where animals are used and often abused, and their nights are spent reviewing documentation that was gathered on the job (i.e., logging photos and watching video) and generating log notes detailing every aspect of the day's events.
- **Ability to travel.** Investigators must have a fly-by-the-seat-of-your-pants attitude with regard to undercover assignments and travel. Investigators spend months on end on the road and on location for undercover jobs, which is a clear area of conflict for those who have families, significant others, or animal companions.
- **Confidentiality.** An investigator's ability to remain undercover is the most critical aspect of any investigation, which means that investigators can tell no one that they work for PETA. This factor, coupled with the geographic distance from friends and family, makes the job of an undercover investigator very isolating.
- **Strong writing skills.** Investigators must draft log notes detailing everything that they experience on the job with coherence and accuracy and without editorializing.
- **Team-player mentality.** Investigators must develop and maintain positive working relationships with co-workers at their undercover jobs. Additionally, investigators work closely with their colleagues at PETA and must follow instructions and communicate openly and honestly.
- **Emotional management skills.** Investigators witness immense animal suffering and must find a healthy balance between masking emotions at their undercover jobs and

acknowledging and working through those emotions after hours. Investigators cannot share their on-the-job difficulties with friends and family but do have access to former investigators who can relate to the emotional hardships of the job and offer advice or simply an understanding ear.

- **Ability to focus on the big picture**. Investigations are intended to document the conditions that the animals would be forced to endure even if PETA were not there. The forceful objections or aggressive actions of a single investigator would probably not do much to help animals — the investigator would merely be fired and thereby unable to continue documenting the lives and deaths of the animals behind the scenes. As a result of investigators' documentation, however, the shocking reality of animal suffering is exposed to the world, campaigns are born and change is effected for the greatest number of animals possible.
- **Investigative mind**. Investigators must pay close attention to — and retain — details and be proactive in their efforts to document conditions for animals.
- **Common sense**. Investigators must work autonomously, make sound decisions under pressure and push through inevitable fear and paranoia while constantly operating under a shield of caution.

"Additionally, of course, investigators must be able to think well on their feet, act quickly, and fit in with employees at their undercover jobs in addition to working well with their PETA colleagues," says Kate. "I recommend that anyone who thinks they have what it takes to work undercover contact PETA to apply for a position as an undercover investigator." Interested applicants should submit their résumé (CV) and a cover letter describing their experience with animal rights and interest in the position, as well as the skills they possess that would benefit them in this job.

Hunt Sabotage

Hunt sabotage (or "hunt sabbing") is a form of direct action in which activists ("hunt saboteurs" or just "sabs") interfere with the progress of hunters—who are often on horseback and may use packs of dogs—in their pursuit of foxes, hares, stags, birds, fishes, or other animals. Sabs use a variety of devices to confuse hunting dogs, such as horns, whistles, homemade whips, citronella oil (to cover animal scents), and something called a "gizmo," which amplifies the sounds of hounds vocalizing and causes the dogs to break off the chase. Because of the complexity of hunts and the potential for confrontation with hunters, this is not an activity for advocates acting alone.

"It's been going on since the early 1960s," explains animal rights scholar Kim Stallwood, "and it's a way in which people nonviolently place their bodies between the hunter and the hunted. It's also a way for people to sabotage and prevent the hunt from being effective or have the opportunity to hunt a wild animal. I think if you're young and fit and willing to run around the countryside and put yourself physically at risk, go ahead."

The best step to take is to join one of the many hunt sab groups that operate throughout the UK, Canada, Ireland, Spain, and the United States (they're not hard to find online). "Don't be scared; just get out there," says Alfie Wood of the Hunt Saboteurs Association in England. "There are 40 autonomous groups of hunt sabs in the UK, and each has a different way of working, so training for new sabs is tailored to their group. To start with, make sure you stay close with the group. Watch and learn. During quieter moments, experienced sabs will let you try out hunting horns and whips and will teach you the voice calls, show you where and how to spray citronella, and when to use a gizmo. I always advise new sabs to look online to see how sabs dress in the field."

Veganism is a key principle in hunt sabbing as well. "Most sabs are vegan, and most groups would not be happy with non-vegan food on the sab vans," says Alfie. As for the dangers, he admits there are risks involved, though being arrested is very unlikely. "New sabs are given a legal briefing. Violence is uncommon, but does occur." New sabs are also given advice on how to spot the warning signs of impending trouble and how to minimize the risk of aggression from the hunters and their supporters.

Activists have a long history of using direct action to expose the atrocities committed against animals. It's an effective method that relies on video and photographic evidence to bring into public discourse the indefensible abuses that animal enterprises work hard to keep concealed. These businesses profit from perpetuating the disappearance of animals into a system of full-scale, institutionalized exploitation—a state that in turn enables corporations to create an alternate reality featuring "happy cows," depict only human faces when promoting medical research, and avoid mentioning what becomes of male chicks in the egg industry. Rescues and investigations directly threaten the status quo, revealing the hidden truth in undeniable detail.

*For an insightful examination of the ALF's tactics, read *Terrorists or Freedom Fighters? Reflections on the Liberation of Animals* (Lantern Books), an anthology of essays by supporters and critics of the ALF from within the animal rights movement, edited by Steven Best and Anthony J. Nocella, II.

Chapter 10

Animal Law: The Legal System

The person who understands what I have to say about justice understands everything I have to say.
Meister Eckhart

She has handled many cases involving animals since cofounding the Animal Legal Defense Fund (ALDF) in 1979, but there's one that Joyce Tischler is particularly proud of. It began in 2004. "A local dog rescuer brought us information about Barbara and Robert Woodley, an older couple running a puppy mill in Sanford, North Carolina, and keeping 500 dogs in the worst possible conditions," she says. Earlier that year, Joyce had discovered a unique and little-used North Carolina law that allows third parties such as ALDF to stop cruelty through a civil lawsuit. "In most states, if a county prosecutor doesn't bring criminal charges against an animal abuser, there is nothing we can do, so we were pleased to find this law." Joyce and her team decided the Woodley case was the perfect testing ground.

"Before we could file our lawsuit," she says, "Mrs. Woodley had some friends 'clean out' the garage and remove 170 dogs from her property. We sued the Woodleys, got the injunction, and the judge gave ALDF possession of the remaining 330 sick and unsocialized dogs, with no money to care for them. And that's when the real magic started."

The commitment of the local people to helping these dogs was inspiring, says Joyce, from the business owner who lent rescuers an empty building in which to house the dogs, to multiple veterinarians who donated hundreds of hours to treat a variety of diseases and injuries, to the many volunteers who fed, cleaned, and socialized the dogs. "It was an extraordinary outpouring of compassion. The Woodleys appealed the case all the way to the North Carolina Court of Appeals, and we won at each level, enabling us to set good precedent and return to North Carolina to rescue other dogs, horses, and even a bear at a roadside zoo. We would like to see a similar law passed in every state. And the icing on the cake was that we found homes for all of the Woodley dogs, including a funny old Boston terrier, Edgar, who turned out to be the love of my life."

While this story had a happy ending, that isn't always the case, of course. Even getting ALDF off the ground was a challenge, and few within the animal rights movement knew what to do with Joyce and her colleagues. "The large animal protection agencies rarely used litigation, and when they did, they relied on local or pro bono attorneys, with no expertise in animal law," she says. "Grassroots animal activists who risked arrest at protests were suspicious of us. With our suits and law degrees, we seemed too mainstream. They informed us that they were doing the real work and our sole purpose should be to provide them with free criminal defense. While we did assist them with pro bono criminal defense on numerous occasions in various parts of the country, we had very different goals in mind. We wanted to bring major-impact civil litigation to protect animals and establish their rights."

Building the organization meant raising funds through marketing and direct-mail appeals, which took time but eventually worked. And as ALDF has grown, the value of litigation to protect animals has become obvious. "Today, most of the large national groups have attorneys on their staffs and are using litigation as one of their approaches," says Joyce.

Though the field of animal law is growing rapidly in the United States and other countries, most animal activists will never see the inside of a law school. Nevertheless, legal means to advance the interests of animals are available to everyone, and indeed some of our biggest victories on behalf of animals are the result of ordinary citizens who care enough to get involved.

As Joyce observes, getting involved can take a variety of approaches. "We need the grassroots activists who will protest, demonstrate, leaflet, and conduct investigations, informing the public about the underlying problems," she says. "Education will also come from writers, as well as animal shelters and sanctuaries, which serve a teaching function, as well as rescuing animals. Groups like mine will litigate, using the common law to achieve decisions that improve the lives of animals." Legislation is another key method—creating new laws to protect animals and fighting against bills that harm them. A recent approach, she says, is innovation, through which alternatives to the use of animals are developed. "A growing industry is inventing and marketing products that take animals out of the equation. There is a fascinating interplay among all of these approaches—one that we at ALDF are keenly aware of. If the lawyers lose a lawsuit on a key animal issue, that may help to mobilize the grassroots to protest the injustice of the law, which may inspire legislation to correct the law's shortcomings."

Legislation

Laws intended to advance the interests of animals are an important tool in generating reform, and countless grassroots activists have campaigned for legislative changes or supported animal rights organizations in their efforts. In fact, assisting animal organizations is probably the easiest way for activists to engage in this form of activism, so check with one of the larger animal rights groups in your country (Animal Aid, Animals Australia, Animal Justice, Animal Legal Defense Fund, Centre for Animals and Social Justice, Compassion in World Farming, the Humane Society of the United States [HSUS], etc.) to ask how you can get involved in current legislative efforts. Such legislation can be used to:

- Ban egregious business practices, such as using confinement crates and battery cages
- Protect wildlife by creating refuges, prohibiting hunting or trapping, etc.
- Advance welfare by setting minimum standards, such as veterinary requirements for rodeos
- Ban specific forms of animal abuse, such as circuses, blood sports, or tethering animals
- Protect farmed animals and public safety by banning the slaughter of "downed" animals or regulating the use of antibiotics in factory farms
- Overturn existing laws that permit cruelty, such as the sale and slaughter of wild horses and burros
- Regulate the sale of exotic animals
- Make animal abusers accountable for their cruelty
- Provide funding for spay and neuter programs
- Strengthen existing laws, such as those regulating the sale of fur from domestic animals.

Before embarking upon a legislative campaign, activists must assess what they wish to accomplish and then decide if legislation is the most effective model for achieving that objective. It may turn out that another strategy would be a better approach. If the goal is a law mandating at least one vegan entrée selection in every school, for example, the activist or group should consider if a law is really necessary. Could the same result be obtained through outreach? Chances are that speaking directly with dining hall decision-makers and school administrators will yield better results for a fraction of the cost.

If legislation is indeed the best course of action, either by trying to create a new law or improve an existing one, activists will want to consider what kind of public support they can expect. This can be achieved through a survey or by collecting voter signatures (which you may have to do anyway). Any changes in the law will come down to a vote of either the citizens or their elected officials, so knowing beforehand what kind of backing your issue will have is likely to be a deciding factor in whether or not you pursue legislation.

"Legal change is absolutely necessary and absolutely crucial in order to codify and enforce increasingly positive social attitudes toward animals," says animal law professor Mariann Sullivan. "And, as society is shifting in those attitudes, we will see greater and greater progress in the courts and legislatures. The forces aligned against us are enormously powerful and wealthy, so the more lawyers who we have out there fighting for progress, the more progress we will see."

Pursuing Legislation

Although they may be protected under certain laws, animals are considered property, which means humans can do pretty much whatever they want with them. Naturally, we'd be living in a very different world if animals were granted rights, the most basic of which may be the right to simply exist for themselves and not as a service to humanity. "Animal rights" do not yet exist, and hence there is no real "animal rights law." Advocates can, however, use laws and regulations to aid animals, since many forms of mistreatment are considered illegal.

Unfortunately, not only do animals not have rights under the law, but not all animals are considered equal; consequently, laws that apply to one species may not apply to another. In the United States, for example, the Humane Methods of Slaughter Act specifies that animals must be rendered insensible to pain before being slaughtered, yet this law does not include "poultry," so there is no federal protection for chickens, who represent more than 90 percent of farmed animals killed in the US. These birds—as well as turkeys, ducks, geese, and rabbits (considered "poultry" by the United States Department of Agriculture, for some reason)—suffer some of the most horrific deaths imaginable.

Through legislation, activists have the opportunity to enhance the protection of animals. Such legislation can cover a spectrum of legal improvements, from the European Convention's efforts to protect pets and stray animals to laws targeting the most egregious industrialized abuses of farmed animals. Legislation may be urged on local or national levels and may even use international agreements, such as those from the International Whaling Commission or the International Air Transport Association, which sets standards for the international transport of animals.

Activist Gene Baur believes that in addition to improving the lives of animals, legislative campaigns help make overall activism more effective. "A large part of what we as animal advocates need to do is determine how to reach out to people who are not animal advocates and communicate in a way that they will listen to us and recognize these issues as important and deserving of

Issues like the environment or human rights are further advanced down the stages than animal rights are. The stages as I understand them are: 1) public education, 2) public policy development, 3) legislation, 4) litigation and enforcement, and 5) public acceptance. Although we do some litigation, legislation and some public policy development, I think the animal rights issue is still very much in stage one—public education. I think that's why media coverage is still the goal. We need to understand that the more we can propel the issue of animal rights into the public policy development and legislation stages, the more that we will expedite the cause.

Kim Stallwood
Satya **magazine**, December 2001

their time and attention," he says. "These campaigns are like a living laboratory of social science, helping us understand how to reach out in the most effective way."

Lobbying

Because democratic governments—including Australia, Canada, Ireland, New Zealand, South Africa, the United Kingdom, and the United States—are meant to represent their nation's people, citizens (especially voters) are an important part of the legislative system. Indeed, the abolition of slavery, child labor restrictions, women's right to vote, civil rights, and other social change owe much to the individuals who exerted pressure on elected officials, and so it is with animal rights and animal protection legislation.

Citizens and organizations in democracies have the right to communicate with elected officials, urging them to support issues that are important to them. By directly targeting lawmakers, activists can help create new legislation or improve existing legislation. You may even find yourself defending recent legislation, as British animal advocates have experienced with the 2004 Hunting Act, which bans hunting with dogs in England and Wales. In the face of efforts by blood sport enthusiasts to overturn the law, activists have worked hard to ensure the hunting ban stays in effect, mostly through lobbying.

This method of trying to influence Members of Parliament (MPs) is called "a Lobby of Parliament," explains Joyce D'Silva of Compassion in World Farming (CIWF). "We hire a big hall near Parliament, have a rally, and then people can queue up to see their MPs," she says. "If you're lucky, they'll come and talk to you; if you're very lucky they'll take you for a cup of tea and talk to you. It's a way of getting issues to a lot of MPs on a quite personal level."

Joyce says that MPs are sympathetic about animal issues, perhaps because they hear about them so often from constituents.

"Many MPs in England have said they get more letters on animal-welfare issues than anything else," she says. "One MP's secretary even said the MP wasn't interested in animal welfare, but he gets so many letters on it that he thought he should show up and vote, because he's representing his people. So, letters really can have an effect." Joyce cites as an example a massive letter-writing campaign they organized with the aid of the Royal Society for the Protection of Animals to encourage MPs to vote for a bill banning gestation crates for sows. The bill passed, and the crates were banned in the UK as of January 1999.

Longtime animal rights campaigner Kim Stallwood says lobbying is all well and good, but people should get active during election season by identifying and supporting political candidates with the greatest commitment to animals, quizzing candidates at public meetings, and developing a platform of issues to lobby with and talk about as candidates stump for votes. "And whoever gets elected, we should hold them to account for whatever pledges they made to help ensure they implement them during the period of time they serve as a publicly elected representative. If they fail to do it, you come back to the next election and make the point that they promised to do XYZ, and they never did it."

For those who favor a political party, Kim also suggests they join that party, develop positions and policies within the party, and raise the topic of animals as an issue of debate. "I think the ideal that we need to strive towards is when we have a national election, the political party with the greatest commitment to animals is elected to form the government so that when that party forms the government, they come ready-made, as it were, with the best pledges and promises to act in that elected cycle," he says. "The most effective way to do that is to work from within the political party. Quietly but firmly assert animal issues and build them into your general political ideology within that party. If you just go in and talk about animals and nothing else, you won't be taken very seriously. But if you go in and talk about animal issues in relation to broader social justice and the environment and public health and so on, then the other people in the party will be more open to taking that position onboard. It's a *long* process."

Hans Kriek of New Zealand-based Save Animals From Exploitation (SAFE) agrees that the legislative process takes considerable time. "The political system is slow-moving, so do not expect instant results," he says, although he adds that accessing politicians in New Zealand is relatively easy, since anyone can make an appointment with their MP and discuss any issue of concern. "Bringing an animal issue up on a politician's radar is important as we cannot expect politicians to be interested let alone make changes to something they have never heard of! When talking to your MP, always be polite and stick to the issue, as you will have limited time to make your case. Leave some very brief reading material behind as you can't expect your MP to remember it all. That said, lobbying can be a powerful tool for animal activists."

While many of us may think that only special interest groups lobby, the reality is individuals can actually hold more sway with their elected officials. "Citizen activism and people being involved in encouraging their elected officials to pass laws and to strengthen laws is at the very root of everything we do," says Steve Wells, executive director of the Animal Legal Defense Fund, which uses the legal system to advance the interests of animals.

"In my experience," says Steve, "the animal protection movement and animal activists individually often don't realize the power we have, and I think we can do a better job, individually and collectively, learning how we can wield that power more effectively." Learning to do that means, in part, recognizing that even though the other side may have pockets deep enough to make substantial political contributions and hire professional lobbyists, he says, we are an influential force that can speak directly to our elected officials. "So when their constituents who care about animals make that fact known by being in touch with elected officials, by paying attention to legislature that's going to impact animals in their state or community, it makes a big difference. I have seen us time after time when we are well organized and people at the grassroots get involved, we are able to do amazing things."

One thing that Steve learned to do is be present at city council meetings, fundraisers, and other events attended by elected officials. "I go to them when I can and wield my own power as a citizen activist," he says. "You don't have to give money, so if you don't have money to give, that should not prevent you from going. These are public officials who are using these events to meet with the public. There's no question that if you show up at these things, introduce yourself, ask them their feelings on animal issues, and let them know of your interests, that this has an impact. If animals are your passion, the more directly involved you can be the better, and face-to-face or talking on the phone are your best bet to have your voice heard."

Canadian activist and animal rights lawyer Camille Labchuk suggests that advocates even support animal-friendly candidates during election season by volunteering to knock on doors and make phone calls. "Legislators remember the people that help them get elected," she says, "and you can use this goodwill to ensure they do the right thing once in office." Camille, who was a Green Party candidate for Parliament in 2014, is also passionate about lobbying, and she suggests meeting with federal, provincial, and municipal legislators often—and bringing as many friends or family members from the community as you can. "Come armed with facts and a specific ask, such as supporting or introducing a piece of legislation. Make sure your legislators know they won't get your vote unless they support animal protection issues. After a meeting, a phone call is your second best option, followed by sending an email. Political staff track the number of phone calls and emails they receive on an issue, and most politicians pay close attention to the mood of their constituents. And don't do this just once—make a point of reaching out regularly to legislators."

Never Too Early
Lest you believe that lobbying is only for voting-age adults, consider the example of Thomas Ponce. Thomas began getting active for animals at age four, attended his first protest at age five, started an animal rights group in the fourth grade, and in 2013—when he was just 12—he founded Lobby For Animals, a web-based resource for training and supporting animal rights advocates in how to successfully lobby their elected officials. "Lobbying is a tool that is often overlooked by many, whether it be from a lack of understanding or an overall fear of the process," he says. "By educating ourselves, raising awareness, and getting involved in the political process, we are leveling the playing field and letting our representatives know we are there and willing to fight for what we believe in: protecting the rights of all animals, our civil liberties, and the environment."

Thomas advises his adolescent peers to not let age be a hindrance—or even a consideration. "Just because you are not old enough to vote doesn't mean that you have no voice. Find an issue you are passionate about and learn as much as you can about it and then get out there and start talking to the right people who can help you reach your desired goal. I am a firm believer that knowledge is definitely power, and when you speak with knowledge and from your heart, people will listen, regardless of your age."

Getting started is as easy as calling the office of your representatives to voice your support for or opposition to a current bill, says Thomas, or simply making an appointment to address an issue that's not yet being addressed. "They will listen to you. It's their job, and they know you will be a voting constituent in a few years, and believe me, they want your vote. There are plenty of bills that have been passed into law that were initiated by citizens. The key is to speak with knowledge and be persistent. Don't ever give up." He adds that young people have the opportunity to forge a kinder future. "We can make this world a better place for animals and human beings alike. By spreading compassion for all living beings and demanding that our laws reflect our values, we can create a better and just world."

Phone Phobia

Just the thought of calling an elected official makes many people nervous. Before picking up the phone, it's helpful to write down what you want to say—and be brief. If you're still nervous when you call, read from your notes. "Virtually everyone gets nervous to some degree, especially if you haven't done it before," says Steve Wells. "The only time that is a problem is when your nervousness prevents you from taking an action." Steve advises anxious activists to remember that animals can't call or speak for themselves in our language. "If you think about that for a minute, it can often give you the power to make the call. To everyone who takes a deep breath and calls their representative on an important issue, I promise that by the time you hang up that phone you are going to feel really good."

How to Effectively Lobby Your Lawmaker

Lobbying is nearly impossible without personal contact, says the Animal Legal Defense Fund, which advises that you call the legislator's office and schedule an appointment. The appointment assistant will want to know what the meeting is about; limit your agenda to one or two topics for discussion. Polite but firm persistence through regular contact with the district's office is essential. While you may feel most comfortable attending the appointment as part of a group, they say, it is advisable to go alone or with just a few others, and dress professionally. Appoint one person to be the main spokesperson.

Here are some additional recommendations, courtesy of the Humane Society of the United States (HSUS):

- Don't be intimidated by the thought of approaching elected officials. State legislators especially are receptive to constituent comments.
- Be concise. Your message should be short and direct. It is fine to express your opinion.
- Use all available resources. Request position papers, fact sheets, or other documentation from animal protection groups. You don't need to be an expert, but the more facts and arguments you have on your side, the better.
- Personalize your appeal. Tell how you are concerned about an issue and how it affects you, your family, and your community.
- Cultivate legislative staff. Establish a positive relationship with staff persons. They are usually more accessible and can have tremendous influence over an issue.
- Be honest. If you don't know the answer to something, admit it and try to get the information later. Also, when working with legislators who sponsor your bill, be sure to be upfront about any potential problem areas.
- Research your legislators. Ask around, talk to others who have worked for legislative change—on any issue—and ask their advice on which legislators are most effective or which committees are most likely to approve of your bill.
- Identify your bill or issue clearly. Whenever you get a

chance to lobby elected officials, don't just refer to your effort by the bill number. And always make it clear whether you are asking for their support or opposition to the matter.

- During the legislative session, constantly check your bill's status. Most legislative entities have a bill status information office. At certain times, action occurs quickly and with little notice.
- Keep things friendly. Maintain a positive relationship with all legislators—they may be in this office or a higher one for decades. Threats and hostile or sarcastic remarks are not productive. Do not create any enemies.
- Avoid party politics. Animals have friends on both sides of the aisle.
- Be flexible. Sometimes compromise is a must. Support legislative strategies that may save an otherwise doomed bill: adoption of sunset provisions, grandfathering clauses, and placing provisions into regulations instead of statute.
- Express gratitude. Thank everyone and let your members know how helpful key legislators were in your success.

Do's and Don'ts of Lobbying

Do's:

- Do know who represents you at all levels of government. You can obtain this information from your local library or board of elections and usually through the Internet. Keep phone numbers and addresses handy. Help others do the same.
- Do identify yourself by name and organization (if any) when talking with an elected official. (Politicians always act like they remember who you are to avoid offending anyone.)

- Do state a clear and concise objective. For example, say specifically that you want to ban canned hunts—not just that you want to stop outrageous hunting practices (which is too broad). Explain the meaning of terms that may be unfamiliar, such as "canned," "pound seizure," "Class B dealers." Broad statements such as "Hunting bears with hounds is inexcusable" may reflect how you feel, but don't convey a message as to what action needs to be taken by the official.

- Do explain why the issue is important to you personally. If possible, link the issue to a personal experience or a situation in the elected official's district.

- Do be aware of previous actions the official has taken on behalf of animals. You can be sure the opposition is aware of the assistance they gave on our behalf.

- Do get to know your elected officials. Make an effort to appear at town meetings and other events, and be sure they hear you ask at least one question on animal issues at each event.

- Do mention how important it is for your elected officials to adequately fund animal programs ranging from local animal control to state enforcement of wildlife protection laws to enforcement of the Animal Welfare Act and others. Let them know that this is how you want your tax dollars spent.

- Do join, create, or revitalize state federations or other state-wide groups to give your cause additional clout. Whenever possible, mention how many individuals your group represents.

- Do get to know and develop a working relationship with key people who have influence over animals. For example, animal control officers, veterinarians, state wildlife board members, prosecuting attorneys, and health department officials have a major impact on animal protection bills.

Legislators listen to their views, so work with them whenever possible.

- Do join forces with other types of groups that may have the same position as you even if for different reasons—groups such as churches, teachers' unions, chambers of commerce, local universities, or specific industries. Whenever appropriate, get school children to support your efforts.

- Do wear many hats—not just your animal advocate hat. When lobbying legislators, identify yourself as a parent, businessperson, campaign contributor, or fellow church/club/team member.

- Do work with legislative staff. They often have more knowledge of the issues, can give you vital background on the legislation's outlook, and have extraordinary clout.

- Do get involved in legislative campaigns—as an individual, not as a nonprofit group. Volunteer to work, place a campaign sign in your yard, hand out leaflets, or otherwise help get someone elected.

- Do learn how to work with your local press by developing a relationship with friendly reporters and editors.

- Do respond to action alerts sent by the HSUS and other groups. Alerts are usually sent when legislation is close to passage or in a precarious position, so your action can make a tremendous difference.

Don'ts:

- Don't threaten or antagonize a legislator even if they deserve it. If an elected official opposes your viewpoint, but respects you and bears you no animosity, you may find common ground in the future on another issue. But if you make an enemy, that person may take extra steps to defeat the bill you support. A legislator who doesn't agree with you on wildlife issues may be great on companion animal issues and vice versa. Don't make enemies. Today's city council member can be tomorrow's governor.

- Don't refer to bills by their numbers alone.
- Don't fail to listen to an elected official's comments and questions on an issue. If she asks how a bill will impact jobs, or medical care, or the budget, you'll know where her concern is focused. Find ways to address those issues.
- Don't ever lie to or mislead a legislator—especially someone who is on your side and needs to know the truth about an issue. Trust is essential for a working relationship.
- Don't overwhelm a legislator with too much information or paperwork. They don't have time for it. Provide them with whatever is key to their efforts and be ready to supply any other needed information.
- Don't be inflexible. Sometimes we have to compromise. As long as such a change won't harm any animals, consider the situation carefully. Learn legislative strategies that might save a bill otherwise destined to die, such as sunset provisions, grandfathering clauses, and placing provisions into a regulation instead of a statute.
- Don't forget to thank someone who was helpful. Whenever possible, let your membership know how helpful the person has been.
- Don't use terms or abbreviations that may be unfamiliar to an official without explaining their meaning, such as WLFA, PIJAC, or even the HSUS.

What Influences a Legislator?

Elected officials are, first and foremost, politicians. When lawmakers are up for re-election, they are often more willing to listen to interests outside their normal concerns. The issues of special interest groups are important to them because they may need that support to win re-election.

One of the easiest and most direct ways to get to know and influence legislators is to help them. You can do so by volunteering to work on a campaign. Although assisting politicians does not ensure that they will always vote your way, it does allow you to spend time with them and their staff. Building and maintaining working relationships is always important.

The following are important questions to keep in mind when lobbying elected officials. The answers to these will influence how a legislator responds to the issue.

The issue:

- What are the merits of the issue?
- What impact does it have on his/her district?
- Does it involve possible job losses?
- What is the cost?
- What is the issue's impact on the economy or business?
- Would the issue create too much government interference?
- Do issue opponents have more clout than proponents?
- Is there a general lack of knowledge about the issue?
- What is the executive branch position?

Political considerations:

- Is there an upcoming election in which the legislator faces tough competition?
- Is the legislator a lame duck?
- Have issue proponents or opponents made campaign contributions?
- Does the issue have the commitment of an interest group? In other words, are there many voters tied to this single issue?
- Does the issue have support from the president, governor, or mayor?

- Does the legislator know that Scorecards (HSUS's annual review documenting how senate members vote on animal rights legislation) are closely monitored on this issue?

Media:

- Have there been many news articles written on the issue?
- Have there been many editorials written on the issue?
- Have readers submitted letters to the editor on the issue?
- Are there more opportunities to gain press attention?

Legislative considerations:

- Is the legislator the chairperson of the committee that would handle the issue?
- What are the legislator's committee assignments?
- What trade-offs has the politician made with fellow legislators?
- What are the positions of others in state or district delegation?
- Are other legislators lobbying for or against the issue?
- What is the staff advice on the issue?
- What is the position of the legislator's political party?

Personal:

- Does the legislator have personal experiences and feelings on the issue?
- What are the positions of the legislator's family members, friends, and (especially) children?
- Does the issue impact the legislator personally or others important to the legislator?
- Does the issue have any connection to the politician's alma mater?

Outside influences:

- Does the legislator have frequent grassroots contact with constituents who could influence him?
- What's the general public sentiment about the issue?
- Do celebrities or sports figures endorse the issue?
- How often does the legislator have chance encounters with the public?

(Source: The HSUS)

Citizens' Initiatives & Referendums

More than half the states in the US allow citizens to submit proposed changes in the law to voters for approval. The initiative process (also called the "ballot initiative" process) allows citizens to gather petition signatures to place a proposed statutory or constitutional amendment before the voters and is most often used as a last resort effort when other means of effecting reform have been exhausted. Citizens' initiatives come with a hefty price tag, making them a last resort. They are worth mentioning, however, since they are another avenue to legislative improvements for animals.

Activist Camilla Fox helped coordinate Proposition 4, which ultimately banned several wildlife traps and poisons in California in 1998. "I think the public ballot initiative process has provided an opportunity for animal advocates to put forth measures to the public where they have not had success in the legislature or through the regulatory process," she says.

Nevertheless, Camilla urges grassroots activists to do their homework and get support from animal-protection organizations. "Ballot initiatives are very expensive, and I do not encourage activists to attempt to pursue a ballot initiative without the backing of major animal-protection groups because of the resources that are necessary to win such a campaign. If you don't have the polling data that shows you have a winnable campaign early on, it can be a tremendous waste of resources, both financially and in terms of activists' efforts."

Before even thinking of embarking on a ballot initiative campaign, Camilla suggests that activists use the other tools at their disposal, such as voicing your concerns at legislative and other public policy hearings or working for change through state and federal wildlife management agency rulemaking processes. "If such efforts fail, you have a better case for taking your measure to the public through the initiative process because you've demonstrated that you've exhausted all other means and now you have no other recourse but to allow the public to weigh in on the matter."

Another tip she offers from the activist trenches: Read the opposition's literature. "These publications often provide an update on the legislation and regulatory agency reform efforts they plan to pursue," she says. Knowing this information beforehand can be extremely helpful when creating your campaign.

New Zealand allows for citizen-initiated referendums, and indeed the first one attempted in the country was on behalf of battery hens in 1993. But according to Hans Kriek of SAFE, the petition to force such a referendum failed to get the required number of signatures. "A referendum like this requires a huge amount of work with little chance of success," Hans says. "Even if enough signatures are collected, the referendum is non-binding and no citizens-initiated referendum has so far succeeded in New Zealand. Other countries do have binding referendums, and they could be effective tools to achieve change for the animals. If promoted well, a referendum can attract a lot of attention and therefore raise the awareness of the issue significantly."

Activists in a number of European countries, including the UK, have campaigned for the European Union to grant citizens the right to create initiatives; if implemented, this would be the first trans-national tool of citizens' participation. In the meantime, activists in the UK lobby lawmakers and sign petitions.

"Petitions to the PM are widely used — and forgotten, as no official system exists for dealing with them," says Joyce D'Silva. "Petitions to the European Parliament actually end up with the Petitions Committee and may get endorsed by the Parliament, so they are much more useful. Our petition to have animals recognized as sentient beings in EU law was endorsed by this European Parliament in 1994."

Joyce says that a proper body such as CIWF can take the government to "Judicial Review" where they challenge their actions as being illegal under a certain law. "CIWF has judicially reviewed the government on at least three occasions and never yet won. The cases were on the export of animals to continental Europe and the welfare of broiler chickens. One case was referred to the European Court of Justice in Strasbourg, but we lost there, too."

Gene Baur of Farm Sanctuary believes that activists who participate in legislation make an invaluable contribution to the process. "As people become aware and take a position against certain cruelties, you have a tipping point where you can pass laws," he says. "And that's what these initiatives do. By passing laws through the initiative process or other processes that garner media attention, you're also continuing to educate. Ultimately, most people agree these practices are cruel and should not be allowed."

Agribusiness is taking notice, too. Just months after Arizona voters banned gestation crates for pigs in that state in 2006, Smithfield Foods — the largest "pork" producer in the US — announced it was phasing out its use of these cruel devices (it completed this phase-out in 2017). One week later, Maple Leaf Foods, Canada's largest "pork" producer, joined the shift toward change and said it was doing the same.

"Activist pressure is where it starts," says Gene. "Smithfield has said McDonald's was a big part of their decision, but the reason McDonald's was pressing Smithfield in the first place was because customers were pressing McDonald's, and that's because of activist pressure. So it all starts with activists raising awareness."

Voting Blocs
Used by all other issue advocacy movements that pursue laws and public policies, the voting bloc is generally a missed opportunity for animal advocates. The voting bloc system comprises a coalition of citizens who are so motivated by a specific concern that it helps them determine how they vote in elections. Julie E. Lewin, political trainer and president of the Connecticut-based National Institute for Animal Advocacy, says the voting bloc system has four components:

1. It organizes supportive citizens by legislative district.
2. Before voting on a piece of proposed legislation of concern to the issue group, lawmakers know that constituents who care will find out how they vote.
3. Before voting, the lawmaker knows that his/her voting record on the general issue will determine whether the political organization endorses him/her for re-election, or endorses his/her opponent.
4. The lawmaker knows that the voting bloc organization will deliver votes on Election Day to its endorsed candidates.

Thus, a voting bloc is an information-delivery system. It coordinates the voting behavior of its members; these citizens hold their lawmakers accountable, and the lawmaker knows that his or her voting bloc organization has the clout to sway other constituents. "That's where the power comes from: the power to use endorsements and political mobilization to swing elections," says Julie. "Voting blocs turn advocates into true power players. Think of the National Rifle Association and Christian Right. In my state, licensed hunters are only one and a half percent of the population, but because they understand all this and use it to their advantage, they control wildlife policy in the state. Animal advocates are huge in comparison but aren't political, so therefore they have no power in the lawmaking arena."

Across the United States, lobbying for animals—when it is done at all—is performed by charitable organizations and concerned individuals, who are largely powerless when it comes to achieving strong legislation; that is, legislation that has organized opposition. Julie defines a strong law as one that bans outright a certain practice, substantially raises the legal minimum standards of care for a group of animals, or makes it easier for humans to gain standing in court to represent animals. For example, Julie does not consider felony cruelty laws strong legislation, because they fail to give animals any additional legal protection. They have no organized opposition, and thus have been won without voting blocs.

Animal advocates, Julie says, are missing a vital opportunity to leverage the legal system by creating voting blocs. "We are a sleeping giant. The tragedy of the animal rights and animal rescue movements to date has been the failure to view *formal* political organizations—voting blocs—as a mandatory component. We must get political, or the animals will continue to pay the price."

You'll find step-by-step instructions for creating a voting bloc for animals in Julie's how-to manual for rights and rescue advocates, *Get Political for Animals and Win the Laws They Need: Why and How to Launch a Voting Bloc for Animals in Your Town, City, County or State.*

No matter how organized we are as activists, using legislation on behalf of animals can be a protracted process. "Be patient," advises Ericka Ceballos, president of Canada's CATCA Environmental and Wildlife Society (formerly Campaigns Against the Cruelty to Animals). "Things don't change overnight, despite your big efforts to change the world or at least stop a specific kind of cruelty. Things in this very ugly animal rights world take months and years to change. Look at the seal slaughter here in Canada. It takes decades. Many people feel so frustrated when things go wrong and their efforts don't make much of a change for the animals, but, hey, perseverance pays eventually."

Animal Attorneys

Although I mentioned earlier in this chapter that most animal activists will never attend law school, many in fact do; indeed, the field of animal law grows every year. Some college students decide as undergraduates to go on to law school, while others know even earlier that they want a career using the legal system to advance the interests of animals—whether that means prosecuting a cat abuser or working to gain animals the legal status of "persons."

If this is something you find appealing, attend an animal law conference, such as those organized by the Animal Legal Defense Fund (ALDF). You'll be able to connect with like-minded advocates, hear talks by leaders in the movement, and speak with attorneys already defending animals in court. If you're a college student and your university is among the growing number of colleges offering an animal law course, enroll in the class.

In the meantime, let's heed some advice from three experts in the field: Joyce Tischler of ALDF; Camille Labchuk of Animal Justice Canada; and Mariann Sullivan, who teaches animal law at Columbia Law School, Brooklyn Law School, and others.

Joyce says there are certain attributes that might make a person more likely to succeed in animal law. "A successful animal lawyer needs to be tenacious, flexible, detail-oriented, creative—because this is a new field—and possess a strong ego," she says, "because we are working within a legal system that reveres the status quo, and, therefore, we lose. A lot. And she will benefit from having a good sense of humor." But of course, that's *after* she's landed a job, which presents its own set of challenges, according to Joyce. "With a few notable exceptions, most attorneys who have tried to make a living in a small animal law practice have not fared well. Most of the large national groups now have attorneys on staff, as litigators, lobbyists, in-house counsel, and in other positions. But the number of jobs is limited. Attorneys should consider working for a local humane society that can afford to hire in-house counsel."

Mariann believes animal law is a great way for activists to use their skills. "But people should become lawyers only if they are fascinated by the law," she says, "or they're absolutely going to hate it. Keep in mind, you certainly don't have to be a lawyer to achieve change. In fact, the law can be a very frustrating form of change-making, because it is slow, and conservative, and legal changes will always be made only in small incremental ways. That being said, legal change is absolutely necessary and absolutely crucial in order to codify and enforce increasingly positive social attitudes toward animals. And, as society is shifting in those attitudes, we will see greater and greater progress in the courts and legislatures."

You might consider the example of Camille, who says would-be animal lawyers must be bold in charting their own courses and seeking out opportunities. "My own path led me to practice criminal law for several years before starting up my own animal law practice," she says. "I volunteered part-time with nonprofit animal law organization Animal Justice at the same time and helped build the organization up from a small team of volunteers into a larger, national organization. This eventually led to full-time employment in animal law."

Although all three women agree finding employment as an animal attorney can be difficult, they are uniformly optimistic about what it can achieve. "I truly believe I have the best job in the world," says Camille. "The law is such a powerful tool for social change, and being at the cutting edge of the new field of animal law in Canada is an honor and a privilege. Sure, constantly watching footage of animal cruelty can be difficult, and it's always crushing to lose a court case or see politicians vote down an important law. But I couldn't live with myself if I wasn't fighting to end animal suffering and bring our legal system in line with Canadian values."

"For those interested in practicing criminal law," adds Joyce, "a job at a prosecutor's offices could offer the chance to handle cruelty cases. On the criminal defense side, the grassroots movement often needs attorneys. Working for the government at the state or local level may offer other opportunities, such as County Counsel positions where one can carve out responsibility for oversight of animal-related matters. More difficult emotionally, but equally important, is working for federal agencies such as the US Department of Agriculture or Bureau of Land Management, and trying to create change from the inside. Consider working for environmental groups and being the dissenting voice on such issues as hunting, trapping, and the connection between meat production and climate." (ALDF has information about animal law opportunities and jobs on its website, aldf.org. Search for "careers.")

Finally, Mariann offers some words of wisdom that cut right to the heart of animal law. "The forces aligned against us are enormously powerful and wealthy," she says, "so the more lawyers who we have out there fighting for progress, the more progress we will see."

The Other Side of the Law

Bryan Pease was 16 years old when he became an animal activist—and when he started getting arrested for his activism. There was the time, for example, when he was holding a protest sign on a public sidewalk in front of a fur store in Syracuse, New

York. "The tactic was first the police would arrest people, and then they'd get a restraining order while the case was pending," Bryan says. "That can take months to be resolved. In effect they were preventing you from going back there, even if the charges aren't valid. So, I was arrested on a charge of unlawful assembly and I received a temporary restraining order. The arresting officer seemed to think 'unlawful assembly' meant a protest he didn't authorize."

He ignored the judge's order and returned to the same spot on the sidewalk, where he leafleted. "So, then they arrested me for contempt of court." At his trial, Bryan was found not guilty of unlawful assembly, but the judge found him guilty of violating his order. "He sentenced me to 13 weekends in jail, but I appealed it and I won," says Bryan, who is now an attorney practicing animal law and cofounder of the Animal Protection and Rescue League.

Being arrested at a protest or for some other animal rights campaign is always a possibility, especially now that governments are cracking down more heavily on animal rights advocates. While an activist who chains herself to the door of a slaughterhouse may have a pretty good idea she'll be taking a ride in a police car that day, other activists are quite surprised to find themselves in handcuffs.

In 2006, activist Adam Durand was convicted of trespassing and sentenced to six months in jail for his part in an investigation and open rescue of hens from a battery farm. A first-time offender, Adam thought he would be getting probation. "But the judge saw otherwise. He decided to give me the maximum sentence times two, because I was convicted on three trespassing counts." Adam and another prisoner shared a ride in a patrol car to begin their sentences. "He said, 'Man, you're a political prisoner. I'm really proud of everything you're doing.' I thought that was a good sign. And that's the way the other inmates treated me. They were very friendly and respectful. The corrections officers were not always as nice. Some of them wanted to see who this vegan guy was and make fun of him."

But being vegan in jail wasn't easy for Adam. "I was not offered any kind of dietary exemption," he says. "I did file papers with the jail. They never responded to them. I think the internal forms in the jail are designed to be ignored. My attorneys tried to get the jail to change their policy, but they didn't offer any kind of exemption for ethical dietary choice—they called it a preference." Luckily, Adam got a job in the kitchen, so he had a little control over what he ate.

"This was a wake-up call to the conditions in which two million Americans are living. I learned a lot. It's definitely a fight I want to include in my future activism: better treatment for prisoners. For example, the Thirteenth Amendment to the Constitution abolishes slavery, but it exempts prisoners who have been convicted of a crime, and I just think that's ridiculous. I didn't realize that until I was in there and I was being forced to work."

In the end, Adam remains proud of exposing the cruelty hens endure in battery cages. "This case is really a classic example of civil disobedience. I don't think anyone really wants to go to jail, but the amount of publicity that this case got because I went to jail was well worth it."

Clearly, open rescues and other tactics that involve sneaking onto private property, removing animals, and even planning such activities may be considered crimes (trespassing, burglary, and conspiracy, respectively). While the chances of getting caught might seem slim, it can happen, so be aware that governments around the world are more likely now than ever to prosecute you.

You will not be arrested for any activities that are guaranteed by your government, however. For example, the freedom of speech (defined as any act of seeking, receiving, or imparting information or ideas, regardless of the medium used) is guaranteed under the First Amendment of the United States Constitution as well as through many human rights instruments, including Article 10 of the European Convention on Human Rights and Article 19 of the Universal Declaration of Human Rights. Thus, leafleting, protesting, or other acts of speaking out for animals are protected under the law.

Jail and prison are life experiences and like any experience it can be pleasant or unpleasant, hard or easy, interesting or boring, depending on the psychology of the person imprisoned. People can adjust to any environment if required. The best thing to do is find a niche and survive and, if possible, find the means to flourish. Prison also provides insight into the state of conditions for all the animals imprisoned on farms, ranches, [and in] zoos, laboratories, game parks and aquariums. Most of the world's citizens spend their entire life in captivity; and the death penalty is the most common sentence given to nonhumans after serving their time.

Paul Watson

Satya **magazine**, March 2004

Laws Targeting Activists

One example of unjust laws that ALDF and others have been fighting are so-called "ag-gag" laws, which forbid the act of undercover filming or photography of activity on farms without the consent of their owner. Enacted in many US states, these laws make it difficult or impossible for whistleblowing employees or animal activists to expose animal cruelty or safety issues.

"Ag-gag laws have already put a chill on factory farm investigations," says Steve Wells, president of ALDF. "Organizations that have conducted such investigations or that seek to do so, including ALDF, are going to avoid states with ag-gag laws so as not to put investigators at risk of prosecution. That's bad news for animals, our environment, public health, and conditions for workers at these facilities."

The most important things we can do to combat ag-gag legislation, says Steve, are to fight efforts to pass such laws in our own states and to contribute to organizations that are carrying on the fight nationally. "Locally, an individual wields the most power in their own legislative district. Get to know your state legislators and contact them to make them aware of your opposition to any ag-gag legislation. If there is a bill in your state, find out where they stand. Get your friends and neighbors to join you in contacting them. Follow any ag-gag bill's progress and be sure to contact your legislators or members of a committee where the bill will be heard every time there is a vote. Contact the governor's office as well and let him or her know where you stand."

Animal Enterprise Terrorism Act
The Department of Justice, the Department of Homeland Security, and the Federal Bureau of Investigation have all cited animal activism as among the most serious domestic terrorism threats in the United States. Lumping animal activists—who have never killed anyone—alongside violent individuals who have murdered abortion providers, gunned down churchgoers because of their skin color, and laid waste to entire buildings filled with people is absurd. Does any nation really feel threatened by a bunch of bunny huggers?

Well, they do when those bunny huggers cause economic damage, which is why a coalition of wealthy animal exploiters from such industries as meat, captivity, fur, research, pharmaceutical, and hunting conceived of and quietly advanced a bill in Congress to bolster the Animal Enterprise Protection Act (AEPA) of 1992. The new legislation, known as the Animal

Enterprise Terrorism Act (AETA), was signed into law in November 2006 and was crafted to repress certain types of activism by branding them "terrorism." It puts an emphasis on the loss of any real or personal property—including animals and records—and economic damage, such as a loss of profits. But the statute was written with such vague language that the AETA potentially paints even peaceful demonstrations with the broad brush of "terrorism," thus having a chilling effect on activities that should be protected under the First Amendment of the Constitution, such as protests, boycotts, picketing, political dissent, and whistleblowing.

The AETA came after the convictions of six members of an activist group called Stop Huntingdon Animal Cruelty (SHAC USA), mentioned briefly in Chapter 6. SHAC USA nearly put the notorious animal testing lab Huntingdon Life Sciences out of business, and even though the actions they used were all legal, the members were charged under the AEPA. "The government was sure that we were responsible for every act of legal and illegal form of protest across the country, despite having no proof to present in court," says SHAC USA defendant Jake Conroy. "We fought them in a lengthy trial and were eventually found guilty of conspiracy to violate the 1934 Telecommunications Harassment Act, conspiracy to commit interstate stalking, and three counts of interstate stalking." In addition, all six defendants were found guilty of conspiracy to violate the AEPA in March 2006 and were sentenced to serve a combined 23 years in prison. As draconian as that may sound, the powerful animal enterprise lobbies believed Jake and the others got off easy, and therefore the revamped law—the AETA—was designed to grant law enforcement agencies expanded powers to repress what should be constitutionally protected animal activism.

Some activists are fighting back. In 2012, for instance, Sarahjane Blum was among five longtime animal activists named as plaintiffs in a lawsuit filed against the US. The unsuccessful lawsuit, known as *Blum v. Holder* (Eric Holder was US attorney general at the time), asked that the federal government strike down the Animal Enterprise Terrorism Act as unconstitutional. Although the activists had never been prosecuted under AETA, they said the law put them in fear of being charged with terrorism for their activities. It had a definite chilling effect on their advocacy work.

"I wasn't sure if it made sense to even show the documentary about open rescue I had produced, *Delicacy of Despair*, let alone engage in dramatic, controversial, or illegal tactics," says Sarahjane. "I stopped everything." She used the time to reflect on her activism and the movement as a whole. "I looked for ways to do work that tackled the moment we were living in, which often led me into spaces doing things that were very different than what had become thought of as 'traditional' animal rights activism." This included challenging the constitutionality of the AETA. "Honestly, I think it's strengthened my thinking as an activist and gotten me to continually question what the best place to put energy into now is, rather than just fall back on the tactic I'm most comfortable with, or known for. Which has been an asset because it's not just the ever-shifting potential of government repression that has made this past decade a slippery period for animal liberation activists, it's also the still-growing power of the Internet as a communication tool."

While Sarahjane is disappointed she and her co-plaintiffs didn't win the case, she says it was still a valuable challenge to bring. "Our loss should stand as a reminder that the best way to challenge laws that limit dissent is to stop them before they get passed. We need to pay attention on the local and state levels to oppose ag-gag and anti-protest laws at every turn. And we need to find a way to do that without falling into traps where we point fingers at other groups of people who are vulnerable to persecution by the government."

In November of 2017, a US appeals court affirmed that the

AETA is constitutional. The ruling followed a challenge by two other animal activists, Kevin Johnson and Tyler Lang, who had been convicted under the AETA for releasing some 2,000 minks and foxes from an Illinois fur farm in 2013 and causing more than US$120,000 in damage. The activists wanted the indictment dismissed, arguing that the AETA is unconstitutional and violated their right to due process. Kevin was sentenced to three years in prison, and Tyler was sentenced to six months of home confinement plus six months in a work release center. (In a move that demonstrates the government's desire to demonize activists, when four teenagers were arrested in 2014 for sneaking into a Foster Farms facility in Fresno, California, and bludgeoning 900 chickens with a golf club, the court refused to charge them under the AETA.)

Activists in other countries have cause for concern, as well: the UK, for instance, has enacted the Serious Organised Crime and Police Act (SOCPA) of 2005—a set of laws to specifically address the "illegal activities" of animal activists. The SOCPA was created in response to a wave of actions against biomedical research companies, and SHAC activists in England have been imprisoned under it. The animal ag industry in Australia, meanwhile, has been agitating for a law similar to AETA, and in New Zealand, the Terrorism Suppression Act, amended since it was enacted in 2002, has targeted environmental activists.

What separates true "terrorists" from animal activists is the activist is out to save lives, not take them. In their pursuit of this goal, animal activists are employing a variety of new tools, from smartphones to cameras mounted on tiny, remote-controlled drones. You can be sure that governments will continue creating legislation to suppress these efforts—or attempt to.

New Technology

Just as activists are using technology for animal protection and liberation, police and other law enforcement agencies are using it to identify and prosecute activists. We explored the importance of digital security in Chapter 4, but let's dig deeper into a practice I only briefly mentioned there: using facial recognition technology — so-called "biometric scanning" — to track and target activists. Not only are police trolling social media posts with software able to identify protesters by their faces, but they are using military-grade versions to monitor anyone they wish to with aerial surveillance, high-powered cameras, and CCTV.

Activist Tino Verducci found this out after he took some photographs of a new laboratory built just outside the St. Pancras railway station in London. "The pictures were supposed to be used to start an awareness campaign about the issues surrounding a Biosafety Level 3-plus laboratory in central London," he says. "On the 15th of August 2013, while I was taking a train at the same station, I was stopped by four plainclothes UK anti-terrorist officers and questioned under Section 43 of the Terrorism Act because they believed that I had in my possession something which may constitute evidence that I was a terrorist. They were looking at the pictures I had taken six weeks before and wanted to know what I was using them for." During a court case, in which Tino was found not guilty, it emerged that he had been recognized from CCTV camera footage as he exited the London Underground station, and he was followed. "They thought that I was carrying 'terrorist stuff' in my backpack."

The widespread use of facial recognition technology is inevitable, and with a huge database of photos from driver's licenses and social media postings at the disposal of law enforcement, police are going to be looking at nearly *everyone*. Not surprisingly, civil liberties groups in England and the US say biometric scanning is an invasion of privacy and discriminatory, tantamount to racial profiling. Like so many other racial disparities in this world, face-scanning algorithms have been shown to be 10 percent less accurate on black faces than on white faces, resulting in more false arrests in communities of color.

Police will tell you that the only problem with facial recognition software is that it takes too long, requiring officers to manually sift through thousands upon thousands of photos to identify someone. New technology—automatic facial recognition, or AFR—identifies a person of interest in real-time: a CCTV camera scans a face, for instance, instantly compares it to a database of mug shots, and notifies local cops if it makes a connection. In 2017, police began making the first arrests based on AFR. Computer programs armed with cameras also can learn "acceptable" human behavior—such as pedestrians crossing the street or hailing a taxi—and alert law enforcement when something "abnormal" occurs. Oh, and this technology is almost entirely unregulated, with police agencies bypassing your civil liberties by using the software without a warrant.

Surviving Prison

The universal sentiment among the animal activists I interviewed who have served time is that the anticipation of going to prison is worse than the reality of being there. "Like many things seen from the outside, it tends not to be as bad as one might imagine," says Roger Yates, who was imprisoned for two years for conspiracy to cause criminal damage. "However, that has to be evaluated on a case-by-case basis. It is a world within a world, with its own rules and norms and values, so that takes some getting used to. I tend to think that the general prison population view animal activists as political prisoners, which can gain one some status inside."

Josh Harper, who as a member of the group SHAC USA served three years for conspiracy to violate the Animal Enterprise Protection Act, says that prison is not how it's depicted on television, and whatever a person fears about prison probably isn't the reality. That said, he urges activists facing incarceration to give up smoking, drinking, drugs, and gambling before going in. "I have nothing against any of those vices, but in prison those things are going to look very attractive," Josh says. "You will be in a stressful place, wanting escape and something to pass the time. The thing is, alcohol, drugs, and cigarettes are all very expensive and all controlled by people you do not want to be in debt to. Same with gambling. If you can avoid doing those four things you have just drastically increased your chances of getting through this situation safely."

Next, he says, remember that for many inmates, prison is their home. "There are people stuck there for 20, 30, 40 years or more. Their entire life is contained in that space, and they want whatever comfort they can have. When you get there, treat the place like it is somebody else's house. Be polite. Say 'please' and 'thank you.' Don't whistle or hum or do anything else annoying, and clean up after yourself. Never, ever walk into somebody's cell without their permission, don't touch anything that isn't yours, and be especially careful with the phones. Making calls is some people's only connection to their families and loved ones. I've seen people nearly get killed because they slammed a phone down when they were done. Again, respect everything as if you were in someone else's home."

Finally, he says, you are going to have to learn new rules. Lots of them. "Learn by observing and asking questions of other inmates when you can. The basics go like this: 1. Don't tell on anyone. 2. Don't be seen talking to staff members—you'll be labeled a snitch. 3. Don't point at anyone or talk behind people's backs. 4. If someone asks you about your charges, answer them quickly and concisely. 5. Do more listening than talking; do not complain about your sentence or the particulars of your case, and don't flash money around. If you have these basics down, you will probably be okay as you learn the other rules."

Josh's SHAC USA co-defendant Jake Conroy was locked up for four years and says that every jail and prison has different rules and security levels and ways inmates carry themselves. "So, while it's nearly impossible to fully prepare for what's to come, getting a general idea of what you can expect is a great idea. If you are lucky enough to self-surrender to your assigned prison, as opposed to already being in custody, I would highly recommend searching out former or current political prisoners and asking them every question you can possibly think of."

Because he served his time in a federal prison, Jake recommends that before turning themselves in, convicted activists headed to a federal institution use the Bureau of Prisons' rating system to get a general sense of what level prison yard you'll be sent to. "In my experience, men's camps and low-security prisons are drastically different from medium- and maximum-security facilities, and you can gather advice accordingly," he says. "Interestingly, the judge often takes into serious consideration the requests you and your attorney can make for what prison to be housed in. Look into prisons that have a better reputation than others in the location you want to be housed in, and make your requests." The SHAC case was in New Jersey, but Jake asked to do his time in California, and that's where he ended up.

"Whether you are self-surrendering or are already in custody, the best things you can do during your first several months incarcerated are watching, listening, and learning," Jake says. "Every prison has different inmate codes on how to carry yourself—and with whom. The more you tune into these 'rules,' the better off you'll be in figuring out how you want to carry yourself as a political prisoner. Practicing humility, street smarts, and respect are vital components to survival, but so is not appearing to be a total outsider. As much as TV and the chow hall might not interest you, investing a couple of hours a week in those places lets others know you aren't a shut-in, and therefore not a target, and it's also a great place to study your surroundings."

Jake's final words of advice are to stay busy. "If possible, make some friends, try to laugh every day, practice self-care, and plan and follow a program. Doing the same routine every day for years sounds awful, but keeping your mind and body occupied and busy makes the time pass much quicker."

"The prison system is confusing, and they don't tell you all the rules," says Amber Canavan, who served a month in jail for rescuing two ducks from a foie gras farm in New York. "Find someone who can show you the ropes—or more likely, they will find you—and hopefully lend you some shampoo to use before your commissary delivery comes in." (Amber explains that the jail she was in only received commissary items once a week.) "Also, before you go in—if you are lucky enough to be turning yourself in—do something that reminds you exactly why you are becoming a political prisoner. Visit an animal sanctuary, go on a hike, spend some quiet time with a companion animal or significant other. Create a book wish list ahead of time. Have your attorney contact the jail or prison informing them of your ethical veganism, and putting yourself down as Buddhist during intake really helps, but be prepared to file grievances. If all else fails, Peanut Chews are often available on commissary!"

Bruce Friedrich, who spent years in various jails and prisons for his peace activism, warns that you should not talk to guards, other prisoners, or anyone about whatever it is they're claiming you did until after your trial is over, since law enforcement may try to get you to incriminate yourself. "Part of their job is to get you to say things that could come back to haunt you. Often if you're arrested, even for something completely absurd like standing on the sidewalk with a sign, in order to get you to talk and say something possibly incriminating, many will tell you that they're going to hold you for a week or a weekend or something; they'll try to scare you about the jail conditions and how 'You don't want to spend a weekend there—those guys will eat you alive.' It's all nonsense. Other prisoners are always nice and respectful if you're nice and respectful to them, and a night in jail is something that you'll be able to tell your friends about later—don't worry about it. So, whatever you do if you're arrested, don't talk with anyone about what you've been arrested for, even though you are certainly completely innocent. It will not help you be released more quickly to speak with the police or other inmates, one of which could be an undercover police officer; nothing you say will help you in any way, but many things can hurt you. Don't do it. Of course, *most* police will not try to manipulate you or be mean to you; they're just doing their jobs and they find the 'good cop, bad cop' duplicity stuff to be beneath them. But some will, so be wary."

Of course, one thing these people have in common, in addition to being activists who have been imprisoned, is they are all *white*. Jails and prisons are notorious for being harsher on people of color, so if you are an activist of color facing incarceration, I am sorry to say that you shouldn't expect the same treatment that Roger, Josh, Jake, Amber, and Bruce experienced.

Black Market Vegan Prison Food

Jake Conroy quickly learned that the inmate-run black market could help him maintain his veganism behind bars. "Anything and everything can be bought and sold, such as drugs, alcohol, tobacco, and tattoos," he says. "I was more interested in the vegetables, fruit, tofu, and textured vegetable protein. By using inmate currency— postage stamps—I could pay kitchen workers to steal the food I wanted and deliver it to me in my cell. With a hot water tap, a microwave, and some creativity, I was able to cook up some great meals and turn a few people toward vegetarianism and veganism. As a vegan inmate, figuring out how the black market works, befriending those who work in the kitchen, and showing respect for this underground system can make eating your ethics while incarcerated so much easier."

Please see "Appendix C—Know Your Rights" for more information.

Supporting Prisoners

There are many ways to help imprisoned activists, and providing a little support to someone facing years in jail can buoy that person's morale and nurture solidarity in the movement. I am going to focus on four key methods: writing letters, sending books, visiting, and providing financial support (sending money, helping with legal expenses, etc.).

The first step is knowing where inmates are, and the easiest place to find addresses for animal activists serving time is the Internet: *Bite Back* magazine (directaction.info) maintains a list of prisoners, the Vegan Prisoners Support Group (vpsg.org) lists prisoners in the UK, or you can simply do a search for a "list of animal rights prisoners" online.

Writing Letters

Write to a prisoner of conscience, such as someone incarcerated for social justice or animal activism. Of course, *any* prisoner, regardless of their crime, appreciates getting mail. Unless you're lucky enough to have unlimited time and resources, commit to writing to just one or two inmates, and do it consistently.

Cards and letters are of paramount importance for relieving an inmate's feeling of isolation; however, all mail is opened and read by prison officials, so don't write anything that may cause problems for the inmate. "Depending on the prisoner, do not discuss the case or anything related to the case," advises attorney Shannon Keith, who has represented a number of animal rights activists and campaigns, including SHAC and Sea Shepherd. "Do not discuss your feelings about whether the person is innocent or guilty." She also says that most prisons do not accept anything other than letters and photos. "So, no stickers—especially no animal rights stickers. No pictures depicting protests."

Dallas Rising, a founding member of the group Support Vegans in the Prison System, cautions supporters not to take it personally if the inmate doesn't respond. "It is *not* about you," she says. "Don't get upset if the person doesn't write back to you, especially if they didn't know you before going in. And even if they did know you, they may not have the mental or emotional energy to write back. Or they simply may not have the time."

Here are a few more letter-writing do's and don'ts.

Do's:

- Write on both sides of the paper.
- Write your address on the letter or card.
- Number the pages of your letter.
- Make sure the content of any photos you send is appropriate; write the inmate's name and prisoner ID number on the back of photos.
- Let imprisoned activists know about animal activism going on around the world.

Don'ts:

- Don't send currency.
- Don't send stamps, envelopes, blank paper, or blank note cards.
- Don't tape your envelope closed.
- Don't include paperclips, staples, or other metal objects inside your letter.
- Don't send food or care packages.
- Don't send photographs larger than 4 x 6 inches. No Polaroid photos.
- Don't write "legal mail" on the envelope or anything in your letter that implies you are an attorney.

"Letters to a prisoner can be like anchors or lifelines to the outside world," says Andy Stepanian, who served two years and seven months in prison for "conspiracy to violate the Animal Enterprise Protection Act" as part of the SHAC USA campaign. "Although my mail was vetted for content, I still received bundles of letters, and every time I did I felt like I could hold my head a little higher. The letters reminded me of where I came from and what I was fighting for."

Sending Books

Most inmates appreciate receiving books, since reading is one way to pass the time behind bars. It's a good idea to write to the prisoner first to confirm they can receive books; you can also ask what kinds of books they would like to read.

Books sent to most prisons must be new and with a soft cover (paperback); hardcover books will either be refused or prison officials will tear off the covers before passing the book on to the inmate. Unfortunately, many prisons will not permit you to mail a book to an inmate yourself; instead, books must be sent either directly from the publisher or through an online retailer such as Amazon.

Prisoners are often able to list books they would like to receive on Amazon's Wish List section (just search the inmate's name), or through a support group website.

Visiting Inmates

Each US federal prison has set up certain days and times— visiting hours—for family and friends to visit inmates. The inmate you plan to visit should tell you what the hours are for that prison. But you can't simply show up and expect to see an inmate. "Most prisons require that you be accepted and on an approved list first, so before you take your trip to the prison, call to make sure you do not have to be approved first," says Shannon. "If so, mail the prisoner and ask them to fill out a form for your visit. You will receive an approval later, and then you can visit as you please during visiting hours. When visiting, know that you are being watched and possibly recorded. Avoid discussing legally sensitive subjects. Dress appropriately." Indeed, pay close attention to the prison's dress code, as it is strictly enforced.

In the UK, visiting a convicted prisoner requires you to first have a visiting order (a "VO"); these are generally issued to inmates once a month, and they will mail it to you. Depending on the prisoner, visits are one to two hours, and prisoners may be allowed between two and four visitors a month. For more information, do an online search for "visiting inmates in the UK." You can do similar searches for visitor requirements in other countries, as well.

A few additional points:

- Bring a photo ID, such as a passport or driver's license
- If your visit is based on a time slot or appointment, arrive at least 30 minutes early
- Do not wear jewelry other than a wedding or engagement ring
- Do not bring gifts
- Be prepared to be searched
- Remember that each jail or prison has rules that must be followed—breaking the rules or arguing with the guards can mean a loss of your visiting privileges and can have a negative impact on the inmate you visit.

Financial Support
Prisoners must pay for envelopes, postage stamps, phone cards, and other necessities. They may even have to buy their own vegan food from the prison commissary. They probably also have legal fees. All these expenses can be offset with a fundraising effort managed by friends on the outside. Some organizations, like

SHAC, set these up and allow people to donate online. Moreover, they raise funds through benefit concerts, film screenings, and product sales.

"Fundraising for costly legal fees is always appreciated," says Dallas. "As a bonus, you automatically have something to write about."

You can also support inmates by sending money directly to their commissary account. The US Bureau of Prisons has a system to maintain an inmate's monies while they are incarcerated. Family, friends, or other sources may deposit funds into these accounts. You might also consider money-transfer services like JPay that allow you to get funds to a prisoner the next business day.

For details on options for depositing funds into a prisoner's account, do an online search for "sending money to inmates."

"Being in prison can be depressing and frightening, but by supporting political prisoners we can make their stay a little easier," says Jake Conroy. "Besides writing letters, putting money onto their commissary account so they can buy vegan food and toiletries is one of the best ways we on the outside can put a smile on the faces of those on the inside. They are in there for us; we need to be out here for them."

Chapter 11

Animal Care: Activists Are Animals Too

Caring for myself is not self-indulgence, it is self-preservation, and that is an act of political warfare.
Audre Lorde

Although it was shocking and sad to see hens being yanked by their fragile legs, necks, and wings from battery cages, it was the vision of thousands of them packed onto a flatbed truck that eventually made me lose it. The tears would come later... after I had helped rescue hundreds of "spent" hens from an avian nightmare known as a battery-egg farm. The owner of this egg farm had decided to convert his battery-cage operation into something less inhumane, and he had invited animal protection groups to take away as many "spent" hens as they could before the birds went to slaughter. (The industry considers a hen "spent" after she's been laying eggs for one to two years—a fraction of her natural lifespan.)

A gloomy shed filled with 160,000 hens greeted us; the stench of ammonia burned our eyes and assaulted our lungs. Carefully removing as many as eight frail hens from each small cage, we worked against the clock, amid dead chickens and curtains of cobwebs, knowing that at some point in the afternoon the "catchers" would arrive and begin their work. The catchers would also be in a hurry. *I don't want any animals to get hurt.*

As we raced in and out of the shed, filling boxes with hens who had never before seen daylight, I grew wearier with each step, having to choose from among tens of thousands of birds. Our actions decided who would end up in a safe home and who would end up in dog food. I cradled nearly lifeless hens in my arms, giving them fresh water, determined they not perish without knowing a tiny bit of kindness. By 3:30 the catchers were removing hens for slaughter, yanking them out of battery cages, stuffing them into even smaller wire crates, and loading them onto a large truck. *Stop doing that! Can't you see you're hurting them?*

Packed into their mobile prison, the traumatized hens awaited a grueling ride. *I'm so sorry I could not save you.* I made it home, got through the front door, and the image of all those hens on the truck caught up with me. My face felt hot and my eyesight blurred, though I could see so many tired faces looking out through the wire, as though imploring me to help them, their used and broken bodies crammed into more cages, waiting hours without food or water to be transported for yet more abuse. *I'm so sorry.* Before long I was sobbing like a freight train, my body and soul consumed by an inconsolable anguish. I felt ashamed to be part of the human species. *What kind of an activist am I, anyway? How can I cope? How can I live?*

With few exceptions, anyone who is active in animal advocacy long enough experiences some form of emotional pushback. Sadness or feeling you're not doing enough is normal; most of us feel that way sometimes. But there's a continuum for activists, caregivers, and those who work with trauma victims: on one end is compassion satisfaction, in which we derive pleasure from our work—the victories, large or small, that remind us how rewarding it is to be a voice for change—and compassion fatigue and its (potential) companion, burnout, on the other. In between the two extremes are painful emotions such as grief, anger, and guilt. Because it's very easy for these emotions to develop into compassion fatigue, taking care of ourselves is critical to help us prevent burnout.

This is not always easy for animal activists. Trying to change consumer behavior can feel like we're drowning as we struggle against the tide of corporate hegemony that keeps most animals oppressed. The result is that we often question our ability to speak out for animals. Even doing nothing can hurt: As Carol J. Adams will explain in this chapter, just *knowing* about animal abuse can cause us to suffer.

So, how do we move past the pain? How do we not just keep our heads above water, but continue to make positive strides amid a potential sea of despair and flourish in our activism? The answer is to be found somewhere in a delicate balance: We have to set boundaries as activists even as we are striving to realize our full potential as human beings. But recognizing your limits — and respecting them — takes practice.

"My best advice is to nurture your joy," says Jo-Anne McArthur, who documents animal abuse with her camera. "I know that it can be hard to do that when there are billions of animals suffering at every moment. How can we be happy when this is going on? The animal rights movement has seen too many people jump in and then burn out only a few years later, because the issues are so distressing, and people aren't taking care of themselves. Yes, there is a global emergency for animals. All the more reason to pace yourself so that you can help animals for as long as you possibly can."

Often, animal advocates hesitate to talk about, or even think about, their own feelings because the suffering of the animals is comparatively so much greater. The motives for this self-suppression are altruistic but the results can be counterproductive.

pattrice jones
Satya **magazine**, June/July 2005

When Helping Hurts

Compassion fatigue is the emotional drain experienced by

caregivers of both people and animals. It's also sometimes called "secondary traumatization," because it impacts people working with the victims of trauma. As such, it can affect not only animal activists, but veterinarians, animal control officers, nurses, doctors, rescuers, firefighters, emergency medical technicians, social workers, mental health professionals, or anyone else who might feel the stress of trauma vicariously. The signs of compassion fatigue often overlap with those of burnout, but they are not the same.

"Compassion fatigue and burnout share a lot of the same symptoms—fatigue or exhaustion; trouble sleeping; feeling sad, angry, hopeless, cynical, or apathetic; loss of joy and/or satisfaction from the work you do; decline in job performance; physical problems—and the two can certainly co-exist," says psychotherapist Jennifer Blough, a certified compassion fatigue specialist (and vegan) who has devoted her practice in Ann Arbor, Michigan, to treating people with compassion fatigue and burnout. "Another difference is that compassion fatigue seems to occur more rapidly, whereas burnout develops more slowly over time."

Other symptoms of compassion fatigue include:

- Nightmares or flashbacks
- Loss of appetite
- Feelings of guilt
- Relationship conflicts
- Low self-esteem
- Poor concentration
- Grief
- Withdrawal
- Feeling isolated
- Suicidal thoughts

Burnout is characterized by three main components: emotional exhaustion, depersonalization (feeling detached or disconnected from your body), and a sense that you are not accomplishing anything. That lack of personal accomplishment—real or imagined—is very important here. A sense of competence and effectiveness bolsters our feeling of self-worth, while telling ourselves that we are not achieving our potential can bring low self-esteem.

In her compassion fatigue workbook *To Save a Starfish*, Jennifer observes another important difference between compassion fatigue and burnout: While anyone can experience professional burnout—plumbers, librarians, teachers, food service workers, writers, and others can all become physically, mentally, or emotionally exhausted because of their jobs—burnout from compassion fatigue is more likely to be the result of witnessing chronic trauma and having empathy for the victims. It occurs when the person is highly empathetic or sensitive and engaged in work that exposes them to the suffering of others. Sound familiar?

Avoiding Burnout

Burnout occurs when we ignore the warning signs of compassion fatigue—the headaches, the depression, the anxiety—and continue to push ourselves too hard. We may want to be superheroes and never stop working for animals, but activists are animals too, at the mercy of bodies, minds, and spirits that need constant nourishing. The threat of burning out follows us like a late-afternoon shadow, casting a dark presence over our efforts to shed light on a world of suffering. Nearly everyone who has been an animal advocate for more than a year has a passionate opinion about burnout.

"Burning out is not an option," declares Kate Fowler. To ward off collapse, Kate recommends a tried-and-true tonic: friends. "Surround yourself with good, committed, and compassionate people, and they will buoy you up. Take a little time to be with animals—at a sanctuary, for example—and they will give you the strength to carry on. Don't wallow in the negatives. There is no point spending hours watching films of abuse if it does nothing more than depress you. You'd be better off spending the time writing campaign letters or organizing demos in your local town."

Clare Mann, a vegan psychologist based in Sydney, Australia, echoes Kate's point about friends and advises animal advocates to talk about their traumatic experiences with their fellow activists. "Having one's story heard by someone who has equally been brought to their knees by what they've found out is in and of itself, I believe, therapeutic," says Clare. "Therefore, that highlights the need to be around other people who are on the same journey. Having your story witnessed and understood is, for a lot of animal advocates and ethical vegans, very helpful."

Among the issues that Clare works on with her vegan clients is effective communication.

"We need the ability to exquisitely communicate issues," she says. "When someone is traumatized, they often attack the meat-eater and other people who don't change their lifestyle." Strategically, and for our own mental well-being, she says, it makes more sense to identify specific issues that interest others, concentrate on them, and later work ethical issues into our conversations. "For example, if people are interested in health, focus on the benefits of a vegan diet rather than trying to discuss social justice." And Clare makes a valuable point about how animal cruelty affects us: "I always say to people, 'What you know about and what goes on behind closed doors is never going to be acceptable. The day you are numbed by it and you don't react is when we've really got a problem.'"

Two of the most important things you can do—not only to avoid burnout, but to stay healthy—are to eat a diet of whole plant foods (at least mostly) and get enough sleep. In addition, following are a few key points to remember as you navigate the often-stressful world of animal activism.

Make Time for Yourself

"One thing I've been seeing in the movement is this attitude that the more you sacrifice, the cooler you are," says Dallas Rising, a personal coach who helps animal activists increase the effectiveness of their advocacy. "People may feel, 'The animals are suffering so much, how can I take time for myself?' They may also have some issues with actually enjoying themselves, because it is so guilt-inducing."

Dallas cautions activists against attempting to turn every hobby or interest outside the movement into an opportunity to help animals, and she uses as an example a time some years ago when she needed a break. "I thought, 'Maybe I should try running.' Then I thought, 'As long as I'm running, I may as well wear a T-shirt that says something about animals because I'm going to be out in public.'" Dallas ended up organizing a group of vegan and vegetarian runners called Team Veg, and it became another form of activism. "So there's a tendency for some to not be able to turn off that part of your brain that says 'How can I turn this into outreach?'"

Taking time for yourself is an aspect of setting healthy boundaries: "I'll do X, and then I will enjoy Y." Without these limits, there is no life beyond activism; you are simply consumed by the struggle. "It's hard," says Mia MacDonald, "but I think people need to set limits: do as much as you can, but don't do so much, think so much, agonize or agitate so much that you get really exhausted, stressed, angry, or despairing." Mia suggests having some regular activities outside of activism: "A hobby, an interest, a spiritual or physical practice that gives you a break, but that might also give you some more energy, some more equanimity when you are doing activism. Talk about being stressed or burned out with others—I think there's still a lot of shame about this—but try not to wallow. Take some active steps to get yourself back from the edge. Even take a nap sometimes if that's what it takes."

"Whatever you need to do to look after yourself, don't neglect doing that," advises Jo-Anne McArthur. "Whether you need community or silence, being active or being meditative, or all of the above, look after yourself so that you have the energy to continue the fight. It's hard to do this. I know this! I've almost burned out a few times, and have needed therapy, and tools, to help myself not focus exclusively on the suffering of animals and stay focused on creating change."

Though it may be counter to your intuition on how best to help animals, giving yourself some time away from activism may be just the thing to enhance your long-term efforts. Julianna Baker was engaged in a number of campaigns and poring over animal rights books while doing her graduate work. After years as an activist, she found herself growing progressively angrier at the egregious abuses perpetrated on the defenseless. She stepped back from activism for a year, avoiding the movement's literature but still advocating compassion and answering the

---

Virtual Burnout

Getting positive reinforcement from social media—in the form of "likes" and comments, for instance—can become an addiction. Spending too much time sitting in front of a computer screen can even lead to feelings of loneliness and depression. If your main form of communication is online, if social media is preventing you from being productive, or if you feel panicked when you don't have Internet access, it's time to take a serious break. Commit yourself to staying offline for a day or two each week. Turn off your phone during meals. Get outside and reconnect with nature—as well as with your family and friends.

---

questions of those inevitably drawn to her calm resolve. "I was actually better at promoting vegetarianism when I wasn't pissed off about what I was reading," says Julianna. "People don't like or respond to the 'angry vegan' or the 'angry activist.'"

Find a Good Fit

One of the best ways to avoid burning out is to match your style of campaigning with your interests and strengths, creating activism that nourishes you. Although Dawn Moncrief recommends pushing past comfort zones to increase your range—especially if you want a leadership role—knowing your comfort zone provides a safe space when needed. "Plus, not everyone wants to be a leader," she says. "Some people are better behind the scenes and some like the spotlight. Some people like to protest, while others like feed-ins or mainstream networking. Regardless, people can use their skills and interests for the cause. If they are working in their comfort zone, they're less likely to burn out."

Indeed, Zoe Weil regards this as the *most important* approach to preventing burnout. She believes too many people sign up for a campaign without first assessing their skills and interests, as she found out the hard way. "When I first learned about animal exploitation, I wanted to do something," she says. "I called an animal protection organization in the city I was living in and asked to be on their activist list." Zoe quickly received a call from the organization asking if she would leaflet. Although she had never leafleted before and didn't think she'd enjoy it, she convinced herself such thoughts were selfish and she should do it anyway—for the animals.

"So I leafleted... and I hated it. People ignored me, or took my flier and threw it on the ground, or sneered at me. I was headed for burnout after my first effort at activism!" Rather than give up on activism altogether, Zoe relaxed long enough to evaluate her talents and passions, imagining what type of activism she would enjoy most. "I realized that I wanted to teach," she says, "and so

I offered some week-long summer courses to secondary school students on animal and environmental issues. I *loved* teaching those courses; I discovered that I'd found my life's work—humane education—and that I could do this work forever. Not only have I not burnt out after 20-plus years, but I am energized, heartened, and enthused by my chosen form of change-making. It feeds me."

Zoe explains that each activist must discover this alchemy for themselves. "Some are energized by lobbying legislators, others by creating and executing campaigns, others by writing books, others by protesting, and others by, yes, leafleting. It's not selfish to consider what your talents and interests are. The animals are served far better by someone doing work they love than by those doing work they think they *have* to do, but which they can't stand doing." It's these latter activists who are most likely to burn out, according to Zoe.

"A lot of times people feel frustrated because they have a preconceived notion of what the most effective form of activism is," says Dallas. "Take leafleting, for example. I'm a huge fan of Vegan Outreach, and I love leafleting—I think it's very effective, and I will recommend it for many activists who want to make a difference and don't have a lot of time; however, it's not for everybody, and sometimes the emphasis on what is effective for the movement can really be counterproductive for an individual. Some people are not comfortable with it or are not ready to do that kind of frontline work. So I work with individuals and ask, 'Okay, what are you really interested in?' I look for ways for them to use their natural talents and abilities and character traits to make a difference for animals in a way that really works and will be sustainable for them, because if you're out there trying to force yourself to leaflet and you're uncomfortable, you're going to shy away from it and there's a danger of losing that activist. For example, there's a guy in our community who is very interested in helping animals, but he's super shy. So he will drive activists to a crowded area, drop them off for leafleting, and then come back and pick them up."

Include Achievable Goals
A longtime activist, pattrice jones recommends remaining wary of spending too much time on problems that don't seem to make a difference—another path to burnout. "To guard against that, individuals and organizations should make sure that their strategic plans include not only long-term aims that might not be achieved for decades, but also achievable short-term goals that can be acknowledged and celebrated when they are met."

Dallas suggests that activists break every campaign down to small pieces. "I mean *really* small pieces," she says. She offers as an example the effort in her hometown of Minneapolis to ban circuses in the city limits. "This is a *huge* undertaking. If the group had simply said, 'Well, we just want to get this banned, period,' that's such a far-off goal it would be really easy to lose sight, and they have a couple of times." So, the group separated each of their objectives. "They took on simpler goals, like 'We really want to make sure that every single council member gets this information. We will have meetings with them, and we want to find out where they stand on the issue either way so that we can work on that.' That is a much more realistic and practical goal to set, and it helps to keep people motivated in the long run."

Even when your goals are achievable—such as handing out 500 leaflets at a busy location in a couple of hours—remember to keep things in perspective and concentrate on the positive changes being made. "It's human nature to focus on the conflict," says activist Freeman Wicklund. "If we leaflet for several hours at a university, what stands out is the one person who flew off the handle and shouted and swore at us, not the hundreds of people who gladly accepted our brochures. As activists we need to see the positive changes that are going on around us every day for animals. Focus on the good conversations on vegetarianism that we had with the person at the bus stop who saw the button on our bag, not the one where our uncle waved away our valid concerns with a flippant 'They're here to be eaten!'"

Learn to Say No

Humans are social creatures, so it is in our nature to be accommodating to requests. And for animal activists—who pride themselves on being compassionate—saying "yes" is practically embedded in our DNA. Because saying "yes" to everything can put you on the fast track to feeling overwhelmed, however, learn to say "no," at least occasionally. This is hard for many people, not just activists. We fear the consequences of making ourselves a priority, such as disappointing someone, damaging a friendship, missing out, or appearing selfish. But too many commitments can lead to stress and burnout. So, set boundaries by learning how to tactfully deny requests and invitations. Practice these phrases:

- "I can't this time."
- "Sorry—not today."
- "Thanks, but I've already got too much on my plate."
- "That won't work for me, but I'll get back to you if anything changes."

When you do say "yes," be sure you're agreeing to something that genuinely reflects your values.

Disconnect from Technology

Numerous studies have shown that spending too much time online can lead to stress, sleeping disorders, and antisocial behavior. Yet we go everywhere with our mobile devices, and we've conditioned ourselves to feel guilty if we don't immediately respond to a phone message or text. As consumers

Compassion Fatigue in Sanctuaries

Although working at a sanctuary for farmed animals has tremendous rewards, it can also expose advocates to a special kind of compassion fatigue, says Susie Coston, national shelter director for Farm Sanctuary. "We are fighting a battle that is not going to be easily won, and we're rescuing animals who have been genetically changed to grow bigger breasts, lay more eggs, produce more muscle, and are designed to live just 36 to 40 days or six months." An animal's death hits sanctuary workers particularly hard, and they often feel they could have done something more. "Recognize that you may fail to save an animal who arrives in a condition that is not fixable—a condition that in many cases is manmade. And even more important, recognize that you cannot save them all. We have to be able to let go of those things out of our control, so we can function in our role as educators and care providers."

of digital media, many of us are literally addicted to the high we get from seeing that someone we don't even know has liked or shared one of our posts—and we experience withdrawal if we're away from our screens for too long.

Activists don't only use social media to be social. We use it for our outreach, to organize events, to promote petitions and animal adoption notices, to announce campaign updates, and a dozen other important things. Clearly, the Internet has become an indispensable tool for us. But as difficult as this might be, we need to set a time each day for a digital detox and turn off social media and mobile devices for an hour or so. Make this a regular practice, not just something you do when you're feeling stressed. You might just find that you get more done.

Think of it this way: Much of our time is spent either creating or consuming. Technology is a time-saving marvel, and it allows us to create in remarkable ways. Still, most of the time, we are consuming technology, and our devotion to screens has only gotten worse and so have the consequences. Before mobile devices became mainstream in the 2000s, for example, the average person had an attention span of 12 seconds; now it's just eight seconds—one second shorter than the average goldfish. Let's make it a goal to create more and consume less. And during those times when you are feeling extra stress, avoiding consuming the news altogether.

Make a Change

And what if you pursue your life's work for animals, do all you can to stay mentally and physically healthy, yet still experience the stress and overwork that can lead to burnout? "It may be that you're ready for a change," advises Zoe. "You don't have to give up on making a difference for animals, but you may need to find a different avenue. We all change and grow, and it's important to allow ourselves to grow in our activism too."

pattrice agrees with this attitude and acknowledges the many opportunities activists have to alter their efforts if burnout creeps up on them. "There's so much work to do on so many problems that you can give yourself a break from one set of problems by turning your attention to another," she says. "If you start to feel like you cannot possibly answer the same old arguments for vivisection yet again, maybe it's time to switch focus and work on factory farming instead. If you need to take a break from direct contact with animal suffering, work on global warming. If you're burned out on working with the public, work on behind-the-scenes research and let somebody else do the leafleting."

One reason activists engaging in a group effort may be reluctant to make a change is the fear of disappointing their peers, Dallas observes. "There's a feeling of scarcity in our movement: there's not enough people working on behalf of animals, there aren't enough vegans—or animal rights groups may feel there aren't enough volunteers or not enough money—so there can be this experience of pressure that says 'I'm going to be letting everybody down if I give up this role.'" Dallas advises her clients who want to make a change within a group to write a detailed guide for someone else to be able to do that job well. "Also, you can make it known that you are available as a resource for anyone else who wants to step up."

Tips for Avoiding Burnout

Since the first edition of this book was published, I've shared the following strategy for beating burnout with countless activists. I call it the "ACTIVE" approach, and these steps are a complement to other steps you should take to keep yourself healthy, such as eating right and getting plenty of sleep:

- **A**llow yourself to be human. Give yourself permission to fail; hard as we try, we are not superheroes, and we are not going to win every battle. Take a real vacation. Try to have fun without feeling guilty.
- **C**reate something tangible to remind you of your victories. This can be a file or scrapbook of your activist achievements to remind yourself of the positive changes you've helped to bring about.
- **T**alk to someone you trust, especially other animal advocates whom you respect; share your concerns and don't be afraid to be honest about your fears. Animal activism is an emotionally loaded endeavor, and as activists it's important that we unburden ourselves. If necessary, talk to a therapist.
- **I**gnore graphic sights and sounds, including animal rights magazines, newsletters, and videos that feature graphic text and visuals, which can trigger depression, nightmares, and even physical illness.

- Visit an animal sanctuary. Better yet, volunteer. Many activists have never met a cow, chicken, pig, rabbit, turkey, goat, or sheep. Treat yourself. These sanctuaries are home to animals rescued not only from slaughterhouses and farms, but from research labs, vet schools, and the entertainment industry. Pet a lamb. Watch a former battery hen spread her wings and enjoy a dust bath. Rub a pig's belly. Get some face time with the faces you're working so hard to help.

- Exercise regularly. Consult your doctor if you're not sure how to begin; otherwise, get out there and sweat. Also consider walking, yoga, or meditation. These will all do wonders for your mental well-being.

Animal advocate Keiko Krahnke spends a little time with Shiro, a rescued goat, at BeakOn Hill Sanctuary in Colorado. Credit: Jo-Anne McArthur / We Animals

Coping with Guilt

"You can bear anything if it isn't your own fault," wrote the novelist Katharine Fullerton Gerould. She obviously was not on a first-name basis with many animal activists. Countless activists suffer feelings of guilt, most often because they believe they aren't doing enough for animals. Perhaps they are comparing themselves to other activists (try reading *Ethics Into Action: Henry Spira and the Animal Rights Movement* by Peter Singer without telling yourself you're not doing enough). Or maybe the constant exposure to animal abuse makes them feel no amount of time and effort could possibly have an impact on so colossal a task.

But unless you're working for an animal advocacy organization, you are likely to be a student or busy with a full- or part-time job outside the movement—or both. The activism you engage in is conducted in your so-called "free time," and every bit you do, whether it's leafleting for 30 minutes a week or devoting several hours a day to corporate outreach, is important. If you're using your time wisely, active in efforts that can make a real difference for animals, then be proud of that! Celebrate your compassion, knowing you are contributing more to making the world a kinder place than most people ever will.

Even if you *are* employed by a group fighting animal exploitation, there is no guarantee you won't experience the pangs of a guilty conscience—however unwarranted that guilt is.

As the founder and executive director of CompassionWorks International, Carrie LeBlanc has precious little time for fun, but she's realized how important it is. "I would say experiencing guilt is a regular part of my day," she says. "Though some days I will work for the animals 12 or more hours, there's always so much more to do." She admits that creating healthy boundaries — knowing when to say "enough is enough" — is one of the biggest challenges. "Every time I do, there is some measure of guilt. I rarely take an entire day off. It's almost impossible since my work is so integrated into my life. I am not sure I physically could take two days in a row off without experiencing enormous guilt about not helping animals, and fear that I am failing as an animal advocate and executive director. But knowing this, I try to take my own advice and have increasingly tried to set boundaries for myself. My goal is to take Friday afternoons and Sundays entirely to myself. I am having about a 50/50 success rate with that so far. I do believe it is enormously important to find those breaks and engage in activities that are unrelated to animal advocacy, but that can be easier said than done, especially if you are the head of an organization."

Dawn Moncrief, founder of A Well-Fed World, knows that feeling well. "I have a lot of guilt," she says. "Not just from the tangible experiences of seeing animals and not being able to save them, but experiencing that sensation on a regular basis—knowing they are suffering and dying and not being able to save them. I also have guilt associated with taking part in recreational activities or other non-advocacy activities. I have guilt from being comfortable in the midst of their discomfort. I have guilt from being upset about my personal, relatively trivial matters."

Matt Rossell documented animal cruelty while working undercover at the Oregon National Primate Research Center, and he says the guilt took a heavy toll. "I couldn't get the monkeys out of my mind. When people were talking about whatever was going on in their life, I was often disconnected and had trouble relating. Also, being undercover meant that I couldn't talk about what was happening, and because it was the only thing that was on my mind and I didn't want to pretend, it was easier just to isolate myself. I had virtually no social life for two years when I was there."

For Monica Engebretson, the North American campaign manager for Cruelty Free International, learning to have fun without feeling guilty has taken time, but it's made her a better activist. "I think that not having any fun makes someone a rather miserable person and ultimately unrelatable," she says, "and so much of making change for animals is dealing with people and relating to them." Still, Monica sometimes worries that she's not accomplishing as much as she could. "Not so much about hours spent but effectiveness. I guess I question whether I could do more or do it better and how exactly I should do that."

Some activists say guilt is simply not an issue. "There is always guilt that you can't do more, but just because you can't do everything doesn't mean you are not being effective," says Kate Fowler. "It is just a measure of how corrupt and amoral this human-run world is. And, even though you may not be able to save every chicken in every battery unit in the world, you can save a handful, and to them, that is everything."

Zoe Weil, president of the Institute for Humane Education, shares a story about driving next to a truck full of pigs, presumably headed for the slaughterhouse: "It was so cold, and going 60 miles [96 kilometers] an hour, the pigs must have been freezing. One caught my eye—literally—and we stared at each other for as long as was safe with me driving my car. When the truck pulled off the highway at an exit, I felt like I should follow it, but what could I have done? I made a promise to that pig that I would continue to educate others and speak out. And that's what I've been doing as a humane educator my entire adult life."

Zoe quotes the singer and social activist Joan Baez, who said "Action is the antidote to despair." "I think that action is also the antidote to guilt," Zoe says. "But when we can't take an action to save specific animals—like all the ones in a factory farm we happen to be visiting—then it's important to take some other action. We can take photographs of those animals and educate others and work for change for all the animals in factory farms. As long as our guilt does not become debilitating, it can be a powerful motivation to action. I'd recommend that people feel their guilt, and let it inspire their work. Doing the work, the guilt abates."

> I regularly visit this wonderful park in the middle of the city and right now there's a whole bunch of baby ducks there. I've been walking there throughout the winter and now the ducks have been born, and I thought, "Everything renews itself—everything." The opposite of burnout, really, is renewal, and to renew ourselves really takes just slowing down and stopping and saying "Okay, I can turn this corner."
> **Carol J. Adams**
> *Satya* **magazine**, July/August 2001

Relieving Stress

We all know that just living can be stressful. Dealing with the frustrations and pressures of life takes a toll on our bodies, minds, and emotions. But the angst of animal activism can easily turn everyday stress into a major hazard—not just for your health, but for your ability to speak out for animals. Moreover, the constant stress experienced by those who investigate abuse, rescue animals, spend time in a shelter, or perform other potentially disturbing work makes these people vulnerable to the crippling effects of Post-Traumatic Stress Disorder. Stress can sneak up on you; therefore, watch for the signs so you can take steps to reduce them.

Physical symptoms of stress include:

- Headache
- Digestive problems
- Muscle tension

- Sore jaw, grinding teeth
- Change in sleep habits
- Chronic fatigue
- Chest pain, irregular heartbeat
- High blood pressure
- Change in body weight
- Nervous ticks (sniffling, nose twitching, foot bouncing, etc.)
- Vision problems (if your stress is this serious, go to the doctor!)
- Excessive alcohol or drug consumption (again, seek help)

Mental symptoms of stress include:

- Memory loss
- Difficulty making decisions
- Inability to concentrate
- Confusion
- Negative viewpoint
- Poor judgment
- Loss of objectivity
- Desire to escape or run away

Emotional symptoms of stress include:

- Depression
- Anger
- Hypersensitivity
- Apathy
- Restlessness, anxiety
- Feeling overwhelmed
- Lack of confidence

"I think it's good to try to pinpoint the cause of the stress," says

Mia MacDonald, whose activism includes work in human rights and the environmental movement as well as animal rights. "Of course, thinking about the state of the world for animals and the breadth and scale of the cruelty is overwhelming in and of itself. Trying to see your way through your role in stopping the suffering can make you feel very tiny and very ineffectual. So it's probably best to try to understand those thoughts but not dwell on them."

In addition to practicing yoga and meditation, Mia unwinds by spending time outside. "I try to realize I can't work all the time," she says. "I try to get enough sleep and eat well and plan ahead." She also emphasizes the importance of friendship. "Circles of support for activists can be good. I think stress is certainly more intense when you're alone and dwelling in and on it. Talking about it with others, seeing others trying to find ways of dealing with stress, can demystify it and let you find more solutions than feeling stuck in it. That said, life is stressful and there will be times when you feel really stressed and the tools to help you with it don't work that well. I have these periods from time to time and kind of have to accept it and believe that it won't last forever, that I'll get some sense of equanimity back."

An Activist's Advice for Relieving Stress
pattrice jones has spent a lot of time contemplating the stress and other issues activists endure. She is an activist and author (*Aftershock: Confronting Trauma in a Violent World: A Guide for Activists and Their Allies*), has practiced clinical psychology focusing on trauma, and she runs VINE Sanctuary in Vermont, where she confesses to suffering her fair share of grief each time a rescued animal dies. Here is pattrice's advice on how animal activists can best cope with stress:

- Be reasonable in your expectations of yourself and others.
- Eat well and get enough sleep.

- Deliberately relax before and decompress after stressful actions or encounters.
- Respect your own animal rights and don't expect your body to do more than it can do.
- In your off time, seek out a variety of pleasurable activities and sensations.
- Have empathy for yourself and others.
- Maintain healthy relationships with your comrades, and be sure to have one or two friends with whom you do not work.

During his two years working undercover, Matt Rossell says he wasn't always consistent with his self-care, and he suffered the consequences. "When I was doing well I was eating right, exercising, doing yoga, getting enough sleep, and focusing on the next thing I needed or celebrating the victories of getting a juicy piece of information or a compelling video clip. Other times I was a mess, barely holding it together at work and then losing it, crying and sobbing all the way home and going straight to bed." Matt credits his wife Leslie with helping him through this very stressful time. "She was my partner and sole support," he

---

Animal groups, organizations and activists come and go, and some stay. The important thing for the long-term is to be a vegan, keep positive, read as much as you can about strategy and history, keep an open mind and set your eye on the battery hen in the seventh tier, thirtieth cage, sixth aisle, or on the scared little pig with the electric prod bearing down upon him at the slaughterhouse—and *don't lose your focus.*

Patty Mark
Satya **magazine,** September 2006

says. "I am lucky she stuck with me through those dark days that rattled the foundation of our relationship." He acknowledges his experiences might be extreme, but adds, "I know many activists have similar struggles, just knowing that the suffering is going on and feeling powerless to change it."

The Curse of Traumatic Knowledge

That awareness of animal suffering can prompt feelings of loneliness and despair—a deep well of sadness that leaves us unable to communicate our pain to others. Activist and author Carol J. Adams calls this awareness "traumatic knowledge."

"Traumatic knowledge makes us feel the suffering of animals acutely," she says. "We are shocked—horrified—as we learn about the treatment of animals: 'I have been a part of that system!' We may feel revulsion at our own complicity. We have a need to forgive ourselves for our enmeshment within a system that daily destroys animals by the millions. We are unable to relate to others, and we are unable to explain what is happening to us. Our desolation cuts us off and amplifies the loneliness the knowledge brings."

Compounding the problem, Carol says, is that our culture shields consumers from the truth about the cruelties animals suffer. We don't witness the horrors of the slaughterhouse; instead, we see only neatly packaged animal flesh in the meat section of the supermarket, so we need not consider where the meat came from. She calls this phenomenon "the structure of the absent referent," and this theory is a central theme of many of her books, including *The Sexual Politics of Meat* and *Living Among Meat Eaters*.

"People are much happier eating some*thing* than some*one*," she says. But that "happiness" is merely the result of being ignorant about the realities of agribusiness—an ignorance not shared by the animal activist, who experiences traumatic knowledge when the referent is restored. "It is very difficult to live with this information. It is painful to know what animals endure. But the response to this is to say, 'I would rather know than not know, and I will find the inner strength to know and not collapse under the weight of knowing.'"

Living with traumatic knowledge requires that we share it. "Sometimes," says Carol, "our friends and co-workers think we are going to drive them crazy saying, 'Do you know about how chickens are treated? Do you know about this? Do you know about that?' We want to be heard, but sometimes indirectly rather than directly is more effective. Give your friends and co-workers pamphlets and books rather than voicing everything yourself. Allow them to hear in their own voice, rather than yours, what is happening to nonhumans."

Carol also emphasizes the need for activists to remember their own needs. "No matter the activism we do for animals, we have to take care of ourselves. We cannot do it all, so as we do what we can do, we must do it with love for our own animal body. We can't exhaust ourselves or we don't end up helping the animals. We have to develop interests outside of the animal rights movement—music, poetry, going to movies—something that meets our needs for nurture and growth. This way we don't ask the animal rights movement to be everything and all things to us. We can come to it with energy rather than feeling overwhelmed. Having healthy boundaries allows for healthy activism."

Traumatic knowledge affects the animal rights movement by fueling activists with an urgent desire to vindicate the suffering and trauma animals experience, Carol explains. "One of the attractions of the more militant activities of the animal rights movement, including targeting someone's home for a demonstration, is that it provides several antidotes to traumatic knowledge: it offers a way to be heard, to have a sense that you are working for change and a way to express anger. But this urgency is dangerous. We sometimes make decisions based on this urgency, losing sight of the need to evaluate. Traumatic knowledge may cause us to see everything in black and white. The problem is we live in a grey world." The key, she says, is to keep theory and activism linked, because theory helps us see this grey world.

"Living with traumatic knowledge, as we all do, means there will always be a crisis. That is because this knowledge causes an inner crisis. We must take care of our bodies because each of our bodies is processing incredibly difficult, demanding, depressing information, and we must be careful and take care as we relate to others. Traumatic knowledge requires that we take care of ourselves, spiritually and physically and emotionally."

Carol suggests that activists acknowledge the pain but not give in to it. "We have to develop an inner capacity, an inner discipline, so that traumatic knowledge doesn't destroy us. We must find ways to say, 'Yes, here you are again, this feeling of pain and hurt and desperation. But I know I can live with it. I can take the time to acknowledge it, take a deep breath, regain my grounding, and then move forward.'"

Finally, she observes that traumatic knowledge causes us to feel needy, and that's okay, as long as we have a good support network. "We need so much," she says. "To win—that would be great—to be acknowledged for trying, to have more time and energy. But sometimes we bring that neediness *to* the animal rights movement. In this sense, the animal rights movement cannot meet our needs. We must be nourished elsewhere. Make sure you have loving, supportive friends who love you simply for who you are. Take time to exercise or develop a spiritual practice. Take time to rest.

"An example of my own traumatic knowledge was the realization 30 years ago that there was a connection between a patriarchal world and animal oppression. This knowledge needed to be expressed. This knowledge forced me to become a writer. Georgia O'Keeffe said that as an artist she lived on the edge of a knife. I live on top of it as well. Traumatic knowledge is sharp, but it is powerful and it can empower us, if we can stay balanced upon it."

The Power of Solidarity

Letting other activists know that you appreciate them and their efforts has enormous power, says activist coach Dallas Rising. "It reminds one another that we're making a difference." Dallas says such encouragement gives both parties more energy and helps sustain their activism. "Write a letter, send an email, make some cupcakes for the next meeting—whatever. People are often surprised others have taken notice, and it can strengthen the bond between people and counteract the peer pressure among activists."

Oppression and Burnout

Because being an effective activist means constantly learning, and because my education since the first edition of this book has included learning more about how activists of color experience the animal rights movement, I think it's important to consider the insights of those outside the dominant (i.e., white) perspective. Aph Ko, for example, identifies as an anti-racist activist who fights for animal liberation. "I don't know how to fight for animal liberation without my lens of being a black woman," she says. She experiences stress and compassion fatigue differently than someone for whom race may not be central to their consciousness.

"Burnout comes with the territory of being a conscious political woman of color, regardless if you're an activist or not," says Aph. "I largely became an activist because I was fatigued with being oppressed and having the dominant class write my narrative and tell my story. That was burnout. I didn't become an activist out of choice. It was an act of survival. I became an activist because I was burned out by racism and sexism in my everyday life."

Aph questions whether she and other people of color can truly avoid burnout while white supremacist patriarchy is still intact. "Most of the time, it helps to get off the Internet, to be completely honest. Having space from the digital world helps in terms of priorities. It's easy to get sucked in and to start stressing about things that don't matter at all. So, I ensure that I spend a large amount of time offline."

She also advises activists of color to stop being impressed that white people like your work. "When you live in a white supremacy, getting white attention as a minority can feel like you're on top of the world—like you're doing something right. However, I would urge minorities to be really cautious of this feeling because it can lead you into exploitation and doing things for free for white folks. I had to learn how to say 'no' to opportunities from white people that were not offering financial compensation for my work. Hollow fame and representation has been used as a tool on brown bodies to get them to believe that doing free work will yield a big payout, and it usually doesn't." Likewise, she's learned to stop listening to and engaging with those in the dominant class who critique her and her work. "As Toni Morrison said, distraction is a large part of racism, so I'm learning how to avoid distraction. Rather than respond to every person who writes a slanderous, untruthful article about my work, or me, I just keep moving forward. I have no need to entertain petty shit."

As daunting as being an activist can be, Aph finds strength in thinking about what lies ahead. "It's really easy to forget why we're working as hard as we are every single day. This is why I love Afrofuturism. It made me realize that there will be a day when I will be able to breathe and relax, but it comes at the cost of fighting hard today, which I will continue to do."

So, it's important we recognize that just as other races experience the animal rights movement differently, they must also cope with compassion fatigue and burnout differently. Aph says white activists can help make a difference for activists of color by sincerely engaging with their ideas. "We are knowledge producers, and we have important ideas to contribute. Oftentimes the mainstream animal rights movement assumes that accommodating people of color means engaging with cosmetic diversity or adding a seat to a table that is already set with white epistemologies and ideas. That's not what a lot of us are fighting for. People of color don't just want to comment on diversity issues in the movement—we have new things to say about animal oppression from our standpoints. We have actual ideas and theories to share!"

Additionally, she cautions against lumping all vegans of color into the same boat. "A lot of times, white folks will view vegans of color as interchangeable," she says. "Just because I'm a black vegan doesn't mean I necessarily subscribe to intersectionality. Just because I'm a black vegan doesn't mean I agree with all other black vegans. Just because I'm a black vegan doesn't mean you can't disagree with my points and theories as a white person. I am not just a bag of melanin to look at. I'm a person with thoughts and ideas."

Other Emotions

Activists are generally motivated by emotion—the love of animals, for example, or rage against companies practicing abuse—so it is axiomatic that they are more likely to be especially sensitive to the pains that accompany the fight against indefensible cruelty. Grief, depression, anger, and despair are all common feelings activists must learn to cope with.

"I think that one of the most important issues that any activist faces is dealing with dark emotions, specifically hatred, sorrow and rage," says Zoe. "We all know activists who are embittered, nasty and so enraged that they push everyone around them away. It's important to realize that this harms animals. We must model a message of kindness, compassion, integrity, honesty, and love." As Zoe observes, no one wants to join a group of angry, hateful people unless they are angry and hateful themselves. "And, unfortunately, the image in many people's minds of animal activists is that they're misanthropes," she says. "We need to find a practice—whether it's meditating, praying, singing, dancing, being in nature, or whatever—that enables us to be whole, joyful, and emotionally healthy. The animals need this from us as much as they need our time and energy directed toward their liberation."

pattrice believes that much of the "burnout" activists feel is actually depression. She advises people to minimize their risk of depression by taking care of their body, maintaining healthy relationships with supportive people, and finding ways to express and work with—rather than ignore or suppress—the natural feelings of anger and sadness that will arise in the course of activism. "If you do start to feel depressed, don't ignore it," she says. "Often something as simple as a vitamin supplement or talking to somebody about your feelings can bring relief."

> We should rage against the dying of the light in every animal's eyes that results from human cruelty and abuse. The thing is to transform that pity and rage into one's case for animal rights. It's hard to burn out once we see ourselves as advocates with a case to put before the public. What matters is making the most of the opportunity of being on the right side, win or lose, while we are living.
> **Karen Davis**
> *Satya* **magazine**, July/August 2001

Sharing Space with (and Even Dating) Non-Vegans

Because it is natural—indeed, expected—for two people in a relationship to have differing tastes and opinions, it is not uncommon for them to disagree on the subject of animal consumption. This has resulted in a longstanding debate in the animal rights community: should vegans date non-vegans? Should they live together? Many vegans, such as Tara Baxter, say no way. "It is such a fundamental ethic for me," she says. "If someone couldn't make those connections, or didn't share the basic belief with me that no living being should be objectified and exploited, then I couldn't connect with them on the deepest heart level. It would be difficult for me to be attracted to them, as well." Tara, who is grateful her life partner is also vegan, says it would be absurd if her family simultaneously included an animal rescued from a meat farm and someone who eats animals that come from meat farms. "It would make no sense."

Many agree with Tara. To them, eating animals is a dating deal-breaker, and few things make a person more attractive than dietary compassion and shared values. Others take a midway approach. "I would not cook meat or change my diet for someone else—at this point in my life—but I would love to date someone who is open-minded enough to date a vegan when they are not there yet," says Michele McCowan. "That does not mean a commitment. It's just a date. It's a good time to help someone become a future vegan. I was not vegan when I was in my last relationship, but he was. I was on the fence. He helped me to get to the other side. I would not marry a non-vegan, though."

Still others hit the jackpot by falling in love with a meat-eater who eventually goes vegan. "My husband was not a vegan when we first started dating but became one," says Lisa Rice. "It took time and patience on my end and his willingness to evolve. He also started feeling and looking better, which motivated his evolution. Now after being with a vegan for so long, I would not be able to date someone who was not vegan."

A few other activists I spoke with are married to non-vegans, and they find it predictably challenging.

Rachel (who asked me not to use her last name) says for more than a year she only dated vegetarians and vegans. "It was rough. Given how hard it is to find a mature, kind, and respectful male partner in New York City, adding the requirement of vegan meant I felt like I was facing steep odds and dating people who were cheating or not really willing to commit or just really not what I would consider a good partner for me." She loves her non-vegan partner, and they keep the peace with separate fridges and cookware. "Maybe it would be different if I'd gone vegan younger and not been looking for a romantic partner at 36," she says. "But even now, I'm kind of horrified at how immature and unkind so many guys are. So, I am happy with my non-vegan—but kind and respectful—partner."

Carrie LeBlanc, who married an omnivore, understands how Rachel feels. "I think that in any relationship, especially in the early stages, it is more important how someone treats you than whether they are vegan or not," she says. "But for most long-term relationships, a difference of ethics on something as important as veganism can really test one's commitment."

In some cases, both people enter a relationship as omnivores, but one person embraces veganism. This can cause tremendous stress, as the other person may feel judged and guilty. They may wonder what happened; what changed the person they used to go out for sushi with or who used to enjoy eggs for breakfast?

Wherever you are on the vegan path, if you're sharing your life and living space with a non-vegan, here are a few tips that might help:

- Make sure your significant other understands the depth of your ethics—and why being vegan is important to you.
- If you like to cook, offer to make most of the dinners so that delicious, satisfying vegan food is the main meal you

share.

- Establish kitchen guidelines and decide what goes where. If your partner is going to keep animal products in the fridge, for example, designate the bottom shelf for that and keep the produce on the top shelf. In fact, consider a mini-refrigerator to be used only for meat, dairy, and eggs. Have separate pots, pans, cooking utensils, cutting boards, and dishes for non-vegan foods.
- Take them to visit a sanctuary for animals rescued from the food system.
- Share with them a book or documentary that may help explain your feelings. Nothing too graphic.
- Show your partner respect. Give them space to consider your point of view and how critical this position is for you.

"I think vegans embarking on relationships with non-vegans need to stay mindful that they are not the only one adapting to a new and uncomfortable situation," adds Carrie. "The non-vegan is also going to experience periods of frustration with feeling that they are being forced to conform to something they didn't sign up for. Remember that going vegan isn't necessarily easy, especially if someone is not quickly influenced by animal suffering." Carrie says that although her husband is not (yet) vegan, he has shifted to a more plant-based diet. "Love plus patience saves lives—in our romantic relationships and in all of our interactions with others."

Roommates and Housemates

With ever-increasing rents and other living expenses, sharing an apartment or house with an omnivore is a real possibility. Many of the tips for couples also apply to living with non-vegan roommates and housemates, such as keeping food storage areas, cooking utensils, and dishes separate. But unlike a romantic relationship, you and your roomie are probably not planning to be together for a lifetime, and other than maintaining a peaceful household, there is little incentive to make a lot of compromises. (Although a roommate becoming a significant other is always a possibility!)

Some vegans will tell you that finding a good flatmate who pays their share of the rent on time is what's important, not what they eat. If you agree, then you'll likely have an easier time living with an omnivore, but here are a few additional tips to better your chances:

- Be upfront about your lifestyle. Make sure your roommate understands what being vegan means and they know the foods and ingredients you do not consume.
- Ask your roommates not to leave animal products out.
- Create a cooking schedule. You do not want to be anywhere near the kitchen when someone is cooking animals, nor do you want to witness the aftermath.
- Don't try to convert. If you're hoping your roommate/ housemates will go vegan, you'll have better luck living by example and sharing some incredible vegan food with them than by preaching to them.
- Be friendly and approachable. Let your flatmate know that they can come to you with questions, whether it's about veganism, the utility bill, or whatever.

Dealing with Family and Friends

Once we know the truth about animal suffering, it is painful for us to watch our family and friends eat meat, eggs, and dairy products, especially when we know these people to be otherwise loving and compassionate. And if you're new to veganism, your feelings—your anger, grief, and frustration—will only be exacerbated. Making matters worse are those who mock our veganism.

Patience and compassion are the key in these situations. Try to take the teasing in stride and remember that few of us are born vegan. Moreover, people who eat animals likely feel some level of guilt, and as a vegan, your presence may make them defensive about their choices. Teasing is often a way for them to cope. In fact, it's probably a sign that they might be amenable to your message at some point.

But not always. Oddly enough, many vegans and animal activists have much greater success guiding strangers toward an ethical lifestyle than they do their own family and oldest friends. Try to not take it personally. There's something about human nature that can make it difficult for people to accept guidance from someone they've known a long time. (Perhaps you've done this yourself, as when you ignore the advice of your partner, only to accept the very same advice from someone else.)

Some occasions, such as going out for meals with non-vegan friends or celebrating holidays with non-vegan family members, can be particularly stressful. When going to a non-vegan gathering, such as holiday dinners, bring a vegan dish. Not only will you be guaranteed to have at least one meal you can eat, but you can share it with others and impress them with how delicious veganism can be. In fact, jokes Brenda Sanders, they might like it *too* much. "No matter how much your family may be against veganism or vegan food, if you bring food, they will eat *all* of it," she says. "They are going to rave about how good it is as they eat all your food and leave you with nothing. If you want to have any of your food that you brought to this family event, bring extra—hide some in your purse or your backpack."

Here are some additional steps you can take:

- Make sure your family and friends understand what being vegan means and that this is not a "phase" for you.
- Explain your reasons for being vegan.
- Emphasize that eating vegan, especially with a focus on

whole foods, is healthy.

- Answer any questions they may have calmly and without any judgment. For example, rather than saying, "I don't want to be an animal killer like you," say, "I've stopped eating meat, eggs, and dairy products because I do not want to support animal suffering."

- Ask them if they are interested in more information. If they are, arrange to watch a documentary with them, such as *Cowspiracy*, *The Ghosts in Our Machine*, or *Vegucated*.

Another suggestion you might try: Instead of receiving presents for your birthday, ask loved ones to go with you to a vegan restaurant or to visit a reputable sanctuary for farmed animals. Both will help educate them without putting the burden on you.

Dealing with Fellow Activists

Here's a hard-learned truth: Sometimes the biggest obstacles to the animal rights movement aren't the industries that exploit animals but other animal activists. I'm not here to name and shame anyone, but infighting within the movement has increased alongside the popularity of social media, where the absence of body language and other social cues—coupled with the guise of anonymity—seems to inspire people to write comments online they would probably never say to someone in person. If you post a story or opinion, and it gains attention, it's all but certain that it will attract negative, even hateful, comments. Sometimes these comments are from animal ag apologists, but often they're from activists who disagree with you.

I try to avoid contemptuous people, but social media is so enormous that it might not always be possible to know who among your online "friends" may be harboring views that are less than compassionate. Admittedly, I've done my share of "unfriending" people who spew hatred and ignorance, but a lot of perhaps more enlightened animal rights activists disagree with that tactic, preferring to send the offender a private message or post a polite comment counter to the poster's intolerant viewpoint. They feel it's better to remain in contact and even engage with them, since comments affirming social justice may have a positive influence on them.

This approach was powerfully articulated in a 2015 *Huffington Post* article called "Dear White Allies: Stop Unfriending Other White People Over Ferguson," in which Spectra, an Afrofeminist social justice activist, observed that because oppressed individuals must deal with the outrage that comes with being marginalized, the more privileged members of the population often have more emotional capacity than the oppressed to talk some sense into the "other side." Writes Spectra: "You're a socially conscious white person? You don't share *their* views? It's disappointing to hear your friends say racist things? You don't wanna talk to *them*? I hear you. I really do. But if you don't speak to 'them,' who will?"

Activist Carolyn Bailey's preferred response to antisocial behavior online is to send a private message. "It avoids a defensive reaction," she says, "something I see all the time on Facebook, and it provides an opportunity for learning in a much more comfortable atmosphere. That said, though, if the issue has been brought to that person's attention before and they continue doing it, or arguing that 'ableism isn't ableism,' etc., I would definitely do it publicly."

Maren Souders agrees and posts constructive comments to help educate, rather than embarrass, them. "I usually do it on the thread, because I want others to see it too," she says, "but I do it in a non-shaming way, like telling the person why I am concerned about what they said, and how I hope they will reconsider their statement or opinion. I have mostly had positive responses. One time I did send a private message, and the person thanked me for opening her mind to this new perspective."

Still others take a middle-way approach, saying it depends on the situation. Elaine Vigneault, for example, says whether or not she ends her connection depends on the comment and context as well as the friendship level. "In certain situations," she says, "I unfriend or unfollow; in other situations, I confront publicly or privately."

Then there are those animal activists who feel obliged to post hateful messages in response to stories related to animal exploitation and cruelty. A Facebook post showing a woman wearing a fur coat, for instance, might elicit comments ranging from "fur hag" to "burn in hell," or even direct calls for violence. Although I understand the anger behind such remarks, I have to wonder: Do the activists who post them really believe they are representing an ideal vegan ethic? Do they think advocating hate is going to win hearts and minds? Is this part of a meaningful conversation? My advice is, do not stoop to this kind of behavior, either online or in person.

Body Shaming

Sadly, one of the most pervasive and painful misconceptions in the animal rights movement is that vegans are thin (or at least *should* be). This myth has been perpetuated both by individual activists and by national groups that have used fat shaming as a way to promote veganism. As if the suffering animals endure isn't argument enough. Besides, using cruelty to promote a lifestyle that tries to avoid cruelty is counterintuitive.

Like racism, sexism, homo aggression, classism, or ageism, body shaming should have no place at the animal rights table. Not only is the "thin vegan" a ridiculous stereotype, but we hurt both others and the movement when we demean, bully, or discriminate against someone we believe does not fit an "ideal" body type.

Activist Andy Tabar knows this all too well. He is the man behind Compassion Co., through which he designs and sells conversation-starting message wear for vegans. One of his boldest T-shirts depicts a smiling hippo saying, "FAT, HAPPY, and VEGAN." It's a topic that's close to home for Andy, who's been the target of fat shaming, and as much as he takes it in stride, it can still hurt. He once posted a photo of himself wearing his latest shirt design, for instance, and the first comment posted about the image was "Fat vegan."

In response, Andy posted that the comment made him sad. "It made me sad for the new or aspiring vegan that saw that comment and decided the vegan community was an unsafe and unwelcoming place for them," he wrote. "That veganism must not be for them." He added that the comment made him sad for all the animals who will continue to suffer and die because so many people within the animal rights movement seem intent on creating what Andy called "a gated community" that only allows in people with a specific body type. "It made me sad because I think as vegans we should be better than that."

Andy described the many times he's done outreach on the streets, and that people who wouldn't be called "thin" would be happy to talk to him because they assumed all vegans were fit and athletic. "By telling people they need to look a certain way to promote veganism, you are doing an incredible disservice to the animals. We need *all* body types in this movement. From the bodybuilders who get ripped and crush it for the animals to all the fat beautiful babes showing off their glorious selves at the beach. Simply put, we need vegans of all kinds to inspire people of all kinds. Fuck your gated community. Get out there and represent veganism, fight for the animals, and love yourself, in whatever body you're in."

Working in the Animal Rights Movement

Many animal advocates want to go beyond the grassroots activism outlined in this book and secure a paid position at an animal protection organization. After all, why not earn a living doing what you love, right? If that is your goal, please pursue it recognizing that there is a side to the movement that is often not discussed: the sexual harassment and objectification of women. Using their position of power, some men who are ostensibly fighting the oppression and exploitation of animals harass female employees, interns, and volunteers. Many of these women fear retaliation if they come forward, or believe that speaking out would be "hurting the movement."

This is an issue Carol Adams has been talking about for years. In a post on her blog in 2017, Carol observes how women are treated—the sexual abuse and harassment, the male "leaders" who take credit for their behind-the-scenes work, the glass ceilings that keep them from advancing within an organization—and wonders what the movement would look like if these women hadn't left and their voices were still a part of shaping the movement's goals and strategies. Finally, she asks, "When will we have an ethical commitment to women's equality in the animal rights movement?"

As Carol observes, sexual harassment exists everywhere, but within the animal rights movement—where women far outnumber men and where men are so often hailed as the "heroes"—the problem is exacerbated. "To begin with, the animal rights movement has a problem about self-care," Carol told me. "And then the animal rights movement has a problem around sexual inequality. Put the two together and what can we say to those who have become victimized by serial sexual exploiters?" Carol avoids using the term "predator" to refer to men who harass and assault women. "Why do we pathologize the behavior of an animal doing what they're meant to be doing? These are deliberate decisions on the part of men, and because they are not held accountable, they continue to do it."

Creating this ability for self-care within the movement has always been a challenge, because too often activists are encouraged to think of their suffering as secondary. "Look at what the animals are going through" is a typical response. "And so we already have a movement that encourages us to get less sleep, to constantly be on the go doing something," says Carol. "I like to say that sometimes the something we need to do is nothing—just stepping back."

Carol believes one of the ways self-care begins is to recognize that we have the right to boundaries, and that's not always easy. "Especially if we're caring, we end up having difficulty with boundaries because we feel responsible for what's happening to cows or chickens or pigs or primates. This openness and caring often might erode the kind of boundary we need to say, 'I stop here and you stop there.' Having this boundary and being able to say 'no' are beginning places. We need to be able to say, 'No, I can't come to that protest—I've got a cold. I need to take care of myself.'"

Moreover, she says, because of the inequality of the movement, men receive a disproportionate amount of credit and even serial sexual exploiters are given a pass. "Someone new to the movement might feel flattered by the attention they are getting," says Carol. "The behavior then shades over as the boundary-violating exploiter takes advantage of the weak-boundaried activist."

Also troubling are the bullies in power within the movement who often make life miserable for the activists who work for them. "Sadly, I know of many animal rights organizations that mistreat employees," says lauren Ornelas, who admits that she's worked for two nonprofits that continue to abuse their workers. "It doesn't change. They are toxic organizations with highly unethical practices and harassment going on. The attitude of the managers is, 'There's this known thing that we shouldn't talk about, because we already have opposition who doesn't like us. So, if it gets out how bad we are, it could be detrimental to the animals and really hurt the movement.' What ends up happening is that a lot of times these people leave and they drop out of the movement, because they're scared and they're scarred and they need therapy, frankly, for the cruel treatment they endured. I encourage these people to be honest with their colleagues and tell them it's okay to tell other people about it. The more people who know, the better."

Being employed by an animal protection group—working alongside like-minded activists and spending your days (and often nights) fighting the good fight—has tremendous appeal. Indeed, you may already work for one, and if you enjoy it, I am very thankful. But if you're considering a career in this field, please talk to others doing the work you want to do, especially if you are a woman. Ask them how they are treated. Do they feel valued? How does their organization handle sexual harassment? What are the group's leaders like? Do they exploit women or people of color, either directly or through their tactics? What are the opportunities for advancement in the organization? You get the idea.

It's not that I believe all organizations are unprincipled. It's that I don't want all your idealism and passion and spirit to get crushed if your "dream job" turns into a nightmare.

To the men working on behalf of animal liberation, I propose you fall into one of two categories: either you genuinely respect women in this movement and value them as colleagues and equals, or you don't. And if you don't, you may even be one of those men who harasses and assaults women. On the other hand, if you *do* value and respect women, then be a strong ally. Believe them when they tell you they've been harassed or assaulted. Ask what you can do to support them. Don't politely tolerate sexism or the objectification of women. Respect women's boundaries. And don't normalize the behavior of abusers by making excuses for them or giving them a platform. Remember that you are fighting injustice; campaigning against one form of domination while participating in or allowing another perpetuates systemic oppression.

Being an effective activist is more than just finding tactics and strategies that work. It often means being able to trust your fellow activists. It means being allowed to express your ideas without fear. It does not ever mean bullying or pressuring your colleagues—or harassing or stalking or touching them in an unprofessional manner. Not only does harassment and assault hurt women, but the entire movement suffers.

Our Call to Action

Shortly after the battery hen rescue that begins this chapter, as I struggled with a variety of emotions, an art therapist offered me some advice. She recommended I take a box, a receptacle for all the pain I experienced on behalf of animals, and decorate it. So, I painted a small wooden box with a chicken, goat, pig, cow, and rabbit. When I am hurting, the therapist said, I should create something to represent the emotional thrashing my spirit is taking—a drawing, a poem, or anything else that might speak to me in that moment of anguish—and place it in the box. The grief, sorrow, or anger then resides in the box and is (in theory) no longer within me. What helped my healing most after the rescue, though, was the national media coverage we were able to garner after saving the lives of 1,800 hens. Many members of the public expressed their shock upon learning how battery hens are treated.

Although the work of the activist can be painful, the potential for emotional pain exists in nearly all rewarding work: firefighters, healthcare professionals, therapists, social workers, and many others experience both the exhilaration and the stress that accompanies helping someone. Engaging in animal activism brings you a profound sense of satisfaction knowing your effort to relieve suffering is the right thing to do. The key to being an effective activist over the long haul is learning and embracing self-care. If you remember only one thing from this chapter, let it be this: *Take care of yourself.* As Zoe says, "If we don't take care of ourselves, we're of no use to the animals, and we're terrible role models. Self-care is part and parcel of activism."

Respect your limits—know how much you can take on and be prepared to take a holiday or shift the focus of your activism, if necessary. Megan Bentjen, who spent a decade at PETA, believes that activists consistently guided by the misery of animals stand the best chance of succeeding. "Keep your eyes on the prize," she says. "Having a sense of humor, taking time for yourself, and not letting your anger overwhelm you are all important, but the activists who have been most successful in not burning out are the people who have kept their focus on the suffering of animals."

Animal suffering is hidden from most of the world. As activists, we offer a gift not only to nonhuman animals, but to the people who live beneath a shroud of ignorance. Most people do not want to contribute to animal abuse—that's your tool. Give a person some knowledge—throw some light into the dark recesses of animal factories, testing labs, puppy mills, circuses, fur farms, rodeos, and all the other sources of misery—and be prepared to answer some questions about what you've shown them. You are the enlightened one, offering information that is both shocking and hopeful.

Unfortunately, those who profit from exploiting animals have tools too, and they see each successful animal rights campaign as a threat to their livelihood. As you read this, businesses with a financial interest in animal suffering are organizing their resources and creating strategies to combat activism. They are quietly attending animal rights conferences to learn more about our tactics. They have the deep pockets and political clout to try to maintain the status quo of consumer ignorance. What they do not have is integrity.

Being not just an activist but an effective activist over the long haul takes an abiding commitment—a conviction shared by each of the more than 140 activists from around the world who contributed their time and thoughts to this book. If you're just beginning your activism, try out what seems comfortable to you. I hope one or more of the models presented here sounds appealing and that you now feel you have the information and resources to begin.

If you're already engaged at the vanguard of activism, I hope this book has inspired some new thinking in your struggle to reduce suffering—and some new approaches to sustaining yourself through the difficult times.

Wherever you are on your path, remember to celebrate each victory you help achieve for animals. Enjoy the successes more than you mourn the losses. If you need to, step back from the movement once in a while. And mind the words of pattrice jones: "Every successful social-change movement has involved a multiplicity of people using a multiplicity of tactics to approach a problem from a multiplicity of angles. Some people push against the bad things that need to be changed while others pull for the good alternatives. Some people work to undermine destructive systems from within while others are knocking down the walls from without. We all need to recognize that and find our place within a multifaceted struggle, being sure to be generous and appreciative of those who are working toward the same goals using different tactics."

Though the abuses of animals are myriad and the battles we must engage in on their behalf appear daunting, our goals *are* achievable. Moreover, if we are to nurse this ailing planet back to health, if we are to bequeath to future generations the promise of a lasting peace, then our vow should be to actively challenge the long-held view that animals exist for us to breed, eat, wear, experiment on, use for entertainment, sacrifice in the name of religion, or exploit for any other human purpose. Their suffering is our call to action, and we must act for them. We must act for ourselves.

Appendix A — Recent Milestones for Animals

- As of 2016, every medical school in the United States has stopped using live animals in their teaching.
- Gucci and Michael Kors joined Giorgio Armani, Hugo Boss, Calvin Klein, Tommy Hilfiger, Ralph Lauren, and other top fashion brands by going fur-free.
- Countries that have banned the use of wild animals in circuses now include Austria, Belgium, Costa Rica, Denmark, El Salvador, Greece, India, Iran, Ireland, Mexico, Scotland, Singapore, and many more.
- Cockfighting is now illegal in every US state.
- Veganism is gaining in popularity: vegan restaurants, veg entrées in other restaurants, and people switching to a plant-based diet are all increasing.
- Bans on veal crates and gestation crates have taken effect in the EU, the UK, and in parts of the US.
- As demand for cow's milk decreases, more and more dairies are planting trees and switching to nut-based milks.
- California became the first state to require that dogs, cats, and rabbits sold in "pet" stores come from a nonprofit rescue group or shelter.
- India declared dolphins to be nonhuman persons.
- Tiger Tops tour company in Nepal ended its elephant-back safaris because of animal cruelty.
- More than 100 high-profile tour operators have stopped selling excursions featuring elephant rides.
- India also banned testing cosmetics on animals.
- France banned the breeding of dolphins and killer whales in captivity.
- In 2018, Illinois became the first US state to ban the use of

elephants in circuses.

- Mary Kay, Revlon, Lush, and other cosmetics firms no longer test products on animals.
- Many school systems offer alternatives to dissection in science classes.
- The US has stopped breeding chimpanzees for research.
- Chimp experimentation has been banned (legally) or abandoned (stopped in practice, but without laws) throughout the EU, New Zealand, and Liberia.
- Ringling Bros. and Barnum & Bailey Circus is no longer in business.
- SeaWorld has stopped breeding orcas.
- Zoos in Detroit, Chicago, New York, Philadelphia, San Francisco, Seattle, and other cities have stopped housing elephants in captivity.
- Live hare/rabbit coursing has been banned in many parts of the world, including England, Scotland, Wales, and in some US states.
- Kmart and Telstra Corporation stopped sponsoring rodeos in Australia.
- Campbell Soup Company and Pace Foods no longer sponsor rodeos in the US.
- Animal law courses are being offered at universities throughout Australia, Canada, New Zealand, and the US.
- Major retail chains have stopped selling glue traps, devices that rip patches of skin off animals' bodies as they struggle to escape and cause them to suffer for days until they die of starvation or dehydration.
- Fox hunting with hounds is banned in England and Wales.
- Cities throughout the world ban rodeos.
- Taiwan has banned eating dogs and cats.
- India's high court declared that birds have the right to freedom and dignity and cannot be kept in cages.
- Vietnam vowed to end their bear-bile industry.

- College and corporate dining halls continue to eliminate the use of eggs from hens confined in battery cages.
- Fur farming is banned in Austria, Croatia, and the UK. Many other countries, including Belgium, Germany, Luxembourg, and the Czech Republic, are considering bans.
- Abercrombie & Fitch, J. Crew, Limited Brands, and many other retailers have stopped buying wool from mulesed or live exported Australian sheep.
- More than 100 jurisdictions across the US, including the entire state of California, have passed legislation restricting or banning the tethering of dogs.
- PETCO agreed to stop selling large birds in their stores and make provisions for the millions of rats and mice in their care—a precedent-setting victory for all animals suffering in the pet trade.
- The Balearic Islands (an autonomous part of Spain) granted great apes the status of legal persons. Other countries are exploring this idea as well.
- The UK halted online sales of puppies.
- The US Coast Guard became the first branch of the US military to suspend the shooting, stabbing, and killing of animals in trauma training drills.
- Nepal's last known "dancing" bears were rescued, ending a cruel practice promoted as street entertainment.

Appendix B—Fifteen Things You Can Do TODAY to Help Animals

1. Go vegan. If you can't, try giving up meat, eggs, and dairy products one day a week, then add another day every week.
2. Set up an account with a site like iGive.com, goodsearch.com, or Amazon Smile, which allow you to support animal groups with a percentage of your online shopping.
3. Contact a local animal shelter or sanctuary and ask about volunteering.
4. Order leaflets from Mercy For Animals, PETA, or Vegan Outreach; begin leafleting when they arrive (see Chapter 1).
5. Ask your school cafeteria or one of your favorite restaurants to carry (more) vegan entrées (see Chapter 6).
6. Write a letter to the editor of your local paper (see Chapter 2).
7. Visit your local bookstore or library and pick up a book on animal rights.
8. Carry a "compassion kit" in your car, which can be used to get an animal to a shelter (see Chapter 7).
9. Visit humaneeating.com, mercyforanimals.org, or peta.org and order a vegan starter kit; give it to a meat-eating friend.
10. If you have companion animals who are not spayed or neutered, make an appointment with their veterinarian to have this done, or ask your parents to.
11. Order buttons, stickers, and shirts with anti-cruelty messages from AnimalRightsStuff.com, CafePress.com, CompassionCo.com, CrueltyFreeShop.com.au, HerbivoreClothing.com, VeganEssentials.com, VeganStore.co.uk, etc.

12. Include a signature line in your email with links to one or two of your favorite animal rights videos or current campaigns.

13. Make sure the cosmetics, cleaners, personal care, and other products you use do not contain animal ingredients and are not tested on animals. Visit leapingbunny.org for more information.

14. Invite a humane educator to speak at your school. (Contact humaneeducation.org for more details.)

15. Support legislation that protects animals.

Appendix C—Know Your Rights

Police powers and a citizen's legal rights obviously differ from country to country. This section offers some basic guidelines and advice from legal groups in Australia, Canada, New Zealand, South Africa, the United Kingdom, and the United States, but this is *not* meant as legal advice from a qualified professional. This is for information purposes only.

AUSTRALIA
(Source: Legal Aid—Western Australia)

Police Powers
The information below sets out the powers of police to arrest, hold, search and question you.

It is important to understand what your legal rights and obligations are in these circumstances.

If you have been arrested, it is important that you speak with a lawyer as soon as you can.

Arrest

When can the police make an arrest?
The police can arrest you without a warrant if they reasonably believe or suspect that you have broken the law. Most arrests are made without a warrant.

An arrest may be lawful even if you have not committed an offence.

What do the police have to do to make an arrest?
When the police make an arrest they should:

- Tell you that you are under arrest

- Tell you why you are being arrested
- Touch you and ask you to accompany them or to stay at a certain place.

If you resist or struggle, you can be charged with obstructing police. A police officer can use as much force as is reasonably necessary to restrain a person, effect an arrest or execute a warrant.

Reasonable Force

If you think that unreasonable force has been used, or if you have been injured by the police, you should:

- Report the matter to the officer in charge of the police station straight away. A written complaint that is dated and signed is best but at least a verbal report should be made.
- Have a doctor examine and document your injuries as soon as possible. If possible, have photographs taken of your injuries.
- Get legal advice about your situation.

What should you do if you are arrested?

If you are arrested, you should:

- Confirm that you are under arrest and ask the police what charges are being laid against you.
- Keep calm and be polite. If you resist arrest and are abusive, other charges may be laid against you.
- Ask to make a telephone call and phone your lawyer, a relative or a friend. It is *not* your right to be allowed a telephone call. However, if you ask, you may be allowed to make a telephone call.

Do you have to answer questions?

Generally you do not have to answer questions, sign a statement or take part in a video interview.

You *must*, however, provide your name and address, date of birth and, if the police request, your current address as well as the address at which you normally reside if they are different.

You should generally get legal advice before answering any questions, whether or not you have been arrested.

Anything you do say or sign will probably be used as evidence in court.

What rights do the police have to search?

The police can stop, search and detain (hold) any person or vehicle, if they reasonably believe that:

- An offence has been committed
- An offence is about to be committed or
- You are carrying something relating to an offence.

Generally the police may search your premises if you agree or if they have a search warrant. In certain circumstances the police may enter premises *without* a warrant.

You should obtain legal advice after the police have conducted a search of your premises.

The police are allowed to search a person and any property in their possession once they have been arrested.

The police can have you body searched and this usually must be done by a medical practitioner or a nurse.

Search Warrants

The laws relating to search warrants and searching a person can be complex. Often different laws will apply, depending on the situation. If the police have searched your body, belongings or premises, and you want to know if it was lawful for them to do this, you should get legal advice.

If the police have a reasonable suspicion that a person has committed a crime, they can enter a property without a warrant to make an arrest.

Once you have been arrested, the police can search you and any property you have in your possession.

If the police have reasonable grounds to suspect that someone has committed certain offences under the Misuse of Drugs Act, they have very wide powers, which include entering onto a premises without a search warrant and searching your person and your property.

CANADA
(Source: The Canadian Charter of Rights and Freedoms)

Section 10—Rights when arrested
If you are arrested or detained, you must be given reasons for this right away. The police must tell you of your right to a lawyer. If you say you want a lawyer, police must stop questioning you until you have a chance to speak with a lawyer privately. If your detention is not legal, you must be released.

Section 11—Rights when charged with an offence
Section 11 rights are basic principles of criminal law—like being presumed innocent, the right to a speedy trial and the independence of the Courts.

If you are charged with a criminal offence you have the right:

- To be informed of the offence without unreasonable delay
- To a trial in a reasonable time
- To be silent (the right not to testify at your own trial)
- To be presumed innocent until proven guilty
- To a fair and public hearing by an impartial and independent court

- To reasonable bail (unless there is good reason to be refused bail)
- To trial by jury for serious crimes (except for military offences decided by a military tribunal)
- Not to be convicted of a crime unless the act was a crime at the time it happened
- Not to be tried or punished twice for the same crime (the rule against double jeopardy).

If the law has changed between the time an offence happened and time of sentencing, a person has a right to be sentenced under the law where the punishment is less.

Section 12—Protection from cruel and unusual punishment

People are protected from cruel and unusual punishment such as punishment that degrades human dignity, is out of all proportion to the offence, or shocks the public conscience.

Section 13—Protection from self-incrimination

If you are a witness, what you say in court cannot be used against you in another court case. But if you are charged with perjury, what you said in court can be used to prove perjury.

Section 14—Right to an interpreter

You have the right to an interpreter in a courtroom if you are a party or a witness in a case and do not understand or speak the language used in the court. You also have this right if you are hearing impaired.

NEW ZEALAND

(Source: The Auckland Council for Civil Liberties)

Questioning, Detention and Arrest

If the police stop you or question you but you are not sure what to say or do: Tell them that you want to contact a lawyer, or your parents, or someone you trust. Stay calm and do not argue with the police.

What personal details should you give to the police?

Although you don't have to give any details to the police in many situations, these days it is advisable, if questioned, to give your name, address, age, i.e., basic identifying information only. If you're driving, you must stop and give your name, address and date of birth. You must also state if you are the owner of the car and, if not, who is. If you are a young person in a place serving alcohol, you can be asked for identification, or proof of age. If you refuse, you may commit an offence.

Should you give other information?

You are not obliged to give any other information to the police. You have a right to remain silent. It is usually better to say nothing in reply to police questions until you have consulted a lawyer, or your family, or a friend. You are not obliged to provide a written statement. If you say anything to the police, they may later use what you say against you. Be careful that any statement you do make is exactly what you mean to say. Don't lie. Make sure you read and correct the statement before signing it.

When do you have to accompany the police?

You do not have to go anywhere with a police officer if you do not want to, unless you are under arrest or are held by the police under a law that gives them the power to detain you. Examples of detention powers are where they suspect you have been drinking and driving, or the police suspect you may have drugs on you.

If the police are questioning your friend, and your friend asks for your advice, make sure your advice is as accurate as possible. If you offer advice without being asked by your friend, you might be arrested for obstructing the police (i.e., if they think your "advice" has made their work more difficult). Always get the officer's ID number.

What are your rights if the police want to arrest or detain you?

You have the basic right not to be arbitrarily arrested or detained. If you are arrested or held by the police, you have the right to be informed at the time of the reason why, and of your right to talk with and instruct a lawyer without delay. The police are required to inform you of that right. If you are arrested or detained, you have the right not to make a statement. The police must inform you of that right. When you are arrested, the police must charge you promptly or release you. If the police do not release you then you have the right to be brought as soon as possible before a court.

You also have the right to challenge whether your arrest or detention is lawful. If your release or detention is found not to be lawful, you must be released immediately.

When you are held against your will in any form of custody (be it by the police or any other enforcement agency), you have the right to be treated decently and with respect to your dignity.

(NZ Bill of Rights Act 1990, sections 22 and 23.)

ARREST

Always ask the police, "Am I under arrest?" If the answer is "No," ask if you are free to go. If they say "No," ask what power they are detaining you under. They have to tell you whether you are under arrest. If you are under arrest or detained under a specific law, you will enjoy the full protection of the Bill of Rights.

If the police arrest you, how much force can they use?

They can use whatever force is reasonable to get you to go with them. If you think the police are arresting you unlawfully, tell them at every opportunity, but go quietly. If you resist arrest, you may be arrested either on a charge of resisting arrest, or for obstructing the police in the execution of their duty.

If you have been arrested unlawfully, you may be able to complain later to the police, or to the Police Complaints Authority, or even bring court proceedings against the police if, for example, they have breached your rights under the Bill of Rights. Alternatively, if the police have breached your rights under the Bill of Rights, they may not be able to use the evidence they have obtained later in court.

AT THE POLICE STATION

If you haven't already been arrested

It's your decision whether you answer any questions or make any written or spoken statement. You don't have to do so. It's always best to contact a lawyer before saying anything or making any form of written statement. You may leave the police station when you wish. (But if you're there for a breath or blood alcohol test and leave before the test has been completed, you will commit an offence and probably be arrested.)

Remember that if you are not under arrest, e.g., you are "helping the police with their inquiries," you may not be protected by the rights contained in the Bill of Rights.

If you have been arrested

You can be searched, fingerprinted and photographed. Palmprints and footprints can also be taken. You must give your name, address, date and place of birth, and occupation. Other than supplying identifying particulars, you have the right to remain silent and the right to consult and instruct a lawyer without delay. Ask to be allowed to contact your lawyer or family as soon as you arrive at the station; keep asking until the police let you.

What are your rights after you have been formally charged with an offence?

Under section 24 of the Bill of Rights, you have the right to:

- Be informed promptly and in detail of the nature of the charge.
- Be released on reasonable terms and conditions unless the police give good reasons for wanting to continue to hold you in custody.
- Consult and instruct a lawyer (under the Bill of Rights, people have a right to consult and instruct a lawyer at the time of arrest. Most people may have exercised this right before they are formerly charged). The police should contact the lawyer you wish to see. There should be a list of legal aid lawyers at the police station. Contact one of them if you don't have a lawyer.
- Free assistance of an interpreter.

Police Rules state that normally a friend or a relative named by you is to be told by the police that you've been arrested. Usually a friend or relative is allowed to visit you.

Can you waive any of the rights given you by the Bill of Rights?

YES, but you should never "give away" your rights without first getting independent legal advice. Make it very clear to the police that you are not waiving any of your rights.

Bail

Ask for police bail, which will allow you to leave the police station. You should always ask for bail. You don't have an automatic right to be bailed by the police, but in many cases bail can be given. You'll then have to appear in court the next day. If denied bail by the police, you should demand to be taken in front of a court as soon as possible.

Privacy of discussions with your lawyer

Any discussion you have with your lawyer should be in private unless the police put forward a very strong reason as to why they need to watch over you (e.g., for security reasons). You do not need to ask for privacy in talking with your lawyer. However, it is better to ask for privacy, because if you don't a court might say that any breach of your privacy was inconsequential. If you are not allowed a private talk with your lawyer, this may be a breach of the Bill of Rights.

Do young persons have any special rights when questioned by the police regarding an offence?

YES. For example, if they are arrested and under 17, they are entitled to have a lawyer and their parent/guardian, or some other adult nominated by them, present during any interview with the police. The young person is entitled to speak to these persons prior to answering questions (Children, Young Persons and Their Families Act 1989, sections 215–232). Ask the police what additional rights you have as a young person.

COMPLAINTS

Try to get a name and badge number of any police officer you wish to complain about. Ask the officer to provide identification. They have to give you this information. If you have been injured, ask to see a doctor of your choice, and obtain photos of your injuries as soon as possible. Write out a full description of what you want to complain about. This statement will be important and valuable. If your complaint is serious you'll want a lawyer to help you. See the lawyer as soon as you possibly can. When dealing with the police over your complaint, take a lawyer or support person with you. You can:

- Discuss your complaint with the senior police officer attached to the main police station in the area.
- Make a formal complaint to the Police Complaints Authority, 7th Floor, Local Government Buildings, 114–118 Lambton Quay (PO Box 5025, Wellington), phone 0800 503 728.

Search

You have a basic legal right to be secure against any unreasonable search or seizure of yourself, your property, or your correspondence (Bill of Rights, section 21).

When can the police search you or your property?

The police can search you, or your car, or your property, if you agree. You should always ask the police what they are searching for and whether you can refuse. A police officer has no general right of search or entry onto private property, without a search warrant. If the police have a warrant, they must show it to you. The search warrant must specify what is to be searched and what offence, or offences, the warrant relates to. The police can only search for and seize items specified in the warrant. The police can use reasonable force to carry out the warrant. If you refuse to let them in, you will most likely be arrested for obstructing them. If they have a warrant, they can even search your home when you are not there.

When can the police search you without a warrant?

The police have the right to search you or your property without a warrant where they have arrested you, or have, e.g., reasonable grounds to believe that you are in possession of drugs or offensive weapons, or they have reasonable grounds to suspect that you have firearms or explosives.

Many provisions give the police and other law enforcement officers, wide powers of search without a warrant. If the police claim they have a power to search without a warrant, always ask them to specify what that power is.

After you have been arrested, the police can search you, your property (e.g., your handbag, your motor vehicle, and even your house), if they think, e.g., there is evidence which could be destroyed, or if they think you could get access to a weapon. (The law is unclear in this area.)

At the police station they will usually ask you to empty your pockets. They can even do a body search in certain circumstances. Where they suspect you may have drugs secreted within your body, they may be able to do an internal search of you (by police doctor). However, you don't need to agree to these searches, although certain penalties may apply if you refuse.

Note: Even if the police act illegally in searching you or your property, this does not necessarily mean that the search will amount to a breach of section 21 of the Bill of Rights. The evidence obtained as a result of the illegal search may still be admissible against you.

SOUTH AFRICA

(Source: Bill of Rights, South Africa; Section 35: ARRESTED, DETAINED AND ACCUSED PERSONS)

1) Everyone who is arrested for allegedly committing an offence has the right
   a. to remain silent;
   b. to be informed promptly
      i. of the right to remain silent; and

ii. of the consequences of not remaining silent;

c. not to be compelled to make any confession or admission that could be used in evidence against that person;

d. to be brought before a court as soon as reasonably possible, but not later than

i. 48 hours after the arrest; or

ii. the end of the first court day after the expiry of the 48 hours, if the 48 hours expire outside ordinary court hours or on a day which is not an ordinary court day;

e. at the first court appearance after being arrested, to be charged or to be informed of the reason for the detention to continue, or to be released; and

f. to be released from detention if the interests of justice permit, subject to reasonable conditions.

2) Everyone who is detained, including every sentenced prisoner, has the right

a. to be informed promptly of the reason for being detained;

b. to choose, and to consult with, a legal practitioner, and to be informed of this right promptly;

c. to have a legal practitioner assigned to the detained person by the state and at state expense, if substantial injustice would otherwise result, and to be informed of this right promptly;

d. to challenge the lawfulness of the detention in person before a court and, if the detention is unlawful, to be released;

e. to conditions of detention that are consistent with human dignity, including at least exercise and the provision, at state expense, of adequate accommodation, nutrition, reading material and medical treatment; and

f. to communicate with, and be visited by, that person's

     i.   spouse or partner;

    ii.   next of kin;

   iii.   chosen religious counselor; and

   iv.   chosen medical practitioner.

3) Every accused person has a right to a fair trial, which includes the right

  a. to be informed of the charge with sufficient detail to answer it;

  b. to have adequate time and facilities to prepare a defense;

  c. to a public trial before an ordinary court;

  d. to have their trial begin and conclude without unreasonable delay;

  e. to be present when being tried;

  f. to choose, and be represented by, a legal practitioner, and to be informed of this right promptly;

  g. to have a legal practitioner assigned to the accused person by the state and at state expense, if substantial injustice would otherwise result, and to be informed of this right promptly;

  h. to be presumed innocent, to remain silent, and not to testify during the proceedings;

  i. to adduce and challenge evidence;

  j. not to be compelled to give self-incriminating evidence;

  k. to be tried in a language that the accused person understands or, if that is not practicable, to have the proceedings interpreted in that language;

  l. not to be convicted for an act or omission that was not an offence under either national or international law at the time it was committed or omitted;

  m. not to be tried for an offence in respect of an act or omission for which that person has previously been either acquitted or convicted;

n.   to the benefit of the least severe of the prescribed punishments if the prescribed punishment for the offence has been changed between the time that the offence was committed and the time of sentencing; and

o.   of appeal to, or review by, a higher court.

4)   Whenever this section requires information to be given to a person, that information must be given in a language that the person understands.

5)   Evidence obtained in a manner that violates any right in the Bill of Rights must be excluded if the admission of that evidence would render the trial unfair or otherwise be detrimental to the administration of justice.

UNITED KINGDOM

(Source: "No Comment: The Defendant's Guide to Arrest")

WHEN YOU HAVE BEEN ARRESTED

You have to give the police your name and address. You will also be asked for your date of birth—you don't have to give it, but it may delay your release as it is used to run a check on the police national computer. They also have the right to take your fingerprints, photo and non-intimate body samples (a saliva swab, to record your DNA). These will be kept on file, even if you are not charged.

The Criminal Justice and Public Order Act 1994 removed the traditional Right to Silence; however, all this means is that the police/prosecution can point to your refusal to speak to them, when the case comes to court, and the court *may* take this as evidence of your guilt. The police cannot force you to speak or make a statement, whatever they may say to you in the station. Refusing to speak cannot be used to convict you by itself.

If you are arrested under the Terrorism Act 2000, the police can keep you in custody for longer. They have already used this against protesters and others to intimidate them. Remember being arrested is not the same as being charged. Keeping silent is still the best thing to do in police custody.

Q: What happens when I get arrested?

When you are arrested, you will usually be handcuffed, put in a van and taken to a police station. You will be asked your name, address and date of birth. You should be told the reason for your arrest—remember what is said, it may be useful later. Your personal belongings will be taken from you. These are listed on the custody record and usually you will be asked to sign to say that the list is correct. You do not have to sign, but if you do, you should sign immediately below the last line, so that the cops can't add something incriminating to the list. You should also refuse to sign for something which isn't yours, or which could be incriminating.

You will also be asked if you want a copy of PACE (the Police and Criminal Evidence Act codes of practice). Your fingerprints, photo and saliva swab will be taken, then you will be placed in a cell until the police are ready to deal with you. DO NOT PANIC!

Q: What if I am under 18?

There has to be an "appropriate adult" present for the interview. The cops will always want this to be your mum or dad, but you might want to give the name of an older brother or sister or other relative or adult friend (though the cops may not accept a friend). If you don't have anyone, they will get a social worker—this might cause you more problems afterwards.

Q: When can I contact a solicitor?

You should be able to ring a solicitor as soon as you're arrested. Once at the police station it is one of the first things you should do, for two reasons:

1. To have someone know where you are.
2. To show the cops you are not going to be a soft target—they may back off a bit.

It is advisable to avoid using the duty solicitor; instead, find the number of a good solicitor in your area and memorize it. The police are wary of decent solicitors. Any good solicitor will provide free advice at the police station. Also, avoid telling your solicitor much about what happened. This can be sorted out later. For the time being, tell them you are refusing to speak. Your solicitor can come into the police station while the police interview you: you should refuse to be interviewed unless your solicitor is present.

Q: What is an interview?

An interview is the police questioning you about the offences they want to charge you with. The interview will take place in an interview room in the police station and should be taped.

AN INTERVIEW IS ONLY OF BENEFIT TO THE POLICE.

Remember they want to prosecute you for whatever charge they can stick on you.

AN INTERVIEW IS A NO WIN SITUATION.

For your benefit, the only thing to be said in an interview is "NO COMMENT."

REMEMBER: They can't legally force you to speak. Beware of attempts to interview you in the cop van or cell as all interviews are now recorded. The cops may try to pretend you confessed before the taped interview. Again say "NO COMMENT."

Q: Why do the police want me to answer questions?

If the police think they have enough evidence against you they will not need to interview you.

Q: But what if the evidence looks like they have got something on me? Wouldn't it be best to explain away the circumstances I was arrested in, so they'll let me go?
The only evidence that matters is the evidence presented in court to the magistrate or jury. The only place to explain everything is in court; if they've decided to keep you in, no amount of explaining will get you out. If the police have enough evidence, anything you say can only add to this evidence against you. When the cops interview someone, they do all they can to confuse and intimidate you. The questions may not be related to the crime. Their aim is to soften you up, get you chatting. Don't answer a few small talk questions and then clam up when they ask you a question about the crime. It looks worse in court.

To prosecute you, the police must present their evidence to the Crown Prosecution Service. A copy of the evidence is sent to your solicitor. The evidence usually rests on very small points: this is why it's important not to give anything away in custody. They may say your refusal to speak will be used against you in court, but the best place to work out what you want to say is later with your solicitor. If they don't have enough evidence, the case will be thrown out or never even get to court. This is why they want you to speak. They need all the evidence they can get. One word could cause you a lot of trouble.

Q: So I've got to keep my mouth shut. What tricks can I expect the police to pull in order to make me talk?
The police try to get people to talk in many devious ways. The following shows some pretty common examples, but remember they may try some other line on you.

"Come on now, we know it's you; your mate's in the next cell and he's told us the whole story."
If they've got the story, why do they need your confession?

Playing co-accused off against each other is a common trick, as you've no way of checking what other people are saying. If you are up to something dodgy with other people, work out a story and stick to it. Don't believe it if they say your co-accused has confessed.

"We know it's not you, but we know you know who's done it. Come on, Jane, don't be silly; tell us who did it."
The cops will use your first name to try to seem as though they're your friends. If you are young they will act in a fatherly/motherly way, etc.

"We'll keep you in 'til you tell us."
They have to put you before the magistrate or release you within 36 hours (or seven days if arrested under the Terrorism Act). Only a magistrate can order you to be held without charge for any longer.

"There is no right to silence anymore. If you don't answer questions the judge will know you're guilty."
Refusing to speak cannot be used to convict you by itself. If they had enough evidence they wouldn't be interviewing you.

"You've been nicked under the Terrorism Act, so you've got no rights."
More mental intimidation and all the more reason to say "NO COMMENT."

Mr Nice (good cop): *"Hiya, what's it all about, then? Sergeant Smith says you're in a bit of trouble. He's a bit wound up with you. You tell me what happened and Smith won't bother you. He's not the best of our officers; he loses his rag every now and again. So what happened?"*
Mr Nice (good cop) is as devious as Mr Nasty (bad cop) is. He or she will offer you a cuppa, cigarettes, a blanket. It's the softly-softly approach. It's bollocks. "NO COMMENT."

"Look, we've tried to contact your solicitor, but we can't get hold of them. It's going to drag on for ages this way. Why don't we get this over with so you can go home?"

Never accept an interview without your solicitor present, a bit more time now may save years later! Don't make a statement even if your solicitor advises you to—a good one won't.

"You're obviously no dummy. I'll tell you what—we'll do a deal. You admit to one of the charges, and we'll drop the other two. We'll recommend to the judge that you get a non-custodial sentence, because you've co-operated. How does that sound?"

There are no deals to be made with the police. Much as they'd like to, the police don't control the sentence you get.

"Wasting police time is a serious offence."

You can't be charged for wasting police time for not answering questions. The cops may rough you up, or use violence to get a confession (true or false) out of you. There are many examples of people being fitted up and physically assaulted until they admitted to things they hadn't done. It's your decision to speak rather than face serious injury. Just remember, what you say could get you and others sent down for a very long time. However, don't rely on retracting a confession in court—it's hard to back down once you've said something.

In the police station, the cops rely on a person's naïveté. If you are aware of the tricks they play, the chances are they'll give up on you. Having said nothing in the police station, you can then look at the evidence and work out your side of the story.

Additional Information
(Source: FreeBEAGLES Legal Resource Centre, UK)

UK laws that could affect animal activists include:

Home Demos

Section 42 of the Criminal Justice and Police Act 2001 enables the police to impose conditions on demonstrations taking place outside someone's home. Much was made of this new law at the time, as it was supposed to be one of the government's "package of measures" designed to stop animal rights extremism. But it has quickly become apparent that this law has had very little impact on home demos, and after intensive lobbying by the pharmaceutical industry and the police, the government have announced plans to make these kinds of demos illegal.

Section 42 confers power on a police officer to impose directions verbally on persons demonstrating in the "vicinity" of someone's dwelling, if he reasonably believes that they are there to protest against the actions of the resident of the dwelling or anyone else, and that their presence amounts to or is likely to cause harassment, alarm or distress to the resident. This includes the power to direct you to leave the vicinity immediately. An officer can ask you to leave even if your behaviour is entirely peaceful, so long as you're in the vicinity of a dwelling. He can also impose conditions on the demonstration stating where it may take place and how many people may take part.

Aggravated Trespass

Section 68 of the Criminal Justice and Public Order Act 1994 (CJA) defines the offence as follows: *A person commits aggravated trespass if he trespasses on land with the intention of disrupting, or intimidating those taking part in, lawful activity taking place on that or adjacent land.*

Notes on Aggravated Trespass

Aggravated trespass can now take place inside as well as outside buildings. The offence was introduced in 1994 to deal with the problem caused to blood sports enthusiasts by hunt saboteurs. However, it has been widely used against other animal rights activists and road protesters as well.

Section 59 of the Anti-Social Behavior Bill has amended Section 68 of the CJA, so that now aggravated trespass can occur inside as well as outside buildings. This amendment was introduced after intensive lobbying of the government by the police and the pharmaceutical industry to give them new powers to deal with office occupations by animal rights activists and others. Previously the police only had the power to remove such protesters from the building or to arrest them for breach of the peace. They now have a specific power of arrest to deal with the trespass itself.

The law states that you cannot commit the offence from a public highway, but you may commit the offence from a public footpath or bridleway. This is because the right to use such footpaths and bridleways generally extends only to the right of passage along them. Any other act can amount to trespass.

Intending something to happen is not the same as wanting it to happen. If the prosecution can show, for example, that you knew that an office occupation would disrupt activity, then this will be enough to show that you intended it, regardless of whether you in fact wanted or desired the disruption.

You cannot be prosecuted for aggravated trespass where no actual activity is taking place to disrupt. The High Court has ruled that Section 68 CJA created a public order offence designed to deal with people disrupting persons actually engaged in lawful activity. It cannot, therefore, be used against activists, for example, who set off unattended badger traps, thus preventing the badger from entering the trap.

Arrest and Punishment

Aggravated trespass carries a maximum sentence of three months imprisonment or a fine. It is not an "arrestable offence," but the act confers a statutory power of arrest on an officer in uniform who suspects you of committing the offence.

The CPS has not been keen on the offence, as they have to show that the accused intended the offence, which is often difficult to prove in court. The police used it extensively during one animal rights campaign and failed to secure a single conviction! However, now that the power can be used to deal with office occupations, protesters can expect it to be used more widely.

Civil Trespass

If the premises are open to the public—e.g., a shop or a bank—then you have an implied license, i.e., permission to enter, and you are not trespassing. Similarly, in the case of somebody's home, you have an implied permission to walk up their driveway and to knock on the front door.

However, if you are asked to leave by the occupier of the house or shop and you refuse, then you become a trespasser. And if you enter a building or part of a building which is clearly marked "Staff Only" or you jump over a security gate in order to gain entry to premises, then there is no implied license to enter and you are trespassing immediately.

The police have been known to demand people's details while they are trespassing, so that they can hand them over to the occupier. They have no right to demand them for this purpose and you do not have to comply with such a request. A landowner may use reasonable force to move you from his premises, and anyone—the police included—may assist him with this.

Burglary

Section 9(1)(a) of the Theft Act 1968 states:

A person is guilty of burglary if he enters a building as a trespasser with intent to either:

i) steal
ii) inflict GBH on someone

iii) rape someone or

iv) inflict criminal damage

This is therefore a much wider offence than many people realize. To justify an arrest, all the police need to say is that they reasonably suspected that you entered as trespasser with intent to inflict criminal damage. They do not have to suspect "breaking and entry" which would be a separate offence of criminal damage.

The police now have far greater powers to deal with aggravated trespass than they did before as this can now be used to deal with activity disrupted inside as well as outside buildings. However, there will be occasions where no-one is actually present when the trespass occurs, and in these cases the police might use burglary when they have little or nothing else to justify an arrest.

Burglary is an "arrestable offence" under Section 24 PACE, and therefore carries all the additional powers conferred by that. Of course, you are unlikely to get charged with burglary unless you actually do steal, or cause criminal damage etc. You may well be able to sue the police for wrongful arrest and unlawful imprisonment afterwards, if the police cannot give adequate reasons for believing that you intended to inflict criminal damage, etc.

Obstruction of the Highway

Section 137 of the Highways Act 1980 makes it an offence to cause a willful obstruction of the highway without lawful authority or excuse.

Many animal rights stalls and assemblies may cause an obstruction, but the key legal point is whether or not there is a "lawful excuse" for the obstruction.

Once it was the case that there could only be a lawful excuse for obstructing the highway where you were using it for passage or re-passage and for ancillary matters, for example stopping to read a map. But more recent case decisions have interpreted the right to use the highway much more liberally, so as to include, for example, the handing out of leaflets, assembling and collecting for charity. Nowadays the courts are much more mindful of the exercise of European convention rights when deciding whether or not an obstruction has been caused.

It follows that it is not necessarily the case that an animal rights stall or a picket outside a shop on the highway is causing an unlawful obstruction, even though the police and council officials often maintain that it is. Leading cases state that all the circumstances must be considered in determining whether the obstruction was unlawful, including the duration, the purpose of the obstruction and its extent on to the highway.

One of the key purposes which the courts must consider in deciding whether or not there is a reasonable excuse for causing an obstruction is whether or not it involves the exercise of one or more ECHR convention rights, for example the right to freedom of expression under Article 10.

Now that the police are legally bound to respect your rights under the European Convention on Human Rights, they have to interpret their powers so as to be consistent with those rights. And the courts must, wherever possible, interpret all legislation so as to be consistent.

In a case that went to the High Court in 2003, an anti-war protester had erected a number of placards in Parliament Square in London. These placards protruded by one and a half feet onto a highway 11 feet wide. The council sought an injunction against him in the High Court prohibiting him from obstructing the highway. The court ruled that he had willfully obstructed the highway, but that the obstruction was reasonable in all the circumstances. The injunction was refused.

You cannot be arrested for obstruction where you are simply walking along the highway, unless you are blocking a main road. The courts have ruled that unlawful activity could never be regarded as "reasonable" for the purpose of the act.

Although breach of Section 137 is not strictly speaking an "arrestable offence," the police can arrest you to prevent an obstruction of the highway using their general power of arrest under Section 25 of PACE.

For more information, visit www.freebeagles.org.

UNITED STATES

Dealing with the Police: General Guidelines for Activists
(Source: The National Lawyers Guild, New York, NY)

I. In General
When dealing with the police, park rangers, health officers or other law enforcement officers (collectively referred to as "police"), keep your hands in view and don't make sudden movements. Avoid walking behind the police. Never touch the police or their equipment (vehicles, flashlights, animals, etc.).

II. Police Encounters
There are three basic types of encounters with the police: Conversation, Detention, and Arrest.

Conversation: When the police are trying to get information, but don't have enough evidence to detain or arrest you, they'll try to get the information from you. They may call this a "casual encounter" or a "friendly conversation." If you talk to them, you may give them the information they need to arrest you or your friends. In most situations, it's better and safer to refuse to talk to police.

Detention: Police can detain you only if they have *reasonable suspicion* that you are involved in a crime. (A "reasonable suspicion" occurs when an officer can point to specific facts that provide some objective manifestation that the person detained may be involved in criminal activity.) Detention means that, though you aren't arrested, you can't leave. Detention is supposed to last a short time and they aren't supposed to move you. During detention, the police can pat you down and may be able to look into your bag to make sure you don't have any weapons. They aren't supposed to go into your pockets unless they first feel a weapon through your clothing.

If the police are asking questions, ask if you are being detained. If not, leave and say nothing else to them. If you are being detained, you may want to ask why. Then you should say: *"I am going to remain silent. I want a lawyer,"* and nothing else.

A detention can easily turn into arrest. If the police are detaining you and they get information that you are involved in a crime, they will arrest you, even if it has nothing to do with your detention. The purpose of many detentions is to try to obtain enough information to arrest you.

Arrest: Police can arrest you only if they have *probable cause* that you are involved in a crime. ("Probable cause" exists when the police are aware of facts that would lead an ordinary person to suspect that the person arrested has committed a crime.) When you are arrested, the cops can search you and go through any belongings.

III. The *Miranda* Warnings

The police do not necessarily have to read you your rights (also known as the Miranda warnings). Miranda applies when there is (a) an interrogation (b) by a police officer (c) while the suspect is in police custody. (Please note that you do not have to be formally arrested to be "in custody.") Even when all these conditions are met, the police intentionally violate Miranda. And though your rights have been violated, what you say can be used against you. For this reason, it is better not to wait for the cops—you know what your rights are, so you can invoke them by saying "I am going to remain silent. I want to see a lawyer."

If you've been arrested and realize that you have started answering questions, don't panic. Just re-invoke your rights by saying "I am going to remain silent. I want to see a lawyer." Don't let them trick you into thinking that because you answered some of their questions, you have to answer all of them.

Arrest Warrants

An arrest warrant is a court order authorizing law enforcement to arrest a specific person, but police and other law enforcement agents often use it as a tool to enter your home. If law enforcement arrives at your home with an arrest warrant, the best thing to do is go outside and give yourself up. If you can, lock the door behind you— don't give agents the chance to conduct a warrantless search of your home.

IV. Questioning

Do not communicate with the police anything other than your right to remain silent. If you are arrested, you may want to give identifying information, such as name, address and driver's license, which will help secure your release by citation or be necessary to be released on bail.

It is a serious crime to make a false statement to a police officer. By talking, you could get in trouble because of two inconsistent statements spoken out of fear or forgetfulness. It is also very dangerous to try to outsmart the police. They are trained in how to extract information and trip people up who are lying to them or even telling the truth. They have learned how to get people to talk by making them feel scared, guilty or impolite. Stay strong and stay silent!

Interrogation isn't always bright lights and rubber hoses—usually it's just a conversation. Whenever the police ask you questions, it's legally safest to say these words: "I am going to remain silent. I want to see a lawyer."

This invokes the rights which protect you from interrogation. When you say this, the police are legally required to stop asking you questions if you have been detained or placed under arrest. They probably won't stop, so just repeat "I am going to remain silent. I want to see a lawyer," or remain silent until they catch on.

Remember, anything you say to the authorities can and will be used against you and your friends in court. There's no way to predict how or what information the police might try to use. Plus, the police often misquote or misrepresent altogether what was said.

One of the jobs of police is to secure information from people, and they often don't have any scruples about how they go about doing so. Police are legally allowed to lie when they're investigating, and they are trained to be manipulative. The only thing you should say to police is:

"I am going to remain silent. I want to see a lawyer."

Here are some of the statements the police might make:

- "You're not a suspect—just help us understand what happened here and then you can go." If you're not a suspect, ask to leave immediately without answering any questions.
- "If you don't answer my questions, I'll have no choice but to arrest you. Do you *want* to go to jail?" No one wants to

be arrested, but regardless of their promises, talking will usually not avoid arrest.

- "If you don't answer my questions, I'm going to charge you with interfering with my investigation." You cannot be charged with interfering or obstructing a police officer by invoking your right not to talk to the police.

- "All of your friends have cooperated and we let them go home. You're the only one left." This is generally a lie— besides, even if that did happen, how does it benefit you to be a witness against yourself?

- "If you don't talk now, we'll come back with a subpoena." Most of the time this is an empty threat. The police do not have the power to obtain a subpoena. In connection with the investigation of a crime, the only subpoena that can be issued is from a grand jury.

- "If you talk, we will go easy on you." Police will promise you the world to get you to talk. However, when they have people sign statements, notice they never sign anything saying the police will keep their promises.

- "You seem to be an intelligent kid with a promising future. You don't want to destroy your life over this, do you?" The truth is, the police don't care about you. This is just another way to manipulate you into making a statement.

- "If you're not guilty, then why don't you talk?" This is one of their favorite tactics. We all have the desire to defend ourselves, especially when we know we are innocent. However, the police will attack and dissect everything you say, continually prying to get more and more information. Even if you are innocent, don't talk! A person's innocence has never stopped the authorities from convicting or jailing them. Furthermore, the more you talk, the more likely you are to mention other people's names, leading the police to them.

Police will often try to trick you into talking. Here are some of the techniques they use:

- Good Cop/Bad Cop: Bad cop is aggressive and menacing, while good cop is nice, friendly and familiar (usually good cop is the same race and sex as you). The idea is bad cop scares you so badly you are desperately looking for a friend. Good cop is that friend.
- The police will tell you that your friends ratted on you so that you will snitch on them. Meanwhile, they tell your friends the same thing.
- The police will tell you that they have all the evidence they need to convict you and that if you "take responsibility" and confess the judge will be impressed by your honesty and go easy on you. What they really mean is: "We don't have enough evidence yet, please confess."

Jail is a very isolating and intimidating place. It is really easy to believe what the cops tell you. Insist upon speaking with a lawyer before you answer any questions or sign anything.

The police do not decide your charges; they can only make recommendations. The prosecutor is the only person who can actually charge you.

V. Searches

Never consent to a search! If the police try to search your house, car, backpack, pockets or other private property, say "*I do not consent to this search.*" This may not stop them from forcing their way in and searching anyway, but if they search you illegally, they probably won't be able to use the evidence against you in court. You have nothing to lose from refusing to consent to a search and lots to gain. Do not physically resist police when they are trying to search because you could get hurt and charged with resisting arrest or other serious crimes.

If the police have a search warrant, nothing changes—you should not consent to the search. Again, you have nothing to lose from refusing to consent to a search, and lots to gain if the search warrant is incorrect or invalid in some way. But remember not to physically resist police when they are trying to search.

VI. Taking Notes

Whenever you interact with or observe the police, always write down what is said and who said it. Write down the names and badge numbers of the police and the names and contact information of any witnesses. Record everything that happens. Be careful—police don't like people taking notes, especially if they are planning on doing something illegal. Observing them and documenting their actions may have very different results; for example, it may cause them to respond aggressively, or it may prevent them from abusing you or your friends.

About Grand Juries

(Source: The Center for Constitutional Rights, www.CCRJustice. org)

In the US legal system, a grand jury is a panel of citizens brought together to investigate crimes and decide whether someone should be charged (indicted) for a serious crime. Grand juries are often used to extract information from activists. Many rights we take for granted do not exist for grand jury witnesses. Grand jury witnesses have no right to be represented by an attorney and no right to a jury trial if they are threatened with jail. Grand jury witnesses do retain the right against self-incrimination but can nonetheless be forced to snitch on themselves and others in exchange for immunity from prosecution and punishment. Immunity only protects witnesses—others can still be prosecuted.

Grand jury subpoenas are served by law enforcement agents, usually police officers or federal marshals. A grand jury subpoena must be personally served on you, meaning it must be handed to you. If you refuse to accept it, it must be placed near you.

A grand jury subpoena does not give an agent the right to search a home, office, car, or anywhere else, nor does it require you to relinquish any documents or say anything at that time. A grand jury subpoena only requires you to do something on the future date stated on the subpoena. If an agent shows up and tries to serve you with a subpoena, take it and do not do anything else. Do not answer any questions, do not consent to a search, and do not invite them into your home for any reason.

Once you have received a grand jury subpoena, you typically have three options: 1) You can comply with the subpoena; 2) you can move to quash the subpoena (challenging it in court); or 3) you can refuse to comply, which could land you in jail. If you receive a subpoena, you should contact an attorney as soon as possible and discuss each of these options in detail.

If you comply with a subpoena, you avoid the possibility of being punished for ignoring it; however, complying with a subpoena may get you into a different type of trouble. For example, if you are a target of the investigation, complying with the subpoena may provide the government with information it might need to charge and convict you. You might also place another activist in jeopardy by complying with a subpoena. If you receive a subpoena, you should speak with a lawyer before taking any action. If the subpoena is politically motivated, it is best to speak with an attorney in your activist circle who does criminal defense or grand jury work. Some non-activist criminal defense attorneys may suggest you become a snitch. It is important to note, however, that many snitches end up serving as many years in prison as the individuals on whom they snitched.

Grand jury proceedings are secret. The activist community often does not know when a grand jury investigation is being pursued. As a result, many activists believe that they should publicize the fact that they have received a subpoena. This may be an effective tactic to explore with your attorney if you receive a subpoena.

Rights of Photographers & Videographers
(Source: American Civil Liberties Union, www.aclu.org)

Taking photographs of things that are plainly visible from public spaces is a constitutional right — and that includes federal buildings, transportation facilities, and police and other government officials carrying out their duties. Unfortunately, there is a widespread, continuing pattern of law enforcement officers ordering people to stop taking photographs from public places, and harassing, detaining and arresting those who fail to comply.

Your rights as a photographer:

- **When in public spaces where you are lawfully present you have the right to photograph anything that is in plain view.** That includes pictures of federal buildings, transportation facilities, and police. Such photography is a form of public oversight over the government and is important in a free society.
- **When you are on private property, the property owner may set rules about the taking of photographs.** If you disobey the property owner's rules, they can order you off their property (and have you arrested for trespassing if you do not comply).
- **Police officers may not confiscate or demand to view your digital photographs or video without a warrant.** The Supreme Court has ruled that police may not search your cell phone when they arrest you, unless they get a warrant. Although the court did not specifically rule on whether

Compassion Fatigue in Sanctuaries

Although working at a sanctuary for farmed animals has tremendous rewards, it can also expose advocates to a special kind of compassion fatigue, says Susie Coston, national shelter director for Farm Sanctuary. "We are fighting a battle that is not going to be easily won, and we're rescuing animals who have been genetically changed to grow bigger breasts, lay more eggs, produce more muscle, and are designed to live just 36 to 40 days or six months." An animal's death hits sanctuary workers particularly hard, and they often feel they could have done something more. "Recognize that you may fail to save an animal who arrives in a condition that is not fixable—a condition that in many cases is manmade. And even more important, recognize that you cannot save them all. We have to be able to let go of those things out of our control, so we can function in our role as educators and care providers."

of digital media, many of us are literally addicted to the high we get from seeing that someone we don't even know has liked or shared one of our posts—and we experience withdrawal if we're away from our screens for too long.

Activists don't only use social media to be social. We use it for our outreach, to organize events, to promote petitions and animal adoption notices, to announce campaign updates, and a dozen other important things. Clearly, the Internet has become an indispensable tool for us. But as difficult as this might be, we need to set a time each day for a digital detox and turn off social media and mobile devices for an hour or so. Make this a regular practice, not just something you do when you're feeling stressed. You might just find that you get more done.

Think of it this way: Much of our time is spent either creating or consuming. Technology is a time-saving marvel, and it allows us to create in remarkable ways. Still, most of the time, we are consuming technology, and our devotion to screens has only gotten worse and so have the consequences. Before mobile devices became mainstream in the 2000s, for example, the average person had an attention span of 12 seconds; now it's just eight seconds—one second shorter than the average goldfish. Let's make it a goal to create more and consume less. And during those times when you are feeling extra stress, avoiding consuming the news altogether.

Make a Change

And what if you pursue your life's work for animals, do all you can to stay mentally and physically healthy, yet still experience the stress and overwork that can lead to burnout? "It may be that you're ready for a change," advises Zoe. "You don't have to give up on making a difference for animals, but you may need to find a different avenue. We all change and grow, and it's important to allow ourselves to grow in our activism too."

pattrice agrees with this attitude and acknowledges the many opportunities activists have to alter their efforts if burnout creeps up on them. "There's so much work to do on so many problems that you can give yourself a break from one set of problems by turning your attention to another," she says. "If you start to feel like you cannot possibly answer the same old arguments for vivisection yet again, maybe it's time to switch focus and work on factory farming instead. If you need to take a break from direct contact with animal suffering, work on global warming. If you're burned out on working with the public, work on behind-the-scenes research and let somebody else do the leafleting."

One reason activists engaging in a group effort may be reluctant to make a change is the fear of disappointing their peers, Dallas observes. "There's a feeling of scarcity in our movement: there's not enough people working on behalf of law enforcement may search other electronic devices such as a standalone camera, the ACLU believes that the constitution broadly prevents warrantless searches of your digital data. It is possible that courts may approve the temporary warrantless seizure of a camera in certain extreme "exigent" circumstances such as where necessary to save a life, or where police have a reasonable, good-faith belief that doing so is necessary to prevent the destruction of evidence of a crime while they seek a warrant.

- **Police may not delete your photographs or video under any circumstances.** Officers have faced felony charges of evidence tampering as well as obstruction and theft for taking a photographer's memory card.
- **Police officers may legitimately order citizens to cease activities that are truly interfering with legitimate law enforcement operations.** Professional officers, however, realize that such operations are subject to public scrutiny, including by citizens photographing them.
- **Note that the right to photograph does not give you a right to break any other laws.** For example, if you are trespassing to take photographs, you may still be charged with trespass.

If you are stopped or detained for taking photographs:

- Always remain polite and never physically resist a police officer.
- If stopped for photography, the right question to ask is, "Am I free to go?" If the officer says no, then you are being detained, something that under the law an officer cannot do without reasonable suspicion that you have or are about to commit a crime or are in the process of doing so. Until you ask to leave, your being stopped is considered voluntary under the law and is legal.

- If you are detained, politely ask what crime you are suspected of committing, and remind the officer that taking photographs is your right under the First Amendment and does not constitute reasonable suspicion of criminal activity.

Special considerations when videotaping

With regard to videotaping, there is an important legal distinction between a visual photographic record (fully protected) and the *audio* portion of a videotape, which some states have tried to regulate under state wiretapping laws.

- Such laws are generally intended to accomplish the important privacy-protecting goal of prohibiting audio "bugging" of private conversations. However, in nearly all cases audio recording the police is legal.
- In states that allow recording with the consent of just one party to the conversation, you can tape your own interactions with officers without violating wiretap statutes (since you are one of the parties).
- In situations where you are an observer but not a part of the conversation, or in states where all parties to a conversation must consent to taping, the legality of taping will depend on whether the state's prohibition on taping applies only when there is a reasonable expectation of privacy. But no state court has held that police officers performing their job in public have a reasonable expectation.
- The ACLU believes that laws that ban the taping of public officials' public statements without their consent violate the First Amendment.

Photography at the airport

Photography has also served as an important check on government power in the airline security context.

The Transportation Security Administration (TSA) acknowledges that photography is permitted in and around airline security checkpoints as long as you're not interfering with the screening process. The TSA does ask that its security monitors not be photographed, though it is not clear whether they have any legal basis for such a restriction when the monitors are plainly viewable by the traveling public.

The TSA also warns that local or airport regulations may impose restrictions that the TSA does not. It is difficult to determine if any localities or airport authorities actually have such rules. If you are told you cannot take photographs in an airport you should ask what the legal authority for that rule is.

The ACLU does not believe that restrictions on photography in the public areas of publicly operated airports are constitutional.

Also see the section "Protecting Yourself at Protests" in Chapter 4.

Appendix D—Resources

ANIMAL RIGHTS GROUPS

This is by no means a comprehensive list—just a few of the national and grassroots organizations out there working on behalf of animals.

Asia

Animal Rights Center
www.arcj.org/en

Animals Asia
www.animalsasia.org

Chinese Animal Protection Network
www.capn-online.info/en.php

People for Animals
https://peopleforanimalsindia.org

Tibetan Volunteers for Animals
www.semchen.org

Wildlife SOS
http://wildlifesos.org

Australia

Against Animal Cruelty Tasmania
www.aact.org.au

Animal Liberation Victoria
www.alv.org.au

Animal Rights & Rescue Group
http://www.animalrights.org.au

Animals Australia
www.animalsaustralia.org

Australian Society for Kangaroos
www.australiansocietyforkangaroos.com

Coalition Against Duck Shooting
www.duck.org.au

Edgar's Mission
http://edgarsmission.org.au

Humane Charities Australia, Inc.
www.humanecharities.org.au

Humane Research Australia
www.humaneresearch.org.au

Southern Cross Wildlife Care
http://southerncrosswildlifecare.org.au

Vegan Australia
www.veganaustralia.org.au

Canada

Animal Justice
www.animaljustice.ca

Canadian Voice for Animals
www.canadianvoiceforanimals.org

EarthSave Canada
www.earthsave.ca

Fur-Bearer Defenders
www.banlegholdtraps.com

The Responsible Animal Care Society
www.tracs-bc.ca

Toronto Pig Save
www.torontopigsave.org

Toronto Vegetarian Association
www.veg.ca

Vancouver Humane Society
www.vancouverhumanesociety.bc.ca

New Zealand
Direct Animal Action
www.directanimalaction.org.nz

Save Animals From Exploitation
www.safe.org.nz

New Zealand Open Rescue Collective
www.openrescue.org/about/orc.html

Wellington Animal Rights Network
www.facebook.com/wellingtonanimalrightsnetwork

South Africa
Activists for Animals Africa
www.activistsforanimalsafrica.org

Animal Voice South Africa
www.animalvoice.org

Beauty Without Cruelty South Africa
www.bwcsa.co.za

UK/Europe

Alliance for Animal Rights
www.afarireland.org

Animal Aid
www.animalaid.org.uk

Animal Equality
www.animalequality.net

Animal Rights Action Network
www.aran.ie

Bite Back
www.biteback.org

Centre for Animals and Social Justice
www.casj.org.uk

Coalition to Abolish the Fur Trade
www.caft.org.uk

Compassion in World Farming
www.ciwf.org

Cruelty Free International
www.crueltyfreeinternational.org

European Anti-Rodeo Coalition
www.anti-rodeo.org

European Coalition to End Animal Experiments
www.eceae.org

League Against Cruel Sports
www.league.org.uk

National Animal Rights Association
www.naracampaigns.org

Vegan Ireland
www.vegan.ie

Viva!
www.viva.org.uk

US

Animal Legal Defense Fund
www.aldf.org

Animal Protection and Rescue League
www.aprl.org

Animal Rights Coalition
http://animalrightscoalition.com

Compassionate Action for Animals
www.exploreveg.org

CompassionWorks International
www.cwint.org

The Dolphin Project
https://dolphinproject.net

Factory Farming Awareness Coalition
www.ffacoalition.org

Farm Animal Rights Movement
www.farmusa.org

Farm Sanctuary
www.farmsanctuary.org

Food Empowerment Project
www.foodispower.org

Free from Harm
http://freefromharm.org

Institute for Humane Education
https://humaneeducation.org

Mercy For Animals
www.mercyforanimals.org

Northwest Animal Rights Network
https://narn.org

Open the Cages Alliance
www.openthecages.org

People for the Ethical Treatment of Animals
www.peta.org

Sea Shepherd Conservation Society

www.seashepherd.org

SHARK
www.sharkonline.org

United Poultry Concerns
www.upc-online.org

Vegan Outreach
www.veganoutreach.org

VINE Sanctuary
www.bravebirds.org

BOOKS

For Activism

The Animal Activist's Handbook: Maximizing Our Positive Impact in Today's World
Matt Ball and Bruce Friedrich

Ethics Into Action: Henry Spira and the Animal Rights Movement
Peter Singer

Get Political for Animals and Win the Laws They Need: Why and How to Launch a Voting Bloc for Animals in Your Town, City, County or State
Julie E. Lewin

Growl: Life Lessons, Hard Truths, and Bold Strategies from an Animal Advocate
Kim Stallwood

In Defense of Animals: The Second Wave
Edited by Peter Singer

Living Among Meat Eaters: The Vegetarian's Survival Handbook
Carol J. Adams

Made to Stick: Why Some Ideas Survive and Others Die
Chip Heath & Dan Heath

Making the News: A Guide for Activists and Nonprofits
Jason Salzman

Meat Market: Animals, Ethics, and Money
Erik Marcus

Move the Message: Your Guide to Making a Difference and Changing the World
Josephine Bellaccomo

Uncaged: Top Activists Share Their Wisdom on Effective Farm Animal Advocacy
Ben Davidow

For Cooking & Baking
Afro-Vegan: Farm-Fresh African, Caribbean, and Southern Flavors Remixed
Bryant Terry

The Artful Vegan: Fresh Flavors from the Millennium Restaurant
Eric Tucker, Renee Comet & Amy Pearce

Eat Like You Give a Damn
Michelle Schwegmann and Josh Hooten

How It All Vegan! Irresistible Recipes for an Animal-Free Diet
Sarah Kramer

The Joy of Vegan Baking: The Compassionate Cooks' Traditional Treats and Sinful Sweets
Colleen Patrick-Goudreau

The Superfun Times Vegan Holiday Cookbook: Entertaining for Absolutely Every Occasion
Isa Chandra Moskowitz

Vegan: Over 90 Mouthwatering Recipes for All Occasions
Tony Bishop-Weston

Vegan Planet, Revised Edition: 425 Irresistible Recipes with Fantastic Flavors from Home and Around the World
Robin Robertson ·

Vegan Under Pressure
Jill Nussinow

Vegan Vittles: Down-Home Cooking for Everyone
Jo Stepaniak

Vegan with a Vengeance, 10th Anniversary Edition: Over 150 Delicious, Cheap, Animal-Free Recipes That Rock
Isa Chandra Moskowitz

For Support

Aftershock: Confronting Trauma in a Violent World: A Guide for Activists and Their Allies
pattrice jones

Animal Grace: Entering a Spiritual Relationship with Our Fellow Creatures
Mary Lou Randour

Even Vegans Die: A Practical Guide to Caregiving, Acceptance, and Protecting Your Legacy of Compassion
Carol J. Adams, Patti Breitman, and Virginia Messina

Healing Through the Dark Emotions: The Wisdom of Grief, Fear, and Despair
Miriam Greenspan

The Inner Art of Vegetarianism: Spiritual Practices for Body and Soul
Carol J. Adams

On Being Vegan: Reflections on a Compassionate Life
Colleen Patrick-Goudreau

Self-Care for Activists: A Guide to Clearing Yourself of Trauma While Working for a Better World
Erik Marcus

To Save a Starfish: A Compassion-Fatigue Workbook for the Animal-Welfare Warrior
Jennifer Blough

Vegan Freak: Being Vegan in a Non-Vegan World
Bob & Jenna Torres

Vegan's Daily Companion: 365 Days of Inspiration for Cooking, Eating, and Living Compassionately
Colleen Patrick-Goudreau

On Veganism

How to Be Vegan: Tips, Tricks, and Strategies for Cruelty-Free Eating, Living, Dating, Travel, Decorating, and More
Elizabeth Castoria

Never Too Late to Go Vegan: The Over-50 Guide to Adopting and Thriving on a Plant-Based Diet
Carol J. Adams, Patti Breitman, and Virginia Messina

The Ultimate Vegan Guide: Compassionate Living without Sacrifice
Erik Marcus

Vegan for Life: Everything You Need to Know to Be Healthy and Fit on a Plant-Based Diet
Jack Norris and Virginia Messina

VEGAN PRODUCTS

Alternative Outfitters (US)
www.alternativeoutfitters.com

AnimalRightstuff (US)
www.animalrightstuff.com

Compassion Company (US)
www.compassionco.com

Cruelty Free Shop (Australia)
http://crueltyfreeshop.com.au

The Cruelty-Free Shop (New Zealand)
www.thecrueltyfreeshop.co.nz

The Cruelty-Free Shop (UK)
www.crueltyfreeshop.com

Ethical Wares (UK)
www.ethicalwares.com

Food Fight! (US)
www.foodfightgrocery.com

Herbivore Clothing (US)
www.herbivoreclothing.com

Meaningful Paws (US)
www.meaningfulpaws.care

Moo Shoes (US)
www.mooshoes.com

Nooch Vegan Market (US)
http://noochveganmarket.tumblr.com

Pangea (US)
www.veganstore.com

PETA Mall (US)
www.petamall.com

Rabbit Food Grocery (US)
www.rabbitfoodgrocery.com

V Word Market (Canada)
www.vwordmarket.com

Vaute Couture (US)
https://vautecouture.com

Vegan Chic (US)
www.veganchic.com

Vegan Essentials (US)
www.veganessentials.com

Vegan Line (UK)
www.veganline.com

Vegan Store (UK)
www.veganstore.co.uk

Vegan Supply (Canada)
https://vegansupply.ca

Vegan Wares (Australia)
www.veganwares.com

The Vegetarian Site (US)
www.thevegetariansite.com

MAGAZINES

American Vegan
www.americanvegan.org

The Animals Voice
www.animalsvoice.com

Barefoot Vegan
www.barefootvegan.com

Black Velvet
www.blackvelvetmagazine.com

Chickpea
https://chickpeamagazine.com/

Driftwood
www.driftwoodmag.com

Laika
www.laikamagazine.com

T.O.F.U.
www.ilovetofu.ca

The Vegan
www.vegansociety.com

Vegan Health & Fitness
www.veganhealthandfitnessmag.com

Vegan Life
www.veganlifemag.com

VegNews
www.vegnews.com

MULTIMEDIA

Animal Law Podcast
www.ourhenhouse.org/animallaw

Animal Rights Zone
www.arzonepodcasts.com

Animal Voices—Toronto
http://animalvoices.ca

Animal Voices—Vancouver
www.animalvoices.org

Animals Today Radio
www.animalstodayradio.com

The Bearded Vegans
www.thebeardedvegans.com

Black Vegans Rock
www.blackvegansrock.com

Brown Vegan
www.brownvegan.com

Colleen Patrick-Goudreau
www.colleenpatrickgoudreau.com

Go Vegan Texas
www.govegantexas.org/index.php

Happy Cow
www.happycow.net

Main Street Vegan
http://mainstreetvegan.net

New Zealand Vegan
http://nzveganpodcast.blogspot.com

Nonhuman Radio
http://kzfr.org/shows/nonhuman-radio

Our Hen House
www.ourhenhouse.org

Toronto Vegetarian Association
www.veg.ca

Vegan.com

The VeganAri Show
https://veganari.com

Vegan Warrior Princesses Attack!
http://veganwarriorprincessesattack.com

Vegan World Radio
http://veganworldradio.org

Viva La Vegan
www.vivalavegan.net

ADDITIONAL ONLINE RESOURCES
http://animalrights.meetup.com
Meet other local animal rights activists in your part of the world.

FoodIsPower.org
Lots of well-researched information for those trying to lead a compassionate life.

VeganMexicanFood.com
Recipes for those who love the flavors of Mexico.

VeganSA.com
Directory of vegan-friendly restaurants, shops, products, and accommodations in South Africa.

WorldOfVegan.com
Recipes, videos, product spotlights, and more.

Index

Other Changemakers Books
by Mark Hawthorne

Bleating Hearts: The Hidden World of Animal Suffering

Comprehensive and hard-hitting, *Bleating Hearts* examines the world's vast exploitation of animals, from the food, fashion, and research industries to the use of other species for sport, war, entertainment, religion, labor, and pleasure.

A staggering investigation into the ethics of animal exploitation around the world, *Bleating Hearts* pulls no punches as it examines the many ways humans use and abuse our fellow creatures. Hawthorne artfully travels to the darkest corners of animal suffering, bringing to light not only the disturbing truth about people's mistreatment of nonhumans, but what we can do about it. Eloquently written and thoroughly researched, this doesn't just belong on every animal advocate's bookshelf—it deserves to be discussed and shared. This is a brilliant, powerfully persuasive book that will inspire you to make a difference.

Ric O'Barry, founder of The Dolphin Project

If there is a place in your heart for animals, this is an important book for you to read. But it is also more than that. If you want to lift the veil of denial, so that you can make your life an effective statement of compassion, you'll find this book to be nothing less than extraordinary.

John Robbins, author of *The Food Revolution* and *Diet for a New America* and cofounder of the Food Revolution Network

A Vegan Ethic: Embracing a Life of Compassion Toward All

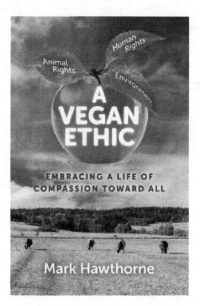

"If veganism is about doing your best to not harm any sentient life, we must logically extend that circle of compassion to human animals as well," writes Mark Hawthorne in this practical, engaging guide to veganism and animal rights. Along with

proven advice for going and staying vegan, an overview of animal exploitation, and answers to common questions about ethical eating (such as "Isn't 'humane meat' a good option?" and "Don't plants feel pain?"), *A Vegan Ethic* draws on the work and experiences of intersectional activists to examine how all forms of oppression—including racism, sexism, ableism, and speciesism—are connected by privilege, control, and economic power. By recognizing how social justice issues overlap, we can develop collaborative strategies for finding solutions.

Concise, accessible, and informative, *A Vegan Ethic* reminds us that compassion is not divisible, and neither should our activism be. Mark Hawthorne's empowering book explores why and how we can achieve social justice goals by working together and treating ourselves and others with compassion and respect. (And don't miss the helpful question-and-answer section!)
Carol J. Adams, author of *The Sexual Politics of Meat*

Mark Hawthorne illuminates a path away from the oppression of animals, humans, and the environment, and toward a more just and peaceful society. *A Vegan Ethic* is food for the soul!
Joyce Tischler, founder of the Animal Legal Defense Fund

About the Author

Mark Hawthorne is an activist and the author of two other books on animal rights: *Bleating Hearts: The Hidden World of Animal Suffering* and *A Vegan Ethic: Embracing a Life of Compassion Toward All* (both from Changemakers Books). He stopped eating meat after an encounter with one of India's many cows in 1992 and became an ethical vegan a decade later. In addition to his work in such publications as *VegNews*, *The Vegan*, and *Laika*, his writing has been featured in *Vegan's Daily Companion* (Quarry Books), *SATYA: The Long View* (Lantern Books), *Uncaged: Top Activists Share Their Wisdom on Effective Farm Animal Advocacy* (Ben Davidow), and *Turning Points in Compassion* (SpiritWings Humane Education Inc.), as well as in the anthologies *Stories to Live By: Wisdom to Help You Make the Most of Every Day* and *The Best Travel Writing 2005: True Stories from Around the World* (both from Travelers' Tales). Mark and his wife lauren live in California. You'll find him tweeting @markhawthorne and posting on Instagram @markhawthorneauthor.

MarkHawthorne.com
Facebook.com/MarkHawthorneAuthor